PROFESSIONAL PHILOSOPHY

THOMAS D. PERRY

PROFESSIONAL PHILOSOPHY

What It Is and Why It Matters

D. REIDEL PUBLISHING COMPANY

A MEMBER OF THE KLUWER ACADEMIC PUBLISHERS GROUP

DORDRECHT / BOSTON / LANCASTER / TOKYO

Library of Congress Cataloging-in-Publication Data

Perry, Thomas D.
    Professional philosophy.

    Bibliography: p.
    Includes indexes.
    1. Philosophy. 2. Ethics. I. Title.
    B72.P38   1986   190.'9'04   85–25684
    ISBN 90–277–2071–1
    ISBN 90–277–2072–X (Pallas Paperback)

CIP

Published by D. Reidel Publishing Company,
P.O. Box 17, 3300 AA Dordrecht, Holland.

Sold and distributed in the U.S.A. and Canada
by Kluwer Academic Publishers,
190 Old Derby Street, Hingham, MA 02043, U.S.A.

In all other countries, sold and distributed
by Kluwer Academic Publishers Group,
P.O. Box 322, 3300 AH Dordrecht, Holland.

Printed in The Netherlands

TABLE OF CONTENTS

PART ONE

PART TWO

PART THREE

INTRODUCTION

Over the past several decades serious work in philosophy has become almost wholly inaccessible to people who do not specialize in the subject. To be sure, the writings of Aristotle and Kant were never easy reading, and even relatively untechnical philosophers like Mill or Santayana demand careful study if we are really to understand them. But during the last generation or two the situation has steadily become worse for readers who may want to know what philosophers of their own time are doing. And this is true even though many writers have been learning to avoid the unnecessary jargon that disfigures so much of traditional philosophy. No matter how direct the English style of recent philosophers may be, their methodic purposes and argument style will remain obscure to anyone who has not gone to considerable trouble to be introduced to them. Then too, the closeness of their analysis and the consequent narrowness of many of the issues pursued make it hard to catch onto the argument without some familiarity with slightly earlier discussions from which those issues emerged. All of this helps to account for the rather common but false belief that professional philosophy is now only a collection of technical exercises that could hardly be of interest to anyone but the philosophers themselves.

New general introductions have of course continued to appear, but these texts and anthologies must stay pretty close to the broadest traditional issues, and they often restrict themselves to a very elementary treatment. While several interesting articles on recent philosophy have been published in general journals of good quality, most notably in the *New York Review of Books*, they usually have concentrated on a single thinker. And with one or two notable exceptions like Searle's article on Chomsky, they do not give sustained illustrations to help us think our way through some of the philosopher's problems and *reasoning*. We are commonly left with only a sketchy acquaintance with his intellectual *style* and major *claims*; or else, hoping to distill much thought in limited space, the writers of such articles often lapse into a specialist idiom which itself can provide no more than a sketch to those who are not at home with it. In any case, it is doubtful that even a lengthy discussion of but one or two thinkers, however eminent, could adequately present that larger development of recent philosophy without which it cannot be well understood. I refer to its methodic origins in, and metamorphosis from, traditional Western thought, and also to the major transformations which have occurred within recent analytic philosophy itself. Even the excellent introductions to subfields of philosophy presented in the Oxford and Prentice-Hall series do not usually fill this need. Finally, the two good book-length accounts of these changes that I know of — Urmson's *Philosophical Analysis* and Warnock's *Philosophy since 1900* — end with the nineteen-fifties and provide more in the way of historical survey than detailed illustration, at least in the case of Warnock's book which is much the shorter of the two. I say all this not by way of criticism but in justification of the present book and the special form which it has taken.

Part One begins by outlining some of the main assumptions and methods of traditional epistemology with which many readers will already be broadly familiar. An illustration from Berkeley is used for this purpose in Chapter 1. Chapters 2 and 3 then illustrate the crucial change in emphasis among the older methods which eventually led to the dominant outlook of mid-20th-century philosophy. This is done by examining three influential arguments published by G. E. Moore, Ludwig Wittgenstein, and P. F. Strawson in 1925, 1953, and 1959 respectively. In these illustrations we see how the project of solving metaphysical problems, or of reconstructing common sense in default of such solutions, gave way to the project of "dissolving" them by uncovering the confusions on which they allegedly rest. But already in Strawson the latter project has begun to serve another: that of *describing and clarifying* the structures of thought more patiently and accurately than philosophers of earlier centuries had normally done. This has proved to be the dominant concern of professional philosophers in later decades, whether they have been occupied with the most elementary and general structures of common sense, as Strawson was in that argument, or with more specialized concepts and thought patterns. But it is now more commonly recognized than it was then that conceptual description can sometimes disclose the need for conceptual reform — not reform in the oldest and most fundamental schemes of thought, perhaps, but in the more recent structures of common sense and (as everyone agrees) in the concepts of science. Chapter 4 illustrates a theory of conceptual change and reform which is designed to avoid the excesses of metaphysical reconstruction and otherwise accommodate the insights of the new philosophy. This illustration builds on the work of several recent philosophers concerning a particular metaphysical puzzle arising from the growth of scientific knowledge. It is put to further use in Parts Two and Three.

A major theme running through most of Part One is the developing influence of G. E. Moore, one of the three giants of analytic philosophy. Bertrand Russell's influence is traced through much of Part Two. The third giant, Ludwig Wittgenstein, has a major role to play in both of these Parts.

After the first Part has contrasted the main assumptions and methods of mid-century philosophy with those of earlier centuries, Part Two traces some major developments within analytic philosophy itself, beginning early in the century and continuing to the present day. In the first illustration of Chapter 5 we consider one of Russell's most famous arguments, his much-admired "theory of descriptions." We then show how, in his lectures of 1918, he built a metaphysical theory upon that argument, a theory which hopes to avoid the sins of traditional speculation by using the methods of modern logic and the results of science. His resulting "ontology" or theory of ultimately real things which language must take account of in describing the world, served to justify the method of analysis which many admirers of Russell pursued during the nineteen-twenties and early thirties. A partly similar theory of reality is embedded in the classic work published by Wittgenstein shortly after World War I. Chapter 6 extracts one of the main arguments of the latter theory and then illustrates Wittgenstein's own dissatisfaction with it during the thirties and forties. For the latter purpose we draw examples from his second classic work, written mostly in the forties and published in 1953. The later Wittgenstein and other mid-century writers achieved a more subtle and complex view of language which seemed to discredit the whole program of exact analysis which had developed in Russell's wake, a program that even Moore had embraced though without accepting the metaphysical underpinnings which Russell and the early Wittgenstein had provided for it. In the eyes of many, this program received its *coup de grace* from Strawson's 1950 refutation of the argument which had launched the whole development, the theory of descriptions itself. Chapter 6 ends with an account of this famous criticism.

Russell's heritage refused to stay dead, however. After being over-shadowed for a decade or two by the influence of Wittgenstein and J. L. Austin, the two most famous of the so-called "ordinary language philosophers," it is again in the ascendancy. At least this is true among prominent American philosophers occupied with such traditional "core" subjects as epistemology and metaphysics, and with the subject now known as philosophy of language. Not that anyone wants to revive Russell's metaphysics or thinks that standard Russellian logic will serve all the needs of philosophical analysis. But a good many people are again ambitious of producing exact analyses, and some continue to look for "best" or "canonical" ways of depicting the world through the resources of natural science and a logically regimented language. W. V. Quine is the best known philosopher of this tendency. The first section of Chapter 7 restates his most influential argument, and we go on to il-lustrate it with materials developed in Chapter 4. Chapter 7 then closes with a section touching more directly on the uses of "regimentation." In Chapter 8 we present a sequence of arguments and illustrations from two younger American philosophers, Keith Donnellan and Saul Kripke, and we end with a criticism of what Kripke has to say about the metaphysical implications of his argument.

These illustrations will suggest that some of the best achievements of present-day writers are actually "elucidations," not "exact analyses," contrary to the program or ambition just referred to. But of course the strict analyst should not be criticized for presenting whatever informal clarifications he may arrive at while traveling toward his more distant goal. The present illustrations are also slightly biased in this regard since they are drawn mostly from the "semantical" rather than the "syntac-tical" side of the literature in order not to presuppose any knowledge of mathematical logic or linguistics on the reader's part. Nor is such prior knowledge required by any of the illustrations in this book, including the one on Russell's theory of descriptions.

Part Three then turns to that other whole side of philosophy which has to do with value theory and specific "value disciplines" like ethics, aesthetics, political philosophy, and philosophy of law. Here the analytic philosophers of the present and recent past belong overwhelmingly to the party of elucidation, both in program and achievement. Hardly anyone thinks that exact analyses of concepts is possible in the departments of thought and action with which these branches of philosophy are concerned, though formal techniques are sometimes useful.

The illustrations of Part Three are organized as follows. Chapter 9 begins by summarizing R. M. Hare's well known account of value standards. Certain points are then added to show why many standards (not all) can provide an adequate basis for "value truth" when joined to ordinary statements of fact. In this way we clarify a conceptual structure which is to be put to use in Chapter 10. That chapter discusses recent ethical theories to see what light they can throw on the problem of moral truth. It is argued that some reform of the notion of truth is unavoidable in morals, and the theory of conceptual reform described in Chapter 4 is used to evaluate the proposals for reform which are found to be implicit in all but one of the theories under discussion. Much attention is given to a type of ethical theory which has variants in the work of Hare, Kurt Baier, William Frankena, John Rawls, and other recent philosophers.

Chapter 11 turns from these abstract concerns of ethical theory to a problem of applied ethics which has become especially acute with the technological developments of recent decades: Do people have a moral and political right to privacy? Philosophers have recently contributed to public discussion of this and many other practical questions by exploring the conceptual issues and doubts which sometime make policy choices more difficult. We trace a series of arguments by Judith Thomson, Thomas Scanlon, James Rachels, and Jeffrey Reiman which throw increasing light on the privacy problem, and we suggest further lines which the inquiry might usefully take. The chapter ends with a discussion of the special qualifications which analytic philosophers can bring to the clarification of public issues.

In the Conclusion we then point out a few other important features of professional philosophy which the illustrations collectively document, and we end by offering a general view of its present condition.

This book should not be mistaken for a *survey* of recent analytic philosophy. Rather, it is an introduction in the etymological sense that it attempts to lead the reader into the subject along three natural routes corresponding to the three Parts. Other writers will prefer somewhat different routes, ending no doubt in rather different conceptions of philosophy and its present worth or worthlessness. Because this is not a survey a good many prominent names go unmentioned except in the Notes and Bibliography. Various branches or "fields" of philosophy receive no illustration at all, e.g. philosophy of mathematics, philosophy of history, aesthetics, action theory. To have tried to represent every major figure or cover every important area would have made the book vastly longer and less coherent in achieving its special purposes.

Despite the chronological development of the illustrations in each Part, and the mainly chronological arrangement of the book as a whole, I have also not attempted to write a *history* with these illustrations. Some topics which would need sustained discussion in any history of analytic philosophy in this century receive only brief discussion and no illustration, e.g. Logical Positivism and Moore's refutation of Idealism.

Something must be said here about the troublesome phrase "analytic philosophy" itself, which I have already used several times and shall continue to use. Many people dislike it because they believe that all philosophy worthy of the name is to an important degree analytic. I am inclined to share their prejudice, or perhaps I should call it a persuasive definition for which *some* good reasons can be given. Thus: Philosophers are not content to leave the great metaphysical questions to poets, dramatists, and novelists, who examine them *primarily* for the purpose of art rather than for the pursuit of literal truth. But when attempting to be rigorous in that pursuit, a good philosopher is forced to give much attention to smaller issues; he must become analytical if he is serious, even at the risk of appearing to lose interest in those great questions. So "analytic philosopher" might seem a redundant phrase that only pseudo-philosophers would use when referring to their more serious rivals. But this is all somewhat misleading. There is more than one way to be serious in philosophy, and we need the expression "analytic philosophy" to distinguish our subject matter – the type of work now carried on by most active philosophers in the English speaking countries and Scandinavia – from the speculative tradition which continues to dominate the scene in continental Europe. Both traditions are historically entitled to the name philosophy, and it would only mislead some readers and needlessley irritate others if I were to reserve it for what is now the mainstream but not the whole of serious work even in the first countries mentioned.

There is another difficulty with the phrase "analytic philosophy" which many readers of this Introduction will already have felt. It was once used almost exclusively as a name for Russell's philosophy and heritage, and it is still often given that sense. Some would prefer that it always be used that way, leaving "conceptual elucidation" or some similar phrase to designate the rest of − the rest of what? Close-reasoning philosophy? That expression is far too awkward, and I do not know of any other handy phrase in common use except "analytic philosophy" itself for grouping the Russell heritage with conceptual elucidation in common contrast to the most speculative styles of thought. There is obviously some danger of confusing the narrower with the broader sense, and on the infrequent occasions when I use it in the narrower way I shall try to make this clear if it is not already obvious from the context.

My title *Professional Philosophy* demands a final prefatory remark. This book is wholly concerned with original work. It does not discuss philosophical scholarship, that valuable activity of a good many professionals who produce original analyses or constructions only as a by-product of their interpretations of past thinkers. (To be sure, some good historical scholars are also creative thinkers who take part in present-day debates.) Nor shall I discuss that other major activity of nearly all professional philosophers: the teaching of undergraduates. I also leave professional organizations and meetings out of my account, and nothing is said about the graduate training and job placement of philosophers. My subject is philosophy itself, not its institutional settings and economics. These have no doubt affected it deeply, but that will have to be a topic for some other occasion.

ACKNOWLEDGMENTS

Chapter 4 of this book grew out of an article which appeared in volume 2 of *Metaphilosophy*, 1971. Chapters 5 and 6 explain the philosophical method which was used but not discussed in my book *Moral Reasoning and Truth*, 1976. Some passages from the article and some illustrations from the book reappear in these chapters. I wish to thank the editors of that journal and the Delegates of Oxford University Press for permission to make further use of these materials and ideas.

I am grateful to James B. Brady, Jorge J. E. Gracia, Peter Hare, John Kearns, Vernon Perry, and John Sutula for commenting on various parts of earlier drafts. Of course, they are not responsible for remaining deficiencies, or for any of the views expressed.

I also wish to thank the National Endowment for the Humanities for supporting my work on this book.

Buffalo, New York   THOMAS D. PERRY

(Professor Perry had completed the manuscript of this book before his death in 1982. It appears here with a few minor revisions made by Kenneth Barber. Margaret Holland compiled the index of proper names, Reidel compiled the subject index, and Jorge J. E. Gracia took care of the publication arrangements.)

PART ONE

CHAPTER 1

FOUR STAGES OF REFLECTION

Most of the great philosophers have used analytical techniques in at least some of their major works, a fact we may be inclined to overlook if we are mainly interested in 19th-century romantic philosophy and its most prominent descendants, Existentialism and Marxism. Writers of the latter schools sometimes suggest that, in attempting to reason coolly and carefully on small or middlesized topics, the analytic philosophers of today have really abandoned philosophy for some other kind of activity. In refusing to engage in large historical speculations or to say whether human existence can be justified, they have allegedly given up the true vocation of the philosopher. But if we run down the list of most famous names beginning with Plato, we find that thinkers like Hegel, Kierkegaard, the early Marx, and Heidegger are really exceptions to the rule, for their great speculative forerunners were powerful analysts as well. Not that the four authors mentioned fail to "'analyze ideas"; indeed they offer very ambitious analyses. But their work is more often brilliantly suggestive than intellectually convincing or even reasonably clear. This is bound to be our estimate if we compare their reasoning with that of Plato's later dialogues, for example, or with the most famous works of Aristotle, Aquinas, Hume, or Kant. So in some sense of the phrase, analytic philosophy has had a distinguished career reaching back two and a third millenia. But in this book we shall only be concerned with a new phase of that career which began in the present century in reaction to romanticism and reached maturity by about the nineteen-fifties.

During the fifties many writers spoke of a "revolution" which had taken place in philosophy. It is possible to view that revolution from two rather different perspectives, and it should be useful for our purposes to do so. The first perspective has a longer time frame, involves fewer technicalities, and connects recent philosophy with older traditions in a more direct way. We shall attempt to develop it in Part One. Here we examine mid-century philosophy not to contrast its goals and methods with those of a generation earlier, but to notice an even more fundamental

3

contrast with some typical attitudes of the philosophers of former centuries. In Part Two we then approach the second perspective by looking at the analytic philosophy of the first quarter of this century. We notice how, despite its logical innovations and sympathy with natural science, it is very much a half-way house between the speculative tradition and mid-century thought. Then we look at the "short frame" revolution by examining some of the great changes that occurred during the period from 1930 to 1950 or thereabouts. More recent developments are considered in the remaining two chapters of Part Two and in the three chapters of the concluding Part.

How does our first perspective "connect" recent philosophy with the speculative tradition while sharply contrasting the two? The answer is that they share certain general "approaches" or "methods," but that there has been a fundamental shift of emphasis in the use of these methods. In the present chapter we shall give a kind of schematic outline which will enable us to say, in a preliminary way, what the change of emphasis was. Then in Chapters 2 and 3 we shall attempt to illustrate that change by discussing a few famous arguments produced by the philosophers who brought it to completion.

1. METAPHYSICAL PROBLEMS AND THEORIES

Before giving our scheme of methods we need to say something about the sorts of problems to which philosophical methods are addressed. The more fundamental and famous problems of philosophy are all metaphysical, which is to say they pertain to the most basic notions we humans use to interpret and cope with the world: the notions of space, time, matter, motion, cause, mind, self, subject and object, other selves, action, responsibility, and some others. These notions are "metaphysical" in the traditional sense (which is not quite exact etymologically) that they are the terms in which our knowledge of *nature*, including human nature, must be expressed *whatever* the content of that knowledge, whatever nature may be found to be like. Thus whatever sorts of material objects the world may contain, it seems that they will have to have spatial and temporal dimensions; whatever laws of matter there may be, it seems that they will have to be laws of cause and effect; whatever the content of our experiences may be, it seems that they must have both subjective and objective aspects, a self which is having the experience and an object of the experience; whatever rules may organize our social world, it seems that we must be responsible for our actions in one way or another. To reflect on these seemingly obvious facts is to reflect metaphysically; it is to think *about* such basic notions rather than to use them, as we do in most of our waking hours. In such reflection we may begin to imagine that we have gained "metaphysical knowledge": knowledge of the essential or necessary features of reality in general (its necessary spatiality, temporality, materiality, and so on), and of the essential features of human existence (our personality, agency, responsibility, and so on).

If we think about these notions very long, however, we will probably become puzzled. We will find in them, or seem to find in them, various paradoxes which we do not know how to clear up, contradictions which we do not know how to avoid. Then we may begin to doubt whether they do correspond to *necessary* features of reality, or indeed to any real features at all. For example, we seem to know that a rapidly moving object can overtake an object moving very slowly. But when we reason carefully about the infinite divisibility of space and time, as in the puzzle of the tortoise and the hare, this seems logically impossible; indeed all motion then seems to be impossible. Thus various of our ideas about space, time, and motion seem to conflict with one another. Or to take another example, the problem of perception and the physical world, we may begin to wonder whether we really have knowledge of anything but our own sensations and thoughts inasmuch as *they* are the only things of which we are immediately aware. We cannot observe the relations in which they stand to objects outside our mind, or even prove that there are such objects. So perhaps there is something wrong with our ordinary notions of perception. Or again, in the problem of other minds, we may wonder whether we really *know* that other human bodies are inhabited by selves; after all, one's usual assumption to this effect is only based on a single observed case of such inhabitation, one's own. Again, in the mind-body problem, it seems obvious that the body affects the mind, as when I feel a pin prick, and that the mind affects the body, as when I decide to take a drink of water and do so. But how is this possible, after all, since the mind has no physical characteristics with which to produce physical occurrences, and the body has *only* physical characteristics with which to produce mental effects? Perhaps common sense is wrong in thinking that such dissimilar things do interact; or perhaps it is wrong, after all, in thinking that they are so dissimilar. Or again, in the problem of determinism, we may begin to wonder whether anyone is ever really responsible for what he or she has done. For it seems that human action, like everything else in the world, is determined by causes, and therefore that a person could never have acted otherwise than he or she did act. So here our common-sense notions of cause and responsibility seem to be at war.

After reflecting on such problems, philosophers have sometimes concluded that one or more common-sense notions cannot be retained if we are to think consistently. Many have held, for example, that the concept of responsibility is essentially mythical, that its usefulness is a function of our ignorance: that the more we learn about the cause of behavior the fewer are the types of behavior as to which we can even go on pretending that we are responsible. They believe they have discovered this startling fact which shows that the world of human relations is vastly different from what common sense takes it to be. Indeed their position has sweeping consequences for our understanding of the nonhuman world as well. If they are correct the notion of *anything* happening which might not have happened must be given up, and so must the notion of something not happening which might have happened.

Let us call such a position a metaphysical theory. The word "theory" is appropriate because a doctrine is being put forth which claims to tell us something true about the world which we cannot observe directly or easily, but which we can come to know about through reasoning. Whereas the scientific theorist reasons from observable events to their probable unobserved causes, the metaphysical theorist reasons from the alleged inconsistency of common-sense ideas to general facts about reality which common sense fails to appreciate because of the defective terms in which we think. Or to be a bit more precise, he reasons from the alleged inconsistency of our beliefs and from certain other considerations allegedly indicating which of the inconsistent beliefs should be retained and which should be given up. Let us also say that a "metaphysical system" consists of one or more metaphysical theories plus whatever parts of common sense the philosopher in question may think are salvageable, all arranged in as neat a package as he can tie together. To illustrate this, consider a philosopher who is a reductive materialist in the mind-body problem; that is, one who explains the apparent interaction of mind and matter by arguing that all mind is really a form of matter. In the problem of determinism he will probably want to deny that we are ever responsible, and if so he will also reject the common assumption that some moral opinions are true while others are false. With respect to the problem of perception and the physical world he will probably hold that sensations and thoughts are physical events in the brain which are themselves very unlike the objects in the environment that impinge on our sense organs to produce them. In other words, he will deny that the sensed qualities of objects are "real." While the position one takes on a metaphysical problem will not usually *force* one to take a certain position on another metaphysical problem, it may well make a given position on the other problem more attractive than some of its competitors. Any metaphysician will argue that his system taken as a whole lends further support to the arguments he has given for the choices he made in the separate problems. He will claim that our thinking on these problems has now been composed into a worldview that is more coherent or "illuminating" than any of its rivals.

It is obvious that any system which takes a position sharply contrary to common sense on even one or two of the foregoing metaphysical problems will present us with a world view radically different from the one we had before turning to philosophy. According to intellectual taste, we may find such a view an exciting revelation or merely "news from nowhere." But if we claim to be intellectually reflective we will need to have some well considered reasons for our attitude, whichever it is. As we shall see later on, recent analytic philosophers have some rather impressive reasons for taking the latter attitude towards all metaphysical systems in our sense of the phrase. But as we shall also discover, this does not mean that they are opposed to metaphysical studies of every kind.

2. THE FOUR STAGES DESCRIBED

Let us now outline four different approaches that one may take to a problem of the kind described in the preceding section. This will give us a scheme, as I said, for understanding the great change that had come over philosophy by the middle of this century from what it had been in former centuries. We shall first state these four approaches in general terms and then go on to illustrate them in the next section. After that we shall indicate which of them came to take precedence over the others. We shall then be in position to put them to more specific use in subsequent chapters.

It seems that we can have a philosophical problem without being quite aware of the fact. We may be vaguely troubled in a way that would turn out to correspond with one or another of the problems mentioned above if we could only bring our troubled thoughts into clear view. We may be plagued by the feeling, for example, that contrary to John Donne's famous phrase each person really is an island; that no one over makes contact with another human soul. If we could put our reason for this feeling into words, we might come up with something fairly close to the problem of other minds, or rather to one of the problems often grouped under that label. We might say that each person's inner life is inevitably private to himself; that we are forever limited to *guessing* about the content of another's mind (assuming that other people do have minds, which is another problem referred to earlier); that although we may sometimes guess correctly, we can only *infer* and never *know*; we can never directly observe or come in contact with another person's thoughts or feelings.

Once we are definitely aware of our problem we can probably say what it is at least that well, which is comparable to the little sketches of problems that I gave a few pages back. But if we want to tackle the problem and try to solve it, or perhaps use it in metaphysical speculation, we must formulate it more carefully. When we do so we will find that it can usually be presented in the form of a skeptical argument which we do not know how to refute. The skeptic, who is more often an imaginary opponent or personage of dialectic than a real philosopher, constructs a formidable argument from plausible premises leading to a conclusion which denies something we thought we knew beyond question. A doubt – at least a "philosophical" doubt if not a real concern – is thus raised as to whether we really do have knowledge of the world through our senses, or whether we really are responsible for our actions, and so on. Or perhaps the problem-generating argument will not deny realities known to common sense but will add to them in ways that seem equally dubious. Thus it may claim, hyper-realistically, that abstractions like goodness or triangularity have a real existence over and above the particular things which are good or triangular. Taking a cue from the character Socrates in Plato's middle dialogues, the argument may insist that these and many other abstractions or "Forms" are even *more* real than the particular things we perceive with our senses, things which exemplify these Forms only imperfectly. But odd and discomfiting as we may find the skeptical or hyper-realistic conclusion, we are at a loss to point out any flaws in the premises from which the argument proceeds, or in the reasoning by which it claims to reach that conclusion.

In order to avoid complex formulations, let us state our four approaches solely in terms of skeptical arguments. As I have said, most of the traditional problems of philosophy seem to be generated by arguments of this kind. But we shall see in Chapters 5, 6, and 7 how these same approaches can be applied to hyper-realist arguments, and indeed to various other types of metaphysical problems and theories.

The FIRST way in which we might respond to a philosophical problem is simply to reject the soundness of the skeptic's argument on the ground that the premises or the reasoning, or both, are less certain than the common-sense belief which the conclusion denies. At this stage of reflection we do not claim to be able to show in any specific way *how* one or more of the premises are false, or *what* error occurs in the reasoning. The premises may be obvious truisms or well known facts, and we may already have scrutinized the reasoning and found nothing to challenge. Or one of the premises may not be a known truth but the conclusion of some other philosophical argument, as in the illustration to be given in the next section. If so, inquiry into the truth of that premise would be reflection on a different and prior philosophical problem. As far as this FIRST approach to the problem at hand is concerned, we content ourselves with saying that there *must* be something wrong with the premises or reasoning or both, though we do not know exactly what. This is not to be confused with dismissing the problem for no reason at all, or because it "strikes use as silly." After all, we seem to *know* that the skeptic's conclusion is false, and we also know that it is possible for an argument to be unsound even though no one has yet explained just how it is unsound.

In a SECOND stage of reflection we try to explain how we do know the sorts of things which the skeptic's argument claims to show that we cannot know or do not know. We try, for example, to explain how we can know about material objects in the "external world," and not merely about our own sensations and ideas. Or we try to show how we can know that there are other minds and not just "behavior" of other human bodies. At this stage, we pretty well accept the problem on the skeptic's own terms and try to solve it on those terms. That is, we try to show how to avoid the skeptical conclusion and justify the sort of knowledge which is under attack by overcoming the obstacles which the skeptic raises. We concede that they are real obstacles and not mere confusions to be exposed as such and brushed aside. We try to explain why, in spite of these obstacles, the skeptic's conclusion is avoidable because of some faulty inference late in his argument, or because of some crucial consideration which he had overlooked.

At a THIRD stage of reflection, to which we may be forced to proceed after repeated failures at the second, we do try to show that the skeptic's whole argument trades on some confusion or distortion of ideas which our earlier scrutiny failed to detect. We attempt to demonstrate that when this elusive error is pointed out and fully understood, his whole argument collapses and the problem vanishes, leaving our common-sense notions and beliefs undisturbed.

If our efforts at the second and third stages are unavailing, we may wish to conclude that the solution is to be found only at a FOURTH stage. Here we are finally obliged to admit that the impact of the skeptic's argument cannot be wholly avoided, that it manages to exploit a real inconsistency or other serious inadequacy in our basic notions and beliefs, our kit of tools for thinking. We therefore go on to propose a correction of those notions or beliefs in order to have a coherent scheme of thought, or one that is otherwise more adequate for our needs. But the new scheme should probably stay as close as possible to the old. If it departs too radically, it can hardly count as a solution to the problem. That is, if it helps us avoid the factually absurd conclusion of the skeptic's argument only at the price of accepting some other great affront to common sense, it will not be of much use to us. We will want to continue looking for a more economical, less revolutionary correction of the existing scheme.

I am not suggesting that we must follow the above sequence if we are ever to make progress with a philosophical problem. Many a philosopher has gained valuable insights while trying to do just one of these things without even thinking of the others. But one could deliberately follow this sequence in successive attempts to solve a philosophical problem, and it is a natural sequence for describing these different approaches. That may be a good enough reason to call them "stages" of philosophical reflection, as we shall continue to do, and we shall actually find the second and third approaches occurring in that order in the classic work to which we now turn.

3. THE FOUR STAGES ILLUSTRATED

Every philosophy student learns that George Berkeley (1685–1753) extended John Locke's critique of the so-called "secondary" qualities of objects to cover the "primary" qualities as well. Locke (1632–1704) had argued that the color, sound, warmth or coldness, taste, and smell of an object exist only as "ideas in the mind," although their *causes* exist outside the mind in the physical properties of the object – its size, shape, weight, microscopic surface structure, motion – and in the physical characteristics of the environment and of our sense organs, such as the presence of light and the sensitiveness of our eyes to light reflected by surfaces. Locke accordingly referred to the mentioned physical properties as "primary" qualities, meaning objective qualities, while those properties which I listed first were called "secondary" or subjective. But Berkeley went on to maintain that all our "sensible ideas" of these so-called primary qualities are also subjective. That is, he argued that there is no reason to suppose that our sensations of the size, shape, rate of motion, or weight of an object correspond with characteristics that exist independently of those sensations. We need not give a full summary of his arguments. It will be sufficient for our purposes to mention the three most important of them.

(1) The sensed qualities of an object *vary with the perceiver and the conditions of perception*, and this leads to logical inconsistencies if we locate such qualities in an external object rather than in the mind of the perceiver. For example, a room will seem comfortably warm to one person and chilly to another; but the air cannot *be* both warm and not warm. An object may look yellow to a person suffering from jaundice, and pale blue to someone else; but it cannot be both yellow and not yellow. We avoid the contradiction by concluding that the warmth and chilliness ex-

ist only in separate minds, as do the yellowness and blueness. (2) There is no reason to think that the sweetness or loudness of a perceived object, for example, could exist *in an unthinking substance*, for after all these are sensible *ideas*, mental contents. The same must be said about all the sensible qualities, both "primary" and "secondary." It will be replied in defense of Locke's position that an object will have an absolute size, shape, velocity or weight even if our sensations of its size, shape, and so on vary with the perceiver, and exist only in the mind. But to this Berkeley replies with (3) his *critique of abstractions*, claiming that the notion of absolute extension is a bogus idea. It is the idea of "extension in general," which we allegedly abstract from all the particular sizes or shapes or distances that we observe or imagine. Berkeley argues that we cannot really form a clear idea to go with these words. All extensions that we can actually imagine are those of particular things. And he also points out that all the values we obtain in measuring objects depend upon our perception of particular extended things, for example our yardstick, and hence upon our perception of the so-called secondary qualities, such as the visible qualities of the yardstick and the object we are using it to measure.

Now we can state a skeptical argument to generate the philosophical problem which we are going to use in our illustration. "None of our ideas of the so-called primary qualities of objects, and none of our ideas of the so-called secondary qualities resemble characteristics which objects really have, as shown by reasons (1), (2), and (3). But our ideas of these qualities are the only ideas of objects and their characteristics which we possess. Therefore, we have no knowledge of objects outside our minds; we only have knowledge of our own sensations and ideas." The problem can be formulated this way after we have read about a third of Berkeley's work *Three Dialogues between Hylas and Philonous*,* and it confronts both characters in the dialogue. Hylas has been led by Philonous from naive realism concerning the qualities of objects to a position like Locke's, and he has then been forced to give up that position as well. (Philonous is Berkeley's spokesman.) Neither character is a skeptic about our knowledge of objects and the world around us. They have been

---

* Bibliographical references and other Notes are collected at the end of the book. The pertinent notes should be read after each numbered section of the text.

debating the issue as to which of them will be able to avoid skepticism – Hylas, who believes that "material substances" exist outside our minds, or Philonous, who denies this. The way we characterized many philosophical problems in the preceding section is thus illustrated; skepticism is not represented as a doctrine that someone seriously accepts, but as a disturbing logical possibility, a threat to the foundations of common sense which must be faced up to and defeated.

While neither Hylas nor Philonous makes the FIRST type of response described in the last section, Hylas seems at times to be on the brink of it, and he might plausibly have taken this line and insisted upon it. He might have said that it is far less doubtful that we do have knowledge of objects than that (1), (2), and (3) are correct. He might have claimed that the alleged inconsistency of locating sensed qualities in objects, and the assumption that the mental content of sensation cannot be distinguished from its objective referent, are debatable theses after all, and that the alleged emptiness of abstract words and phrases is also highly debatable. If (1), (2), and (3) really do entail that we have no knowledge of objects, then so much the worse for one or more of them since it is *far* less debatable, if not absolutely certain, that we do have such knowledge. Theoretically, Philonous might also have responded this way, being a professed anti-skeptic. But for dramatic and dialectical reasons he could not, since he is the one who had just argued for (1), (2), and (3). We draw the skeptic's premises but not his skeptical conclusion from Philonous's arguments up to this point in the *Dialogues*.

What Hylas actually does is attempt to show how we do have knowledge of objects, even though he is now convinced that the skeptic's premises are true. (Or at least he admits that all his criticisms of them have been effectively answered.) Thus he takes our SECOND approach to the problem, and he does so in three distinct arguments. First he appeals to Locke's idea of a "material substratum." He argues that although we cannot perceive a material substance underlying and producing the sensed qualities of an object, we need to suppose its existence in order to explain the order and coherence of our sensations. The hypothesis is highly confirmed, and we may therefore claim to know that there are material substances existing outside the mind even if what (1), (2), and (3) say about the subjective character of all the *sensed* properties of objects is true. And we may also claim to know a great deal about such

objects through their effects upon us and their effects upon other
objects.

Philonous demolishes this argument by forcing Hylas to admit that he
really has no clear idea in mind when he speaks of a material substratum.
(I shall not summarize their reasoning on this point.) Hylas must
therefore admit that the hypothesis lacks any definite meaning. So next
he appeals to the idea of distance, claiming that we directly see the
distance of objects: their "outness" from our minds as he puts it. But
Philonous proceeds to convince him by several arguments that distance
is not properly a sensible quality but a learned sequence or order of
transformation among the sensible qualities of objects, all of which
qualities exist only in the mind in view of (1), (2), and (3).

After that Hylas plays his last important card, the "representative"
theory of perception. This theory concedes to the skeptic that the only
thing of which we have *immediate* knowledge is our own ideas, but it
holds that "real things or external objects [are] perceived by the media-
tion of ideas, which are their images and representatives." Philonous
then attacks this theory by pointing out that one thing cannot serve as
our image or representation of something else where the latter is a kind
of thing which we *never* directly observe. There is more to this argument,
but again it is not our concern to give a full summary. It is enough to
point out how these three arguments of Hylas all illustrate our second
stage of reflection on a philosophical problem. They all accept the skeptic's reasoning to the effect that we can have immediate knowledge only
of our own ideas; they all admit that it is at first difficult to see how we
can get beyond such knowledge to knowledge of external objects; and
they all attempt to overcome that difficulty rather than claiming that it
is a mere confusion. They attempt to show that the skeptic's conclusion
does not follow, after all, from the many true points he has made.

Philonous's solution (and Berkeley's) is that there is no real problem
of getting past our sensations and ideas in order to have knowledge of
objects and the world. For he holds that objects just *are* collections of
sensations. The table before me consists of the various sensible qualities
which I now perceive it as having, plus other qualities which I would
perceive it as having under altered conditions of perception. There is no
need to postulate an experience-transcending, unintelligible "substance"
which exists over and above these sensations.

Two aspects of this attempted solution show how it exemplifies our THIRD stage. First, it points out that the skeptic's argument assumes throughout that there is such a problem of getting past our sensations and ideas if we are to have knowledge of objects, an assumption which Hylas also accepts without challenge when he argues as above. Philonous-Berkeley claims that this is a false assumption and a fundamental misconception because what we *commonly mean* by an object is *nothing other* than a pattern of experience of a certain kind. The second and closely related aspect is Berkeley's claim that as soon as we recognize that we are making such an assumption, and proceed to reject it, the problem vanishes and common sense is left undisturbed. For he repeatedly insists that his theory of objects (that an object exists only if it is "perceived," i.e. sensed or thought of) is no real departure from what everyone commonly thinks. He claims that it merely clarifies common sense and refutes the *philosophical* doctrine of the unobservable substratum. Notice how this illustration underscores the distinction between stage two and stage three, a distinction which may have seemed unreal or unimportant because at both stages one attempts to explain why the skeptic's argument fails to prove its conclusion. To say that at stage two we try to solve the problem "on the skeptic's own terms" means that we accept practically all of his reasoning *except* the conclusion, and then look around desperately for ways to avoid it. But at stage three we attack some unexpressed assumption which underlies the whole argument or some major part of it.

Berkeley's alleged solution will not be a *successful* effort at stage three, however, if he really departs significatly from common sense. He probably does, and we shall briefly explain how. The explanation will be sketchy but it will serve its only purpose here, which is to lay some groundwork for a brief illustration of stage FOUR.

It is common sense that real objects, as distinguished from imaginary or hallucinatory objects, continue to exist when no human or other animal is perceiving them, in Berkeley's broad sense of "perceiving" mentioned above. And it is part of Berkeley's solution that they are perceived by God in these intervals, just as God (according to Berkeley) is the cause of the ideas we have whenever we do sense or think about objects. He gives reasons why God must be the cause of those ideas which we do not seem to produce by ourselves. These reasons are not impressive, but let us refer to a different trouble that can be stated as follows. Give Berkeley his God and his story of how the tree in the quad manages to exist when no one *but* God is perceiving that tree. It is still common sense that the tree *would* go on existing if no one, including God, *were* perceiving it. To be sure, many eighteenth-century Englishmen and Anglo-Irishmen like Bishop Berkeley believed that God *always* is perceiving everything that exists, a point on which he explicitly relies. (The Book of Common Prayer says that God is "the Maker, and Preserver of all things.") But if we asked people then or now whether trees unperceived by men or animals would exist if God did not exist or were not perceiving them, most would no doubt have replied, or would now reply, "Of course! What an odd question!" The only exceptions would be people who had come to embrace as literal truth the theological doctrine that God not only created the world and everything in it but sustains the world and each thing at each moment by the attentive exercise of his power, and that without such attention the world (or perhaps just the tree in the quad, if he neglected to support *it*) would cease to exist. Far from believing this doctrine, most people on earth during the past few centuries probably never heard of it, and it is certainly contrary to what hundreds of millions of polytheists and atheists have believed. So it can hardly claim to be a common-sense belief, something nearly everyone takes for granted as obvious.

No one who thinks this criticism is sound will be able to accept Berkeley's account as a successful stage-three solution to our problem. But such a person might still wish to maintain that Berkeley's account is nevertheless *the* solution. He might think there is no other choice if we are to escape the skeptic's factually absurd conclusion. This neo-Berkeleyan might argue as follows. (1) We surely do have knowledge of objects that exist independently of human or animal perceptions of them. But (2) we have shown that there is no reason to think that anything but minds and their thought exist. Therefore, (3) God must exist to support with his thoughts the existence of real objects otherwise unthought of, and we must accept this even if it does force a revision of the common-sense assumption referred to in the last paragraph. Our neo-Berkeleyan would add that this is a small price to pay in order to avoid both the conclusion that objects pop in and out of existence with our perceptions of them, and the conclusion that we have no knowledge of objects.

That would be an extremely weak argument because the second step is highly doubtful. But it does illustrate stage FOUR. Notice also that it illustrates two features of a metaphysical theory in our sense of the term. It claims to discover a new way of thinking which we must use in place of older ways if we are to think coherently or adequately. And it claims to disclose a startling general fact about reality: the dependence of each finite thing on God's continuing creative attention.

In Sections 7 and 8 we shall discuss some thoughts that recent analytic philosophers have had on this same general problem of philosophy, including an attempt to solve it at stage THREE.

4. A CHANGE OF EMPHASIS

We can now use our scheme of approaches or stages to describe very broadly the change that philosophy had undergone by the middle of the twentieth century, although we shall hardly be able to appreciate the revolutionary force of this change until we consider some illustrations in the next two chapters.

From the seventeenth century until well into the twentieth, Western philosophical thought was predominantly carried on in the second stage and, somewhat less clearly, in the fourth stage. Metaphysical problems were taken very seriously since it was considered a distinct possibility that the skeptic's conclusion could not be avoided, at least not without some important reinterpretation of human experience, some striking new outlook on the world arrived at through the critical re-examination and reconstruction of basic notions. Philosophers would try hard to escape from the skeptic's toils (stage two), but there was never a consensus that anyone had succeeded in that way, and many a thinker would go on to propose such a reconstruction (stage four). From the time of René Descartes (1596–1650) through the career of the distinguished American philosopher C. I. Lewis (1883–1964), some dozens of famous thinkers and hundreds of lesser known people have tried unsuccessfully to devise such escapes in the problem of perception and the physical world, which is perhaps the central problem of modern European philosophy. In light of this failure, and similar failures in other problems, many philosophers have constructed metaphysical systems which intentionally or unintentionally revise some of our fundamental concepts. One could mention the system of Spinoza (1632–1677), who held that there is really only one substance, one real thing as distinguished from the attributes of a thing; or the system of Malebranche (1638–1715), who held that mind and matter do not interact at all; or the system of Hegel (1770–1831), who held that all reality is a great mind getting to know itself better, a process in which the distinction between subject and object is finally abolished; or the philosophy of Bradley (1846–1924), who held that all our basic notions are full of contradictions.

It must be admitted that metaphysical theorists of the past were often not *clearly* engaged in stage four work; that is to say, *intentional* revision of concepts *to solve a problem* or problems. Some were more concerned to express their new vision of reality (Hegel) or to bemoan our alleged inability to know reality (Bradley) than to offer clear solutions to specific metaphysical problems. Others, who did try to solve problems, and with reasonably clear arguments (Berkeley), did not intend to depart from common sense when doing so. It may therefore appear that in distinguishing stage four we are only pointing to a *possible* approach to metaphysical problems which no philosopher has actually taken. But in fact the most famous theory in the history of modern philosophy is a rather clear illustration of stage four. Immanuel Kant (1724–1804) was trying to solve specific metaphysical problems (in our sense given in Section 1) which had been formulated by David Hume (1711–1776) and others. These included the problem of perception and the physical world, the problem of personal identity, the problem of induction and causal necessity, the problem of our *a priori* knowledge of the properties of space in Geometry, and several others. To solve them he offered one fundamental correction of common sense, a "Copernican revolution in philosophy" as he called it. According to this metaphysical theory (again in our sense of *that* term), the main structural features of "nature" – of the world as it is understandable by human beings – are determined by the structure of the mind himself, so that we can never know objects "as they are in themselves." He argued that we must give up the ordinary assumption that space and time, cause and effect, and so on, are features of reality that exist quite independently of our perceptions.

One likely reason why the history of philosophy does not illustrate the fourth stage as clearly or as often as it does the second is that traditional metaphysicians have usually not decided whether they meant to spell out the picture of reality which is already embedded in common thought, or to show how that picture must be revised to make it coherent or adequate. Perhaps this is due to their tendency to use the "material mode" of speech rather than the "formal mode," which is twentieth-century jargon for, respectively, (1) talk about reality, and (2) talk about the *language* we use to talk about reality. They were mainly attempting to spy out the most general features of the world rather than to construct a consistent set of basic beliefs and language conventions — a consistent conceptual scheme, as we would now say. Understandably then, it did not usually strike them as important to decide whether they were revising or merely clarifying the conceptual scheme humans already possess.

When we come to the middle of the present century, we find that the second and fourth stages have receded into the background, especially in the work of the most influential authors. Much greater emphasis is placed on stage one, which was rarely used in earlier philosophy, and especially on stage three. The following pattern of thought occurs again and again: stage one quickly prepares the way for stage three where most work on philosophical problems is then carried on. This change of emphasis can be understood most readily, perhaps, if we focus on the point that the skeptic's toils are not taken seriously *except* as a puzzle for stage three solution. Because we surely *know* his conclusion is false, and because his argument looks all right on the surface (there would be no problem otherwise), we do not expect to find the trouble in some technical error of reasoning but in an underlying misconception or confusion which vitiates his argument as a whole. Since we do *not* accept practically everything in the skeptical argument *but* the conclusion, we never enter those toils; hence we never find ourselves desperately casting about for ways to escape from them, whether through epistemological theories at stage two or metaphysical theories at stage four. Instead of thinking in the skeptic's own terms we try to uncover that hidden misconception or confusion. We hope to dispose of the problem not by solving it but by "dissolving" it, as the point was often expressed. When and if we finally see throught the skeptic's confusion (and thereby overcome our own confusion), the problem will "vanish." That is, even though no one has been able to explain how we cán avoid the skeptic's conclusion after accepting his premises and most of his reasoning, we will then realize why it was wholly unnecessary to give such an explanation.

Work at stage three was considered important because if it reaches its goal it not only gets rid of some tough old intellectual puzzle, at least in one formulation; it also clarifies and maps our concepts and basic beliefs in a way they never were clarified and mapped before. Discovering the skeptic's subtle distortions and tacit misanalogies cannot help but give us a better understanding of the proper shape and fit of our ideas. As in other studies, pathology was expected to give instruction in normal functioning.

This brief characterization of analytic philosophy at mid-century is of course very sketchy. It tells us little or nothing about how or why such a change occurred, or whether it represents real progress in philosophy. These are questions to be pursued in the next two chapters.

CHAPTER 2

DEFENDING COMMON SENSE

In order to illustrate the emergence of the "ONE and THREE" pattern, we shall first discuss an article, famous among philosophers, that was published by G. E. Moore in the middle nineteen-twenties. Moore's piece makes certain assertions that obviously belong to stage one of our scheme, and it also foreshadows the later emphasis of stage three without clearly exemplifying that stage. We shall then give a clearer illustration of stage three from a well known argument by Ludwig Wittgenstein. Although Wittgenstein was teaching in this vein from the early thirties onward, his best known stage-three writings, the *Philosophical Investigations*, were not published until 1953, after which they became the single greatest force in the transformation of philosophy on both sides of the Atlantic. Our illustration will be drawn from that work.

5. MOORE ON COMMON SENSE

To say that Moore's article, 'A Defense of Common Sense,' was highly original would almost be an understatement. The more traditional thinkers whose work appeared with it in a pair of co-operative volumes called *Contemporary British Philosophy* (First and Second Series) must have found it rather absurd if they could stand to read through it. Today that is still the reaction of most people encountering it for the first time. This is partly due to unfamiliarity with its methodic approach. Elementary philosophy is still taught in the traditional idiom of stage-two epistemology and stage-four metaphysics, while Moore's article, a stage-one classic, is likely to be among the first things we read when moving on to contemporary work. Another reason is its dogmatic format in which Moore for the most part simply states his opinions without arguing for them. But the really outrageous quality of the piece results from Moore's subjecting his opponents, and any reader who may symphatize with them, to a most unsettling stage-one *attack*. He is not content to list his opinions and remark that many philosophers have held theories incompatible with them, although he does both of these things. He also says he *knows* these opinions are true, that we all know they are true, that even philosophers holding those incompatible theories know, at least when they are not philosophizing, that opinions like Moore's are true.

I say that Moore's article is unsettling because any honest reader will feel great pressure to admit that Moore's opinions in the relevant section of the article (the first) are certainly true and known to be true by all normal persons. What are they? Well, things like the following (I abbreviate Moore's list). There is a certain body, namely Moore's body, which was born some time ago and has existed ever since on or near the surface of the earth; that during all that time there have been many bodies located here and there in space, sometimes in contact with Moore's body; that there are also other human bodies; that the earth existed for many years before Moore's body was born; that Moore is a human being, and has had many thoughts, dreams, imaginings, feelings, and other experiences, including awareness of his own body and many other bodies, both animate and inanimate; that very many other bodies have also been the bodies of human beings who have had mental experiences of many kinds. Not only does Moore think he knows these things with certainty, but he also claims to know that, of the great many human beings who have existed, most though not all of them have at various times in the past known a great many things closely similar to the statements in the foregoing list.

Why do I say that readers will feel *pressure* to admit they know such things? Will we not all simply agree to them straight off? Many of us will, but I am thinking especially of philosophers. As we saw in Chapter 1, philosophers have often found common sense puzzling and partly unacceptable. To such readers it may seem that Moore, a philosopher, is refusing to play by the rules when he simply *asserts* the truth of the foregoing common-sense beliefs and says they refute all philosophical theories in conflict with them. Yet, are we not forced to admit that we all do know the things Moore says we know? If we have some favorite theory which seems to deny or question one or more of these truisms, are we not obliged to give it up if we cannot show that it is really compatible with them?

Let us take a closer look at one of the ways in which Moore makes his point. He notes that the statements in his list presuppose that there are such things as bodies, selves, space, and time. And he reports that some philosophers have undertaken to show that one or more statements in the list are false because they entail a contradiction. He gives no example of this, but let us supply one from our discussion in Chapter 1. A philosopher may argue that our beliefs about bodies, space, and time are inconsistent because they entail both that a hare can catch a tortoise and that it cannot. Now Moore thinks he has a conclusive proof that all such arguments are incorrect, that none of the statements in his list entail a contradiction. The proof is this: Every statement in the list is true; no true statement can entail a contradiction (nor can any combination of true statements, he might have added); therefore no statement (or conjunction of statements) in the list entails a contradiction. People who know some traditional philosophy but to whom Moore is brand new will invariably show great contempt for this proof, which they regard as pure question begging and empty dogmatism. Their reaction is understandable, but Moore's proof does not beg the question in any objectionable way, as we shall see, and his dogmatism is far from empty or silly.

Question begging is harmful when we *surreptitiously* assume the very thing we are claiming to establish by arrangement, or when we do so *inadvertently* but unobtrusively. No one will be taken in by *obvious* question begging as in the following example. "God exists because it says so in the Bible, which is the word of God, who never lies." Of course, if someone is so lacking in intellect as to present such an argument seriously, we ought to try to explain to *him* why it is worthless. But Moore, in begging the question so obviously as he does, is not the sort of person who needs this service. What is his point, then, in assuming statement S (the statement "Every statement in my list is true") when the very issue between Moore and those who would claim to derive a contradiction from statements in the list is, precisely, whether S is true? Would it not be better for Moore to explain if he can where their derivations go wrong, showing the specific errors of reasoning they commit? Well, that would no doubt be interesting and valuable if it could be done, but there is still a great point to Moore's insistence that every item in the list is true, and that every such derivation *must* therefore be unsound. For the items of knowledge in his list seem to be the sorts of things we certainly know if we know anything at all, and the statements used to express them seem to be the sorts of statements we clearly understand if there are any statements we clearly understand. The premises of any argument seeking to show their falsity, whether by deducing a contradiction from them or by other means, cannot possibly be more certain than they are, and such premises are likely to be a good deal less certain. There may also be room for error or uncertainty in the reasoning which purports to take us by valid steps from those premises, whatever they are, to the conclusion that some statement in Moore's list is false. But surely there is no possibility of error or uncertainty as far as the latter statements are concerned. Or at least Moore is being very reasonable when he says that, in his opinion, he certainly does know them to be true. So he is also being very reasonable when he says "It seems to me I have an absolutely conclusive argument" that none of them entails a contradiction.

Now such a defense of Moore will undoubtedly provoke another objection, an objection which can be directed to stage-one reasoning generally. This is the complaint that it would "justify" something which is obviously unjustifiable, namely, the disregard of future evidence or arguments against things one claims to know. We will be in a better position to consider this complaint towards the end of the next chapter. It has to be answered, and I believe we only begin to appreciate the full force of stage one in the basic problems of philosophy when we see how it probably can be answered.

Moore does not tell us who those philosophers are who have held opinions contrary to his truisms, but one readily imagines that he had Berkeley in mind among others, and he does mention Berkeley in a later part of the article. Did Berkeley deny anything in Moore's list, so that he is open to this kind of refutation? A defender of Berkeley will argue that he did not; that he never said or implied that there are no bodies existing in space and time; and that he certainly never denied that there are selves and experiences. It was only a philosophical theory about matter (Locke's material substratum) that Berkeley denied. He never questioned that there are material bodies in the everyday sense of "material" and "body": real things that we can see and touch and knock about. To be sure, he did have a surprising metaphysical theory of his own as to their ultimate nature, and as to the ultimate nature of space and time, namely, that they are all patterns of perceptions and possible perceptions.

Such a defense of Berkeley is rather shaky, however. There is good reason to hold that Berkeley's theory really is incompatible with statements in Moore's list and is therefore false if everything in the list is true. Moore takes pains to explain that in making the statements in the list he is using words just as they are normally used, and hence that philosophers who give extraordinary meanings to their words may very well be disagreeing with him even though they seem to be saying the same things. Now Berkeley also tends to use words in their plain everyday meanings, and when he sometimes uses them in a technical way (as he admits he does), he still intends to preserve the *content* of common sense. But does he always succeed in doing so? We can use the criticism already sketched in Section 3 to suggest that he fails crucially in this regard. In the ordinary meaning of "tree," "table," or "stone," a tree or table or stone is something that could exist even though no one, including God, were sensing it or thinking about it. So in the ordinary meaning of these words (which Moore does seem to adhere to) Berkeley really denies that there are trees, tables, and stones, and thus he denies that we know there are, and that we know that any particular tree, table, or stone exists. For he holds that *no* object can exist when no mind whatsoever is "perceiving" it, that is, sensing it or thinking about it.

So much for our illustration of how Moore makes use of the stage one approach to philosophical problems, and how that approach can have significant weight against metaphysical theories propounded as solutions to such problems. If we wished to explore his philosophy in detail, we might go on to ask whether we really do know the sorts of things he has in his list. Or if we are as convinced as he is that we do know them, we might be more interested in trying to explain *how* we know them. In that case we would be doing epistemology in the manner of Berkeley and most other important philosophers from Descartes down to quite recent years. That is, we would be trying to explain how our ideas or "mental contents" relate to the world and give us knowledge of it. We shall not pursue such inquiries here, but we should mention that Moore himself did a good deal of this. Even in "A Defense of Common Sense" he insists repeatedly that, while he knows that every statement in his list is true, he does not know "how to give the correct analysis" of a single one of them. By the correct analysis of a statement he apparently means an accurate and complete explanation of its meaning, from which it would be clear *how* we know that such a statement is true or false. He tells us in the later sections of the article that as far as he can see the analysis of statements about material things would have to be made in terms of "sense data," i.e. Berkeley's "sensible qualities" or something rather similar to that. But while Moore worked hard at this several times during his career, he never thought that he or anyone else had managed to give the correct analysis of such statements.

6. MOORE AND LATER PHILOSOPHY

There are certain features of "A Defense of Common Sense" that might lead one to interpret Moore as arguing at stage three as well as at stage one. But I think this is a mistaken interpretation that results from reading too much of later philosophy back into Moore. Stage-one arguments, which were rare in Western philosophy before Moore and are now commonplace, appear regularly by the nineteen-fifties as preambles to stage-three "dissolutions," as we have already mentioned. The typical movement of thought might be put somewhat crudely as follows. (1) With the possible exception of some traditionally minded people who manage to confuse themselves and perpetuate old sophistries, anyone can see that we do know such and such a thing. And (2) the alleged puzzle about how we know it is itself based on such and such mistakes and can therefore be dismissed, except perhaps as a vehicle for clarifying our concepts by exhibiting those mistakes. That pattern became so familiar in the philosophy of the last generation that when we find Moore arguing two generations ago in a way that illustrates the first half of the pattern we may falsely assume that the whole pattern is there even if he does not bother to make the second half explicit.

Another cause of this misinterpretation is Moore's repeated reminder that he means to use words in their ordinary plain meanings. A great many philosophers in later years who reasoned in that whole pattern also thought that it is important to avoid technical jargon and other departures from the ordinary use of words (especially unnoticed departures) because the conceptual mistakes on which traditional puzzles rest are often the result of them. These philosophers believe that the problem-generating arguments (and the qualms preceding their formulation) often arise from the misuse of ordinary language, and that we can hope to get rid of such puzzles by clearly identifying the linguistic mistakes involved. But Moore himself was not an "ordinary language philosopher" in this now-familiar sense. All analytic philosophers beginning with Plato have insisted that we must try to be clear about how we are using words if we are to understand each other and know when we are agreeing or disagreeing. When Moore insists that the safest way to do this is to use words in their everyday meanings he is not maintaining the further thesis that philosophical problems are based on conceptual errors resulting from our failure to understand the logic or conceptual structure of ordinary language.

Finally, there is a somewhat more plausible reason for believing that Moore "came close" to arguing at stage three, or that he did so "in effect" though without clearly intending this type of argument. One can easily find statements in this article which might be useful if one did intend to argue that way. Let us cite some examples before briefly commenting on them.

He says that if material things do not exist, or if selves do not exist, or if space does not exist, or if time does not exist, then no philosopher has ever existed, since after all a philosopher is a person or self with a material body existing in space and time. So, says Moore, there is no reason why he should give any weight to the fact that some eminent *philosophers* have denied or doubted one or another of these things. He also points out various inconsistencies that philosophers have fallen into when maintaining theses incompatible with the truisms in his list. For example, some have forgotten themselves and said "*We* believe there are other selves but *we* do not know there are; *we* only know there are other human bodies that behave in certain ways" (emphasis added to their words). Or again, some philosophers have said that it is *common sense* that there are many human selves, but that it is at least doubtful whether common sense is correct about this. As Moore points out, if there are common-sense beliefs then there are many people holding them in common. He also says that philosophers who deny or doubt things in this list "have repeatedly, even in their philosophical works, expressed other views inconsistent with them; i.e., no philosopher has ever been able to hold such views consistently."

This last remark suggests that even though a skeptical philosopher can, with care, avoid the more obvious sorts of self-contradiction illustrated above, there are other kinds of inconsistency which he cannot avoid. For one thing, he cannot avoid acting on ordinary nonskeptical beliefs in his everyday affairs, thus giving the lie in practice to his philosophical theories. (This does not show the falsity of the philosopher's theories, but it is substantial evidence that he does not really believe them.) As famously remarked by Hume, the most eminent skeptical philosopher, it is psychologically impossible to retain one's skepticism when one is not engaged in philosophical reflection. But the words "even in their philosophical works" suggest the stronger claim that a skeptical philosopher's reasonings will always be *deeply* incoherent, and necessarily so, even if they have the superficial appearance of self-consistency. This *would* express a stage three approach to problems founded on skeptical arguments which look consistent and formidable. It is not clear, however, that Moore intended to make this stronger claim. It seems more likely that he only meant to suggest that a skeptical philosopher will at some point *fail* to take sufficient care, that common-sense beliefs and habits of thought are so deeply engrained that somewhere in a skeptical work they are bound to gain expression. Then the philosopher will inadvertently say something which is plainly incompatible with his skeptical doctrine.

Anyone familiar with more recent philosophy who takes Moore to be making the stronger of those two claims will probably find in his remarks something like the following critical stance towards skepticism. (1) Our philosophical beliefs and doubts cannot be sealed off from our other beliefs, some of which they even claim to correct. (2) If we really took seriously our skeptical doubts about the existence of bodies, selves, space, or time, this would be so deeply incompatible with our existing system of thought and language as to tear that system down and turn our discourse, as skeptical philosophers, into logical gibberish. (3) Our discourse would then only seem to make sense as long as neither we nor our audience noticed this consequence. In propounding our skeptical doubts we would go on plausibly but inconsistently using a language that embodies the very scheme for thinking which our doubts, if seriously entertained, would render impossible. Hence (4) the skeptical arguments cannot formulate genuine problems because they do not succeed in saying something coherent.

To *show* that this is true about even one of the famous old problems of philosophy would no doubt be exceedingly difficult, requiring great deal of patient analysis if it could be done at all. But let us attempt to sketch in extremely broad terms how someone might proceed with the task. He might begin by trying to say what he means by "basic" concepts and beliefs, and indeed by "concepts." He might then try to identify the most basic of our concepts and beliefs, and show how they support our whole "conceptual scheme," or certain major conceptual schemes that we use in thinking, communicating, acting. Of course, he would also try to get clear on what is meant by a "conceptual scheme." Then he might try to show how this scheme, or these schemes, are reflected in the standard use of our language, and in our everyday activities. And he would attempt to explain how the skeptic's doubts or denials are inconsistent with the retention of certain basic beliefs, or the continued use of certain basic concepts, without which the system or scheme collapses in ways that can be convincingly exhibited. If he could do all this and also explain how the skeptic's doubts or denials only seemed arguable in the first place because of seductive misinterpretations or distortions of our scheme, he would have effectively disposed of the skeptic's argument.

Much of the philosophy written in the decade or two immediately following World War II can be located somewhere in that broad program. While it probably was not Moore's program, his ideas had a great influence on many thinkers who in various ways attempted to carry it out: Wittgenstein, John Wisdom, Gilbert Ryle, J. L. Austin, P. F. Strawson, R. M. Hare, and H. L. A. Hart, to mention only a few of most prominent names.

7. PRIVATE LANGUAGE

Perhaps the one most striking feature of the later philosophy of Wittgenstein is that he reasons quite intentionally, and almost continuously, in the "ONE and THREE" pattern. He believes that most of traditional philosophy and much of his own earlier work has been concerned with problems that only arise from failure to understand the "logic" of our language. Since the main burden of his thought during the last two decades of his life is to lay bare the specific sources and occasions of this failure, so that we might all escape at last from philosophical puzzlement

and useless theorizing, it would not be too great an exaggeration to say
that the whole of his later philosophy − that of the thirties to the early
fifties − adds up to one grand stage-three project. And it proceeded
from the stage-one conviction that there is nothing wrong with the ordinary ways of speaking and thinking which the problems and theories
of philosophy call in question and often seek to discredit.

For our next illustration let us consider his famous argument against
"private language." If this criticism is sound it effectively undermines
more than one skeptical problem, "external world" and "other minds"
being the most obvious ones. But his attack is not primarily directed
against skepticism. Its main targets are certain false assumptions about
the relation between language and the world, assumptions that give rise
not only to skepticism but to various other views inimical to common
sense. Let us confine our attention, however, to the same problem that
figured in our illustration from Berkeley: How, if at all, can we have
knowledge of a world lying beyond our sensations and inner experiences?
And let us attempt to extract the most direct argument that Wittgenstein
makes against private language, so that we can see how it would apply
to that problem. By being this selective we should be able to obtain a
somewhat manageable illustration, but we shall not do justice to the full
force of his attack, which is much longer and more subtle than this one
argument will suggest. Some efforts to repair the injustice will be made
in later sections.

As applied to the problem of the external world, the thrust of Wittgenstein's criticism is as follows. We would need to possess a certain
kind of private language if that problem were even to be coherently formulated; but such a language is impossible, and therefore the problem
may be dismissed as nonsense. In order to see the kind of language that
he has in mind it will be helpful to mention two other kinds first. (1) Suppose I make up a code for translating English words and sentences into
strings of letters or other signs that are mere gibberish as far as any
known language is concerned. Then I use this code when writing in my
diary. But you might "break" the code and then translate the diary into
English and other public languages. (2) Suppose I devise a private
language which includes many words for things of which no one else has
any knowledge or experience. Then I use such words to refer to those

things in my diary, and I take care not to describe them in terms for which there are equivalents in other languages. For example, I list some new empirical effects that I have obtained in certain experiments, but without explaining the experiments or describing the effects in any way. I simply wish to record, for my own future reference, which effects I obtained on which days. In these circumstances it is extremely unlikely that anyone will be able to understand my diary, but it is not impossible. Someone else might come to have the same experiences I have had and named, and to discover my arbitrary verbal conventions for referring to these experiences. Then he could translate and understand the diary. But in a third kind of private language, the kind that Wittgenstein has in mind, I would talk and write about things which no one else could even conceivably be acquainted with, namely, my own sensations and inner experiences − my own pains, sense percepts, joys, and so on, considered purely as objects of my inner life. In a word, I would talk and write only about my own "ideas," in the special sense of the word that Locke and Berkeley employed in our first illustration.

It does seem that we would have to use this third kind of private language if we were to formulate the problem of the external world in a fully explicit and wholly consistent way. When we use English or some other public language, as in practice we must, we are using verbal instruments which presuppose in a thousand ways that there is such a world and that we do know a great deal about it. This need for a private language is a little less obvious in Berkeley's *Dialogues* than in Descartes' *Meditations on First Philosophy*, the first classic statement of the problem in modern times. This is largely due to a difference in literary form. In Descartes' work we are not presented with two philosophers "already in the world" talking to one another. We encounter the reflections of a solitary mind asking itself whether it can know anything beyond its own sensations and thoughts, including its *belief* that a world of matter and space exists outside of it. But in fact Berkeley's characters must ask the same question, each for himself. And after all, here *we* are, "already in the world," reading Descartes' book! Its contents lead us to ask whether these book-like sensations (and all our other sensations) give us knowledge of anything beyond themselves, or beyond our "mind" which "contains" them.

The only thing a soliloquizing philosopher can do in attempting to describe the private objects of his private world and then ask such a question about them, is to adapt words from some public language and then give them a subjective twist. "I have the experience of *seeming* to see a red object" is a typical device. But this is hardly satisfactory. It not only adapts "red" and "object" from English, but uses several other words of that public language, along with its syntax. Indeed the sentence in quotation marks just *is* a sentence of the public language. And of course it has to be if the philosopher is to write something down for other people to read. Even when he is engaged in wholly private reflections, he must use some public language because he has not actually invented a private one, and his topics are certainly too abstract and difficult to be dealt with in non-linguistic thought. Descartes and other philosophers have not been unaware of this situation, but they have commonly assumed that it poses only a technical problem. They thought they *could* devise an artificial language to formulate the problem in a strictly consistent way, but that this would require a great deal of unnecessary labor. The problem could be indicated *well enough* in ordinary language, and they wished to get on with their attempts to solve it.

Wittgenstein thinks they were deluded in that regard. He maintains that the linguistic aspect of the problem is no mere technical difficulty but an obstacle which cannot possibly be overcome. His simplest argument to this effect, and the one his critics have tended to focus upon, can be summarized as follows. In order to have any language, public or private, you must have rules for the correct use of words. And how would you lay down such rules for a private language of the third type referred to above? Presumably, you would say to yourself, "Here is a certain kind of sensation that I am having; I will call any sensation of this kind 'E'." And you would go on and make a list of such private common nouns, each standing for a certain inner experience. And it seems that you could keep a calender and write 'E' on it for any day during which you had sensation E; and similarly with other sensations. But how would you know that you had correctly remembered the connections between sensations and names? You could not have made a dictionary, for there is no way to list sensations opposite the signs 'E,' 'F,' 'G,' and so on. (Nor could you have listed words from the public language, e.g. 'red,' 'warm,' 'joy,' opposite 'E,' 'F,' 'G.' For if they were not arbitrary signs but carried their ordinary meanings the language based on this dictionary would not be private. And if they *were* disconnected from their ordinary meanings, serving as purely arbitrary synonyms for 'E,' 'F,' and 'G,' nothing would be accomplished by this list.) For the same reason, you could not set up *any* public criterion for correctly applying 'E' to a sensation or other inner experience. For example, you could not list 'the color sensation that fire engines usually cause us to have' any more than you could list 'red.'

So it seems (to continue the argument) that you would have to look up the meanings of 'E' only in your memory as it were, consulting the conventional connection between sign and sensation which you had previously made. You would bring the connection back before your mind's eye, somewhat as you might verify the departure time of a train by recalling the appearance of some part of the printed timetable. But how would you know that you had remembered these connections *correctly*? There would be no way to determine that you had; there would be nothing comparable to the printed timetable to fall back on. So really there would be no criterion for remembering the meaning of 'E' correctly and using it correctly to name a sensation that you are now presently having. But if there is no criterion of correctness in the application of a rule, then there really is no rule at all, or so Wittgenstein maintains. Thus he concludes that there can be no rules for the use of 'E,' 'F,' 'G,' etc., and that it cannot make sense to talk about applying these words correctly or incorrectly. We are not even making sense when we say, "Suppose you used 'E' for the *wrong* sensation one day." And since there can be no *rules* in this private language which we have attempted to imagine, there can be no such language.

What conclusions should be drawn, then, as to the problem of the external world? First, the philosophers who continue their somewhat incoherent discussions of this problem should not be allowed the excuse that they *could* be coherent if they had the time to create the necessary linguistic tools. Second, we need not bother to challenge them to create their private languages and teach us how to devise such a language for ourselves, so that we might come to understand their problem. We know this is impossible, so we may dismiss the problem as no problem.

8. A CRITIQUE AND A PROMISSORY NOTE

The longer discussion of which the foregoing argument is a part is so densely packed with illustrations that one could hardly "summarize" it without taking a good deal more space than the fifteen pages of the original text. The whole discussion adds up to extremely powerful argument or series of arguments to the effect that language by its very nature is a product of the interactions of many human beings, and that it would not be merely difficult but conceptually impossible for one person to devise a private language of the type described, even if that person could use existing public language as his guide. As I have said, it is rather unfair to Wittgenstein to concentrate on the single argument which I have summarized above, and we shall return to this topic in Chapter 6 (Section 21). But it may be worthwhile to take a brief critical look at the foregoing argument, if only to convince ourselves that the traditional problems of philosophy are not *easily* overthrown in stage three attacks.

The argument obviously is based on the principle that memory cannot be the last court of appeal on the question whether we have used a word correctly. But if this principle is intended quite universally, it is a rather doubtful one. Of course we do use words all the time without checking the dictionary, and sometimes we would be *unable* in fact to cite any public criterion. For example, if I am discussing the meaning of a word with someone, can I *prove* that the word I am now mentioning is the same word we were discussing two minutes ago? One can argue plausibly that it is even *theoretically necessary* at *some* point in the use of language, even public language, that we should rely finally on memory. In order to use words correctly we have to remember *how we have been* using them, and all knowledge of the past rests finally on memory. Even when we have public evidence of what went on in the past, e.g. a magnetic tape which records what was said two minutes ago, its value as a basis of knowledge depends on inductive inference, and induction itself rests finally on memory. This general point can be brought out with one of Wittgenstein's own illustrations.

'Let us now imagine a use for the entry of the sign 'E' in my diary. I discover that whenever I have a particular sensation a manometer shews that my blood-pressure rises. So I shall be able to say that my blood-pressure is rising without using any apparatus. This is a useful result. And now it seems quite indifferent whether I have recognized the sensation right or not. Let us suppose I regularly identify it wrong, it does not matter in the least. And that alone shews that the hypothesis that I make a mistake is mere show. ...' (*Phil. Invest.*, I, Sec. 270)

Wittgenstein's thought in the second-last sentence of this passage must apparently be taken as follows. "Let us suppose that I regularly say to myself 'Ah! There is E again; my pressure must be rising', when in fact I had called this sensation 'F' in the original baptism ceremony. It does not matter in the least, since I am still able to tell that my blood-pressure is rising without using the manometer."

But how am I able to know on a given occasion that this is the *same* sensation that goes with the pressure rise except by recognizing it as such? To be sure, I have *previously* discovered the regular co-occurrence of a certain sensation and a pressure rise; so I *could* gather confirming evidence for my present memorial belief (that this sensation is the same one) by proceeding to use the apparatus. But in the quoted passage Wittgenstein rightly assumes that I need not do this. Furthermore, how was I ever able to discover and verify that regularity in the first place? I did it by testing on a number of occasions and observing that a certain sort of sensation was accompanied by a pressure rise. Yet, in order to do *that*, I had to remember correctly that the sensations which I had experienced on those occasions were *the same*. And I had to do this independently of the apparatus.

If this criticism is sound (and I shall not pause to examine *it*), one cannot prove the impossibility of private language merely by pointing to the fallibility of memory. But private language may still be impossible for all of that. And if so, the problem of the external world may be dissolvable on that basis. One thing is sure: even if metaphysical problems *are* based on confusions, they are not to be gotten rid of with short snappy arguments, as Wittgenstein would be the first to point out. Let us conclude the present discussion by quoting a passage which vividly confirms his sense of the frightful difficulty of philosophical problems. Its final sentence also points in the direction our discussion will take in Section 21.

'What reason have we for calling 'E' the sign for a *sensation*? For 'sensation' is a word of our common language, not of one intelligible to me alone. So the use of this word stands in need of a justification which everybody understands. – And it would not help either to say that it need not be a *sensation*; that when he writes 'E,' he has *something* – and that is all that can be said. 'Has' and 'something' also belong to our common language. – So in the end when one is doing philosophy one gets to the point where one would just like to emit an inarticulate sound. – But such a sound is an expression only if it occurs in a particular language-game, which should now be described.'' (Sec. 261)

CHAPTER 3

DESCRIPTIVE METAPHYSICS

If anyone succeeds in a stage three attack on a metaphysical problem which has really troubled him, he may rid himself of the vague qualms and fears that accompanied his intellectual confusion. This seems to be one of Wittgenstein's principal objectives in his later philosophizing, although he seldom gains more than temporary relief. Some less neurotic but also less profound philosophers of the fifties and early sixties had a rather different objective. They were out to poke fun at traditional metaphysics by readily dissolving its puzzles and the pretentious theories of reality which these puzzles, unsolved at stage two, had been used to construct and justify. As my concluding remarks in the last chapter will suggest, the "ready dissolutions" they produced did not usually survive careful study. But perhaps the most enduring and valuable function of stage three work, even when it fails to produce a definitive solution, is to help us gain a deeper understanding of the existing structures of our thought. It does so by highlighting certain features which skeptical arguments, and other anti-common-sense arguments, obscure and trick us into distorting and violating. Part of this improved understanding is a better sense of how immensely difficult it would be in theory, and impossible in practice, to replace or radically revise the most basic concepts of common sense, as metaphysical theories commonly demand. In order to illustrate these last points, let us see how Sir Peter Strawson uses stage three reasoning as a device of purely descriptive, nonrevisionary metaphysics in his book *Individuals*, 1959.

9. IDENTIFICATION

In that book Strawson sets out to describe the oldest structures of human thought, those having "no history − or none recorded in the histories of thought": the categories and concepts that are "the commonplaces of the least refined thought; and are yet the indispensable core of the conceptual equipment of the most sophisticated human beings." His description proceeds "ontologically." That is, he wants to consider the more basic kinds of things we recognize as real. And more specifically, he wants to "exhibit some general and structural features of the conceptual scheme in terms of which we think about particular things" — as distinguished from qualities, properties, numbers, and species of things. At the beginning he means to deal with "objective" particulars, those which are different from the self and states of the self, such as particular pains. Now to say that we admit particulars of a certain type to our ontology presupposes that we are able to identify particulars of that type.

'For what could we mean by claiming to acknowledge the existence of a class of particular things and to talk to each other about members of this class, if we qualified the claim by adding that it was in principle impossible for any one of us to make any other of us understand which member, or members, of this class he was at any time talking about.'

Strawson goes on to describe in a straightforward way how a speaker does make an identifying reference to some particular, and how his hearer may succeed in identifying the particular to which the speaker refers. This includes the theoretically easy though sometimes practically difficult task of picking out a particular thing which lies within the range of the speaker's and the hearer's present experience. ("The man in the sixth seat from the left end of the twelfth row in Section E.") And it includes the more complex case of identifying things outside that range through the use of "definite descriptions"; for example, "the tallest building in New York before the construction of the World Trade Center." In explaining the scheme by which we successfully make the latter sort of identifications, Strawson uses his first metaphysical problem, admittedly one of the easiest ones: a certain "old worry which is both practically and theoretically baseless."

The problem-generating argument in this case goes somewhat as follows. We can never really *know* that a definite description has *unique* application. It is logically possible, after all, that there is some other region or regions of the universe which duplicate this one, so that no matter how much detail we put into our description it may still apply to two or more things, not just one. There may be another New York with another World Trade Center and another Empire State Building constructed some forty years earlier, and so on. To be sure, we have no reason to think there actually are such duplications in the universe, but we cannot rule them out as logically impossible. Thus we cannot be absolutely sure that our description succeeds in its role of referring to one and only one real thing lying beyond our present experience.

The solution is not hard to find. In order to make sure that our description applies only to the particular we have in mind, all we need do is add to it in such a way as to relate that particular to some other particular which *can* be identified demonstratively. For example, we can explain to our hearer how to get from the spot where we are now standing to the formerly tallest building in that City of New York which we have in mind. Easy as this "problem" is, its dissolution does something to help describe the structure of our conceptual scheme. It calls attention to the fact that a vast number of our nondemonstrative identifications are made with the aid of a system of space and time, and that the speaker and the hearer are themselves located within that system and know their place in it.

Now it is true that there are ways to make nondemonstrative identifications without giving spatial directions. Some other relationships figuring in our descriptions do uniquely refer by their very "grammar," and we know that they must have application. Consider the description "George's paternal grandfather." Neither the speaker nor the hearer need know the where or the precise when of the particular person thus referred to, or anything else about him, in order to make the same identification. Yet, as Strawson explains, the space-time system is peculiarly comprehensive and pervasive, so that it has better qualifications than any other system within which to organize our "individuating thought about particulars." "Every particular either has its place in this system, or is of a kind the members of which cannot in general be identified except by reference to particulars of other kinds which have their place in it. ..."

He proceeds to defend the claim that the spatio-temporal system is indeed the general unified framework of our knowledge of particulars, the basis of our single picture of the world of particular things. One major point is the following. We do have some individuating thoughts about particulars in which we make no use at all of the spatio-temporal system − not even the sort of use we make of it with the phrase "George's paternal grandfather," where we mention George, whom the speaker and hearer *have* located in space and time. Consider the phrase "the first dog born at sea" which, unlike the phrase "the first dog born in England in the 19th century," does not contain a spatio-temporal reference. But descriptions like the first of these cannot really succeed as identifications unless they draw on our other knowledge of the world, in which case we must rely on the spatio-temporal system after all. The claim of a speaker and hearer to have identified a particular without doing so would be frivolous. They could not be confident that the expression *uniquely* referred; after all, the first two dogs may have been born simultaneously. To avoid that risk we might wish to make the description considerably more specific, as in the phrase "the first dog born at sea who later saved a monarch's life." But this would greatly increase the chance that the expression has no application at all. The only way to eliminate or reduce both risks is to elaborate the description by drawing on our knowledge of the world and its history. And if we do that we cannot sincerely claim to avoid connecting the particular with items belonging to the space-time framework.

So much by way of preparation for our main illustration in this chapter.

10. RE-IDENTIFICATION

A little later in the discussion Strawson turns to a second metaphysical problem, one which is far more difficult to solve, as we shall see. It runs as follows. We seem to operate with a *unified* spatio-temporal system, i.e. a system in which we can inquire about the spatial relations of any one spatial thing at any moment of its history to any other spatial thing at any moment of *its* history, where these moments may be different. For example, "I am now standing ten miles due north of the place where Caesar crossed the Rubicon in 49 B.C." But in order to operate with such a system it is necessary that we be able to *re*identify particulars as the same individuals encountered on another occasion, or described in respect of another occasion. For we have to use the same framework on different occasions, and in order to do that we not only have to pick out some stable elements to fix the framework within which other items are then located (for example, the topographical features and rivers of Italy and cisalpine Gaul), but we also have to identify them as the *same* elements in a single continuously usable system of elements. Now, it is easy to construct a skeptical argument "proving" that we can never know that we have succeeded in such re-identifications. Let us state the argument in four steps before considering Strawson's answer to it.

(1) There is a distinction between qualitative identity and numerical identity. When we say that two things are "the same" we sometimes mean that they have the *same qualities*, such as the same shape, color, and so on; but sometimes we mean that the two particulars which have been referred to in different ways are really the same individual, the *same one*. (2) It is common sense that we can use this distinction successfully when our experience of the things in question has been interrupted, just as we can when it has not been interrupted. In the latter case we continuously observe a certain particular and notice that it undergoes no qualitative change, or only gradual change; thus we can know that the particular we are observing at one time is the same one we observed earlier. But we normally assume that we can often know this even when our observation has not been continuous. (3) Yet all we can really have after the interval of non-observation are *qualitative reoccurrences*. We really have only different kinds of qualitative identity. For example, if I go back to the auto dealer's showroom today, I may find a model of the same make, year, body type, color, and so forth, as I saw there yesterday. In these respects the two particulars are qualitatively the same. But how can I be sure that this one is physically continuous with the one I saw yesterday if I have not been able to observe that continuity? Common sense assumes that we can make sure of this by checking some further qualitative reoccurrences, for example by noticing that this machine has the same number stamped in the engine block. But this only gives a more detailed qualitative identity. It is perfectly possible that this is *not* the same car numerically or even the same engine that I saw yesterday. (4) So it is never possible to be sure that we have re-identified the same individual unless, indeed, we are willing to admit that all we *mean* by "the same one" is this more detailed qualitative identity between particulars on different occasions, with no requirement of physical continuity between the two.

Strawson's reply to this kind of argument attempts to catch the skeptic out by explaining how, in order to express his doubt, he incoherently uses the very scheme for thinking which his doubt would render impossible. Let us quote the reply at some length before commenting on it.

'There is no doubt that we have the idea of single spatio-temporal system of material things; the idea of every material thing at any time being spatially related, in various ways at various times, to every other at every time. There is no doubt at all that this *is* our conceptual scheme. Now I say that a *condition* of our having this conceptual scheme is the unquestioning acceptance of particular-identity in at least some cases of non-continuous observation. Let us suppose for a moment that we were *never* willing to ascribe particular-identity in such cases. Then we should, as it were, have the idea of a new, different, spatial system for each new continuous stretch of observation. ... Each system would be wholly independent of every other. There would be no question of *doubt* about the identity of an item in one system with an item in another. For such a doubt makes sense only if the two systems are not independent, if they are parts, in some way related, of a single system which includes them both. But the condition of having such a system is precisely the condition that there should be satisfiable and commonly satisfied criteria for the identity of at least some items in one sub-system with some items in the other. ... [The skeptic] pretends to accept a conceptual scheme, but at the same time quietly rejects one of the conditions of its employment. Thus his doubts are unreal, not simply because they are logically irresoluble doubts, but because they amount to the rejection of the whole conceptual scheme within which alone such doubts make sense. So, naturally enough, the alternative to doubt which he offers us is the suggestion that we do not really, or should not really, mean what we think we mean, what we do mean. But this alternative is absurd. For the whole process of reasoning only starts because the scheme is as it is; and we cannot change it even if we would.'

The skeptic "pretends" to accept the ordinary scheme − or more likely just does accept it automatically − when he says "we can never be sure they are the same one." For it does not even make sense to speak of them as *possibly* being the same one unless a single spatio-temporal system is taken for granted, just as in the ordinary scheme. Yet if we should take the skeptic's advice and *never* be willing to say that an object encountered on one occasion is the same one encountered on an earlier occasion, that system would be impossible.

A critic might ask the following question. "Which step in the skeptic's argument does Strawson mean to reject? Or if he does not bother to reject any particular step, which one should he have rejected? The skeptic's *argument* is not refuted by pointing out that he must adopt the very scheme in question in order to express his doubts." An answer to this is suggested by our four stage breakdown of philosophical method, namely, that a stage three attack does not purport to single out a factual or inferential error at some one point of the skeptic's explicit reasoning. Rather, it tries to call attention to a confusion or misconception underlying the whole argument or some major portion of its (see Section 2). To be sure, we *could* single out step (4) if we liked, saying that it is *implicitly* inconsistent in recognizing the *possibility* that today's car is the same one as yesterday's while denying that we can ever be sure that we have reidentified something – inconsistent because even that possibility lapses if such a denial is true. But it is more natural to say that the whole argument overlooks the latter point. The whole purpose of the argument is to show that we can never be sure; yet it is expressed in a way which presupposes that we can sometimes be sure. And this does seem to refute it.

But have we really arrived at a final solution? It might be suggested that the skeptic could avoid Strawson's attack by saying that he is quite aware of this logical situation but wishes to do away with the existing conceptual scheme. He is indeed using it, but only to call attention to an inconsistency within it. The inconsistency would be that *we* pretend to have a unified spatio-temporal system when a condition necessary for having one is never satisfied. It is never satisfied, he might argue, because no matter how complex and circumstantial the description might be of object O at one time and object O' at another, we can imagine circumstances under which they nevertheless are not one and the same object. To use the example of the car in the showroom again, suppose that on Monday I secretly make tiny nicks on the car at various hidden places, and that on Tuesday I find similar nicks at all the same places. Unscrupulous salesmen may have brought in another car of the same year, model, body color, trim, upholstery, accessories, and so on, and then they may have gone over both cars with magnifying glasses and duplicated every nick and mark of every kind. This is of course highly unlikely, but it is possible. It is also possible, though even more unlikely, that my car of yesterday was sold and replaced by another one that just happened to have tiny nicks at all and only the same places, and so on.

In one way this suggestion might seem to reinforce Strawson's point. For even in the skeptic's *explanation* of why our existing conceptual scheme is incoherent, he is still forced to use it. Consider his statement of further circumstances under which the extremely similar cars are numerically different. That statement itself takes for granted the unified spatio-temporal system in which the same unscrupulous salesmen exist from day to day along with the same streets by which I get to the same showroom, the same house and bed in which I went to sleep last night, and so on.

This last point need not put the skeptic to rout, however, as we shall see in the next section. In the meantime, let us ask what change in our existing scheme the skeptic means to propose. Presumably his suggestion is that, in cases of interrupted observation, "numerical identity" would only *mean* a certain degree of complexity and circumstantiality in qualitative reoccurrences. There would be no requirement of physical continuity between material object *O* and material object *O'* . Or rather, in light of the last paragraph, the skeptic might say that the very notion of physical continuity would be entirely out of place in such cases. But could we get along with such a change? Certainly it would require a vast revolution in our thinking, and little reflection is needed to see that we humans could not in fact make such a change. It would be psychological-ly impossible. The innocent looking suggestion that we change the mean-ing of the words "numerical identity" and "the same one" contains the destruction of the unified system of spatial and temporal references by which we organize all our knowledge of particulars and all our actions, the system in which we "live and move and have our being" as the kind of intelligent beings we are. Intelligent *clams*, permanently embedded in coral but possessing some means of instantaneous communication, might not need such a system or any spatial concepts at all. But it seems entirely obvious that we humans cannot get along without it, even for the task of imagining those clams and their situation.

Let us conclude this section by glancing back at our discussion of Moore in Section 6, especially the remarks we made there about more re-cent philosophy. We saw how Moore caught certain unnamed skeptics in patently inconsistent positions, as when they doubted whether there are any minds but their own while conceding that "common-sense belief" assumes there are. Such obvious inconsistencies could be avoid-ed, but the question was raised whether the skeptic is nevertheless involv-ed in some deeper inconsistency which he cannot avoid, some attack on the conceptual scheme which he is nevertheless forced to use in that very attack. In a sketchy and wholly programmatic way, we suggested how a philosopher might try to follow up such a possibility. But now we have seen how Strawson does follow it up. He claims that skeptical conclu-sions are necessarily avoidable because they are only obtainable through conceptually incoherent arguments. And he attempts to explain in some detail just what the scheme of ideas is that the skeptic in a particular argu-ment both uses and violates, and just how he uses and violates it. Strawson also goes a step beyond the program sketched in Section 6 when he helps us see why certain skeptical arguments apparently turn discourse into gibberish even if we take them as proposals to reform the existing scheme. For what they propose is that we should begin to think in certain ways that are in fact impossible for us, however possible they might be for beings of some radically different construction and experience.

11. A SKEPTICAL COUNTERATTACK

Since "the skeptic" is a device of conceptual exploration and description, we should place no limits on his resourcefulness. Indeed, he may be able to produce new skeptical arguments which escape our answers to earlier ones, thus showing that we have failed to produce a fully satisfactory solution to the problem at hand. But even if we never reach a complete solution we may expect to add to our philosophical knowledge each time we uncover some new distortion or violation of existing concepts. Now, we saw in the last section how the skeptic sought to turn to his own advantage Strawson's point that his doubts undermined the very scheme which he used to express them. His tactic was to say that he *intended* to undermine that scheme. We may now imagine him responding as follows to the third-last and second-last paragraphs of the preceding section.

'*Naturally* I continued to use the existing scheme in order to explain that no qualitative reoccurrences, however detailed and circumstantially convincing, can guarantee reidentification. After all, I never *claimed* to possess a coherent conceptual scheme of my own with which to express myself. I only claimed to point out that the scheme we all use is incoherent. Furthermore, it was not incumbent upon me to propose a change in that scheme which would be psychologically possible for humans to adopt. It is enough for my purpose if I can manage to call attention to the inconsistency of the existing scheme. And this I claim to have done in the fourth-last paragraph of the preceding section. To sum up what was said there, it simply does not *follow* from *any* descriptions of O at time *t* and object O' at *t + n* that they are the same particular. This was shown by the fact that we can always imagine further circumstances under which they are *not* the same one in spite of all the similarities and circumstances tending to indicate numerical identity.

If it will ease your mind, however, let me explain how a statement of those further circumstances *need not* take for granted the existence of a unified spatio-temporal system in which the same salesmen, streets, and so on, exist from day to day, a system which presupposes successful re-identifications. It is logically possible that there is a numerically distinct but qualitatively identical second universe into which I was suddenly thrust last night as I slept, and that my counterpart in that universe was likewise thrust at the same moment into my home universe. In such a case the salesmen, streets, and so on, which I encounter today would have only a qualitative identity to those encountered yesterday. Since this is all logically possible even if no one believes it happened, I have now circumvented

Strawson's refutation. I have done so even if (as I deny) all inconsistency must be avoided if we are to succeed in calling attention to the incoherence of a conceptual scheme we are using.

That way of avoiding inconsistency suggests a more general argument why we can never know that we have re-identified the same particular after an interruption of experience. Here it is:

(I)   You do not know that you have successfully re-identified the same object A unless you know that the object before you is *not* a certain other object B, namely A's counterpart in a duplicate universe.

(II)   You do *not* know that the object before you is not B unless your usual criteria for re-identification (whatever they are in the existing conceptual scheme) serve to distinguish A from B.

(III)   Your usual criteria obviously do not serve to distinguish A from B.

Therefore, you never know that you have successfully re-identified the same object A which you identified on an earlier occasion.

So ends the skeptic's counterattack.

Our stage one response to the skeptic's latest argument is the same as before. We simply remind ourselves that *of course* we know how to re-identify objects, and that we do so successfully many times every day. On innumerable occasions we know that some object A which we are then observing is the same one we observed on certain earlier occasions. Thus we *know* that it is not B, even granting for the sake of this response that "A's counterpart in a duplicate universe" is a coherent concept. Thus we also know that there *has* to be something wrong with the skeptic's reasoning leading to the conclusion indicated above. And we are justified in saying this even before we know what the trouble specifically is.

How shall we go on then, at stage three, to put our finger on the conceptual distortion or abuse underlying the skeptic's argument? My suggestion is that since we *can* often know, the abuse must lie in some false assumption which deviates from our existing conceptual scheme and seems to force the conclusion that we can never know. Now one assumption that seems to be implicit in *all* the skeptical arguments which we have noticed in this problem is the following: A mere *logical possibility* that object O at t and object O' at $t + n$ are not numerically identical is enough to prevent our knowing that they *are* numerically identical. The two-universes possibility seems but one more variation on this theme. In other words, it is assumed in all of these skeptical argument that we have, or ought to have, as our criterion for re-identification, that a statement of the empirical data – the observed similarities and other circumstances – must *strictly entail* the numerical identity of O and O'. But of course this assumption is false. We have no such requirement in our conceptual scheme, and the skeptic offers no reason why we ought to have it. Nor does it appear that he could offer any good reason for such a claim.

It is the mentioned assumption which gave color to the skeptic's doubt and made us feel that his arguments needed answering. It is an assumption which we are likely to accept automatically until we fix our attention upon it. Why is it so seductive? The question may call for psychological as well as conceptual inquiry, but one might speculate that its attractiveness is due to our desire for simplicity and certainty. As matters are, we cannot state a *general* empirical test for the numerical identity of O at t and O' at $t + n$; the best we can do is say that at all events *there are* cases in which we unquestioningly and properly accept particular-identity even though continuous observation is lacking, and of course we can cite innumerable examples where this is so. But suppose *per impossibile* that we had in our conceptual scheme the requirement of entailment by the empirical data. Then we would have a single test for every case, and in theory at least we would never have to be in doubt about any case.

Whatever truth there may be in this speculation about the seductive power of the skeptic's assumption, it is remarkable that many metaphysical problems seem to depend *at least in part* on the same kind of distortion of ordinary ideas: the assumption that to know something is either to be immediately aware of it or to see intellectually that it is strictly entailed by something else of which we are immediately aware. In the problem of perception and the external world, the skeptic relies on the fact that with a little imagination we can always describe a set of logically possible circumstances under which we would not be observing the realities we think we are observing, no matter how many precautions we may have taken to avoid being deceived. Thus Descartes, in the skeptical phase of his argument, supposed that a malevolent deity might be deceiving him at every turn, while a typical contemporary formulation of skepticism supposes that one's brain might be wired into an electronic device which a mad scientist uses to produce all one's sensations, feelings, and thought, none of them corresponding to external realities. It is pointed out in this way that none of our beliefs about external objects are strictly entailed by what we know about our own sense experience; from which it is supposed to follow that we can never have knowledge of such objects. In the problem of other minds, similarly, it is pointed out that statements about a person's external behavior do not strictly entail statements about his inner life, so again it is supposed to follow that we can never know that someone else is in pain, for example. In Hume's problem of induction, to cite another famous example, it is pointed out that statements describing all the events we have observed or are presently observing do not strictly entail any statement about an unobserved event, whether past, present or future. So it is supposed to follow that we can never have knowledge of unobserved events. In each of these problems the friends of common-sense are entitled to reply that the reason given does not warrant the conclusion since it is no part of our concept of knowledge that we can only know what we observe or what we can infer therefrom by valid deductive reasoning.

The same point was made by J. L. Austin in his important article, 'Other Minds' (1946), which focuses on the problem mentioned in its title but also deals with metaphysical problems of knowledge generally. The article concludes with the following summary:

'The gist of what I have been trying to bring out is simply:

(1) *Of course I don't* introspect Tom's feelings (we should be in a pretty predicament if I did).

(2) *Of course I do* sometimes know Tom is angry.
Hence

(3) to suppose that the question 'How do I know that Tom is angry?' is meant to mean 'How do I introspect Tom's feelings?' (because, as we know, that's the sort of thing that knowing is or ought to be) is simply barking our way up the wrong gum tree.'

Notice that step (2) of this summary illustrates what we have been calling stage one, while step (3) illustrates stage three as if it were cut to measure. The words in parenthesis call attention to the false assumption on which the skeptic in the other-minds problem relies. And of course the skeptic had also pointed out, with Austin's assistance, that no statement about

Tom's behavior strictly entails any statement about his feelings. (When he yells and holds his finger after striking it with the hammer, there is at least a logical possibility and indeed a physical possibility that he is not in pain at all.) It is instructive as well as amusing to adapt Austin's summary to fit the problem we have been discussing:

(1) *Of course* I *cannot* observe the physical continuity of material object O' at $t+n$ with material object O at t when experience has been interrupted.

(2) *Of course* I *do* sometimes know that they are numerically identical even though experience has been interrupted.
Hence

(3) to suppose that the question 'How do I know that *this* object O' is numerically identical with *that* object O?' is meant to mean 'How do I observe that continuity or something else which strictly entails it?' (because, as we know, that's the sort of thing that knowledge of numerical identity is or ought to be) is simply barking our way up the wrong gum tree.

12. A FINAL PARADOX

What we really learn from the foregoing skeptical arguments, it would appear, is not that there is always room for doubt about our alleged re-identifications, but that strict entailment of numerical identity by the observational data is simply not required for re-identification. To sum up the whole inquiry thus far, we surely *know* that we can often re-identify objects, so the skeptic's arguments have to be mistaken; and we seem to have found the mistake in his tacit assumption that such an entailment *is* required.

This result will hardly seem secure, however, unless we now answer an important objection that we mentioned in connection with Moore (in Section 5) and postponed for later discussion. It will be said that the form of inquiry just summarized is irrational in a way pointed out by Saul Kripke and Gilbert Harman. After expressing his indebtedness to Kripke, Harman formulates the following paradox:

'If I know *h* [some statement] is true, I know that any evidence against *h* is evidence against something that is true; so I know that such evidence is misleading. So, once I know that *h* is true, I am in a position to disregard any future evidence that seems to tell against *h*.'

This is paradoxical in that a truth (that we do know some things) seems to commit us to the falsehood that we are entitled to disregard all future evidence against those things. It may be that for practical reasons we *are* entitled to disregard *some* evidence against things we know, perhaps attributing it to unreliable reporters or to experimental error. But it is surely false that we are entitled to disregard *all* future negative evidence relating to such items of knowledge. Now, our defense of Moore and our response to the skeptic in the present chapter seem to run along similarly objectionable lines. To avoid confusion, let us use the remainder of this paragraph merely to underscore the point before going on to formulate a specific objection in the next paragraph. We said that since Moore knows that certain things are true, he is in a position to disregard any argument against these things – to reject it even without examining it. And we said that since we know that we can re-identify objects, we are in a position to reject any argument which the skeptic can possibly give to the contrary. We said we were entitled to do so even before discovering his deviations from the existing conceptual scheme. And now let us boldly add for good measure that we are entitled to reject in advance any argument in which he may attempt to show explicitly that (1) "genuine" knowledge really does require either direct observation or strict entailment by a statement of what we have directly observed, so that (2) the existing scheme ought to be changed.

Harman offers to explain how anyone can escape from the above paradox. He says that we can and should reject the principle that we are entitled to disregard misleading evidence. A sufficient accumulation of seemingly misleading evidence can *change* the fact that we know a certain statement to be true. That is, we may no longer be *justified in our belief* that it is true, which is necessary for knowledge. Here then is the objection we must answer: Moore's certainty about some item in his list may be undermined by some future argument if he will only examine it. His knowledge, or rather his justification in claiming to know, gives him no intellectual right to reject all future arguments. And similarly, we have no right to disregard all future skeptical arguments in the re-identification problem merely on the ground that they deny something we justifiably claim to know.

There is probably no good answer to this kind of objection at higher levels of knowledge, evidence, and argument; but there seems to be a very good answer that can be given at the most fundamental level of common-sense knowledge, the level represented by Moore's truisms and by our knowledge that we can often re-identify objects. Let us first state the answer dogmatically before attempting to explain and defend it. Harman's way of getting rid of the paradox is too general; the statement that I am in position to disregard any future evidence, etc., is false only for non-fundamental knowledge claims. At the most fundamental level the statement is actually true, so that at this level there is no paradox to begin with. At this level it is entirely proper to insist that we really do know and therefore cannot be mistaken, so that all future evidence and arguments to the contrary are known in advance to be misleading or wrong. Indeed, they are entirely *out of order*, and *this* is a more fundamental principle of reason than the principle that we must not disregard future evidence or arguments against things we justifiably claim to know.

It will be easier to state our reasons for this position if we first look at a somewhat similar but weaker claim. Suppose Mr. Smith asserts that the thing on his wrist is certainly a watch, and that he knows this to be so, and hence that it cannot turn out the next day, on further evidence, not to have been a watch. One thing to notice is that it would be inconsistent for him to say he knows it is a watch while admitting that it could so turn out. Secondly, it would also be inconsistent for anyone else to say, in the third person, that Smith knows this but can also (at the same time) be mistaken. Thirdly, if we are present when Smith makes his statement, we shall undoubtedly be convinced that he *does* know, on this occasion, that the object on his wrist is a watch. But in spite of all this, it is still possible that he does *not* really know. Whatever our convictions might be as witnesses, and whatever would be a consistent thing for him to *say*, or for us to say, it is possible that the object on his wrist is not a watch, so that it *can* turn out the next day, on further evidence, not to have been one.

A crucial difference between that example and the assertion that we *know* we can *sometimes* re-identify objects is that the latter assertion makes a *general* rather than a *particular* knowledge claim, as do many of the statements in Moore's list of truisms. These general claims are of such a kind that if they are not true and known to be true, then our whole conceptual scheme collapses and we can know nothing or next to nothing. Suppose that on some occasion I should sincerely speak as

Smith did, saying that I certainly know that something on my wrist is a certain kind of object, and that later on it should turn out to have been of some other kind. This would only be a cause for personal embarrassment; or even if it made me fear for my sanity because I had just been carefully examining and testing the object, it would be no catastrophe for other people. But if we do not really know that we can *sometimes* properly classify the objects we are looking at, or if we do not really know that we can *sometimes* re-identify objects, or if we do not really know that there have been many other human beings who have had thoughts and feelings (and so on through various other general statements in Moore's list), then all our knowledge is in ruins. The point seems fairly obvious even without any explanation, but we have sketched the explanation given by Strawson in the matter of re-identification. This was his account of how re-identification is essential to the existence of a unified spatiotemporal system of reference, and of how that system is essential to the organization of all our knowledge of particular things.

For these reasons we apparently must recognize a principle of reason which can be formulated in three parts as follows: (1) we know that we can *sometimes* identify and classify objects correctly; (2) we know that we can *sometimes* re-identify objects; and (3) we know that we can never turn out to be mistaken about (1) and (2). Such a principle will take precedence over the principle that we must not disregard future evidence or arguments against things we justifiably claim to know. At the most elementary and fundamental level of knowledge, we apparently are entitled to reject out of hand all arguments to the contrary; it seems that we *must* reject them on pain of destroying our conceptual scheme. If we do not, then none of the other levels of knowledge, where we usually are *not* so justified, can even exist. At the most fundamental level the very notion of "evidence to the contrary" would appear to be incoherent. For such evidence would have to be evidence that we can never know that we have properly classified or re-identified an object, and how then could we know that we had properly classified objects when gathering that evidence? But if the very idea of evidence to the contrary is not impossible here, then it seems that all such evidence must be dismissed on pain of utter chaos in all our thoughts and actions.

Before ending this discussion it may be well to mention one last objection. Have we really managed to produce an adequate defense for

Moore-like reasoning (stage one), seeing that we have had to resort to stage three in order to do so (arguing that if Moore's claims are false then our conceptual scheme collapses and all knowledge is in ruins)? The answer, I believe, is that Moore *is* somewhat vulnerable until stage three is brought to his aid. To be sure, the mere assertion of apparently fundamental beliefs does carry *some* important weight, as we have suggested all along, because even without any analysis we have reason to *suspect* that chaos would result from seriously doubting or denying them. But a substantial stage-three argument must be given to *show* why this is probably so if Moore's point is really to take hold of philosophical minds. And perhaps we have now seen such an argument, focusing on the Moore-like claim that we know we can often re-identify material objects. The argument has had four parts: (i) Strawson's quoted response to the skeptic, pointing out (among other things) that the ability to re-identify such objects is essential to our possession of a spatio-temporal system of references; (ii) his explanation that the latter system is essential to our knowledge of the world of material things; (iii) our own response to the skeptic's attempts to circumvent Strawson's criticism; and (iv) our answer to the claim that Moore and everyone else ought to remain endlessly receptive to further skeptical attacks, however inane, at this fundamental level of knowledge.

CHAPTER 4

CONCEPTUAL REFORM

The foregoing answer to Kripke's and Harman's paradox not only helps to indicate the strength of the "ONE and THREE" pattern of philosophical reasoning; it also suggests the proper limitations of that pattern. For stage one has its full force only with respect to the oldest and most elementary structures of thought. Once we leave off studying that old city of the mind, a city whose streets have been worn into a coherent usable network from the earliest times, any presumptions favoring common-sense belief must be a rebuttable presumption. It may be that some less basic structural beliefs laid down in cultural history have conceptually disparate origins and do not yet form a wholly coherent scheme. And it may be possible to reform them without disrupting all thought. When the skeptic presents an argument attacking an apparently crucial piece of common-sense in these suburbs of the mind, we cannot simply read off his error from some violation of existing concepts. We must construct a stage three criticism giving clear reasons why the argument is incoherent, and it may turn out in some cases that it is not incoherent but calls attention to a real inconsistency in existing thought (or some other serious defect) which ought to be removed through conceptual change.

The now familiar distinction between descriptive metaphysics and the older revisionary metaphysics is helpful in one way but possibly misleading in another. It reminds us that our fundamental everyday concepts – our most metaphysical concepts if you will (see Section 1) – need not revision and in practice can have none. But it may also cause us to overlook the point that a careful description of *some* of our existing concepts – a more careful description than traditional philosophers typically made – might itself show their incoherence, their need to be revised. The topic is an important one if we are to gain a consistent overview of philosophy as it has continued to develop during the last couple of decades. For there is increasing recognition that conceptual reform may be necessary if we are to resolve *some* of the problems of philosophy;

but it is not clear, on the one hand, why a proposed solution which *changes* the ideas giving rise to a problem should be regarded as a solution to it. Nor is it clear, on the other hand, how this kind of solution would differ – if it would differ at all – from the metaphysical theorizing or conceptual reconstruction which has supposedly been discredited in analytic philosophy.

In this chapter we shall attempt to show how conceptual revision can be part of a larger philosophical method that also preserves the important insights of mid-century philosophy which we have been studying in the preceding chapters. Three tasks confront us. First, we must try to become clear on what we mean by "incoherent concepts" needing "revision." For there is an established philosophical usage according to which a "concept" is coherent by definition, even if people sometimes use it confusedly or incoherently, or even if no one has yet become entirely clear about it. In this connection we must explain the theory of revisionary solutions (stage four) more fully than we did in Chapter 1. Second, we must show how, in recognizing the possibility of revisionary solutions, we do not throw the door open again to revisionary metaphysics. We must try to say something tolerably clear about the standard of *good* revisionary solutions, and why it rules out any attempt to reconstruct our most fundamental concepts. Third, we must show how that standard for good analytic philosophy is really no different from the one we recognize in our attempts to dissolve conceptual problems (stage three). In pursuing these objectives we shall make illustrative use of a fictional problem. But in Chapter 10 and 11 we shall consider revisionary solutions to real and important problems.

13. TIME GAPS

Let us begin with a puzzle or former puzzle which is perhaps less a problem for philosophers than a bit of the history of conceptual change in science. It will serve to introduce some material which we can use in our fictional problem of philosophy in the next section. Often called the time-gap or time-lag problem, it runs as follows. The visual experiences we ordinarily take to be perceptions of the present states of things are really only the effects or traces of their past states. This is obvious in the case of stars, some of which may well have ceased to exist hundreds or thousands of years before the present moment when their light strikes our eyes. If a star under observation in our century were "seen" to explode, we or our descendants would know that the object we had supposedly been seeing had in fact ceased to exist long before. But the result is the same whether a star we "see" has ceased to exist or not. For the state of an existing star that we presently "see" is not its present state. And if we cannot see its present state we cannot really see the star at all. Our eyes only register some of the effects of stellar states and events of many years ago, or ages ago. Now the same considerations apply in the case of such nearer objects as the sun, which is roughly eight light-minutes distant, and the moon, which is roughly 1.3 light-seconds distant. They apply in fact to all the objects about us and even to those parts of our own bodies that we can "see." This is because *there is no non-arbitrary cut-off point* after which it can be allowed that although a state or event is in the past we can nevertheless see it. Therefore, since we can never see the present state of things, we can never really see them at all.

Most writers on this problem seem to think that the best solution is to allow that we *can* see in the present some past states of things, namely, those states in which objects emitted or reflected light directly to our eyes in present times. The problem depends on the assumption, which I made rather explicit, that whenever we see an object or state of an object, or an event in which an object is involved, that object must exist and be in that state or involved in that event at the time we see it. I shall call this assumption *A* hereafter. If we give up this assumption there is nothing in the finite speed of light to prevent our saying that we see distant stars, objects in the room around us, and our own hands. Nor are we then forced to admit that we can never see anything *but* the past states of things. For as two recent writers on the problem have pointed out, there really is a non-arbitrary cut-off point at which we can allow the present some slight duration in visual contexts. That cut-off point is at the lower limit of our capacity to discriminate temporal differences in visual stimuli. Suppose that people in general cannot distinguish visual stimuli that are less than one-tenth of a second apart. Then our visual experience of any object less than 18,600 miles away (one-tenth of one light-second in distance) will be indistinguishable from what it would be if the speed of light were infinite. So in visual contexts it is reasonable to allow the present a duration of one-tenth of a second (or whatever the general limit approximately is) and to understand that when someone reports that he is seeing such and such an event occurring "now" he is committed only to the belief that it occurred within the current one-tenth of a second.

Nearly all recent writers on this puzzle agree that the solution does lie in rejecting assumption A, but they differ on whether A is a conceptual truth – on whether it is "part of the concept of seeing." Here is how one might argue that it is, so that the foregoing solution would involve a conceptual change. Before we learn in school that light does not travel instantaneously from point to far-distant point as it appears to do, the notion that we can see any past state or event will seem absurd if anyone suggests it to us without any mention of light or its velocity. And before it was discovered two and three centuries ago that light has finite velocity, people would surely have thought it absurd if anyone had suggested that we can see things or states of things which no longer exist. In fact it still seems a very strange thing to say, no doubt because in the overwhelming majority of our visual experiences (seeing things on earth) we only do see objects, states, and events in the present (allowing a *very* brief duration to the present). This experience no doubt affects our thought and verbal understanding in such a way that if anyone were to say that he was seeing an event happening yesterday we would take him to mean that he was imagining it happening yesterday or inferring that it happened yesterday. Otherwise we would have to conclude that he was joking or perhaps had just begun to learn English and did not know what the word "seeing" means. Until we learn about the speed of light, the correct use of "seeing" is perhaps always restricted in this way.

Even when we raise the time-gap problem with people who do know about the speed of light we often find them reluctant to give up that universal restriction, which I have called assumption A. From this I think it is apparent that their concept of seeing has not changed as a result of this knowledge. So perhaps a philosopher can help to change it by explaining to them why assumption A must be dropped if we are to avoid the outrageous conclusion of the argument given above. Since the concept of seeing is part of the system of concepts with which we organize our experience and cope with the world every day, it might seem to follow that science and the need to think consistently have here forced a change in that system.

Another possibility, however, is that the discovery that light has finite speed forces a change only in scientific concepts, not in those of everyday thought. Here are some reasons for taking such a position. While there has to be a change in the *theory* of the time location of objects seen in present time, this requires no practical change in the ordinary use of "seeing" and related words and thoughts. In our everyday thought about seeing, including our everyday thought about seeing stars, we can totally ignore the theoretically required change. As far as the stars, sun, and moon are concerned, our everyday experience *is* the same as if the speed of light were infinite; and so, of course, is our experience of nearer objects. There is no practical advantage in the conceptual change sketched above, and it carries some psychological disadvantage if only because it interferes with settled ways of thought which we get along with very well. So if one takes the position that our ordinary conceptual schemes are practical schemes whose sphere is common experience and the everyday purposes of thinking, it follows that no change in the ordinary concept of seeing is required. Even though seeing is an empirical concept – one having to do with experience rather than with theoretical entities never experienced – we can distinguish two concepts of seeing: the pragmatic one of everyday thought and the one that properly figures in the context of scientific thought where the logical consequences of the finite speed of light must be taken into account. These latter include contexts in which observations and tests are being made and described with the aid of existing theories.

Some readers may object that this is arbitrary, that we can have but one conceptual scheme for our visual experience of the world, and that by insisting on having two schemes a person who argues this way is guilty of obscurantism and reasoning *ad hoc*. That is, he refuses to accept all the logical consequences of new knowledge, and he does so merely to save his thesis that there is no need to change the common-sense scheme. But this objection will lose much of its force if people in fact do retain the old schemes for everyday purposes, and without inconvenience, even when they are aware of new theoretical knowledge and are prepared to use *its* schemes on appropriate occasions. We cannot now undertake the extensive inquiry that might be required in order to determine whether this is so, but let us consider at least two pieces of evidence.

The early development of astronomy, and the later discovery that the earth has axial and orbital motions, must have forced a change in the very concept of space. After all, the primeval core of common-sense which Strawson has attempted to describe conceives of the earth less as something *in* space which may or may not move than as a landmarked surface which, together with the vault of the sky, helps to *constitute* space as a usable system. But in spite of this change, when I watch the sun in late afternoon I think of it as literally going down. Only on rare occasions, for theoretical fun as it were, do I think of myself as standing on a ball which is turning me away from the sun. Still, I always *know* that I am standing on a turning ball, and I accept all the consequences of this fact. So it seems that I operate with both the old scheme and the new, depending on the occasion, and this causes no trouble that I am aware of. It is true that until only a few centuries ago there was not so vast a difference between the spatial scheme of astronomy and the more ancient common-sense scheme; but the fact that there now is a great difference between them does not imply that the common-sense scheme ought to be given up for all purposes.

I have already mentioned the second piece of evidence, namely, the fact that people who understand the time-gap problem are nevertheless often reluctant to admit that we can sometimes see into the past. I have found this to be the case when discussing the problem with people who are scientifically literate and philosophically sophisticated. I take this as a sign that they have two schemes for two different purposes, and assumption *A* remains firmly lodged in one of them.

The following discussion reflects my present opinion that the solution of the real or historical time-gap problem requires no change in our everyday concept of seeing. But this fictional illustration should go through reasonably well even if the reader disagrees with this opinion, or wishes to reserve judgment about it.

14. A PREFABRICATED PHILOSOPHY PROBLEM

Now we have the materials we need to construct our problem. Let us attempt to imagine a group of people who have actually incorporated the finiteness of the speed of light into their everyday conceptual scheme. This will require some anthropological science fiction, and it will be poor science fiction. Good fiction of any kind must be psychologically plausible, and the one we are going to indulge in is highly implausible because it supposes that the people in question are always taking account of this fact about light. As I have just noted, there is nothing in our ordinary visual experience to require this, and it is surely contrary to the most ancient thought habits of human beings to do so. But crude as the illustration may be as fiction, it will serve its purpose if it enables us to say more clearly what we mean by "concepts," "incoherent concepts," and "conceptual revision to solve a philosophical problem." The illustration should also help us clarify the criteria of a good revisionary solution.

It will be convenient to have the following list of abbreviations for describing concepts clearly and concisely, although we shall often spell out our descriptions in words. The reader can always refer back to this list to refresh his or her memory as to the meaning of an abbreviation, but let us also use a mnemonic device. Let the capital letters in the left hand column below correspond with the initial letters of key words in the statements standing to the right. (The exception to this is A, the meaning of which should be easy to remember from the last section.)

$A =$ Whenever we see an object, or state of an object, or an event in which an object is involved, that object must exist and be in that state or involved in that event at the time we see it.

$D =$ In visual context, the present has some slight *d*uration; let us say one-tenth of a second.

$E =$ We can see objects on *e*arth.

$H =$ We can see the *h*eavenly bodies.

$O =$ We can see *o*bjects, material things.

$P =$ In the present, we can see some *p*ast states of some objects, namely those states in which objects have emitted or reflected light directly to our eyes in the present.

$T =$ We can see at *t*ime t the visible states that terrestrial objects have at t.

$V =$ The *v*elocity of light is 186,000 miles per second.

$Z =$ The Present is a boundary of *z*ero duration separating the past from the future.

Now let us tell the following story. The members of a certain island tribe have been in contact with modern culture for several generations and admire certain aspects of it, or rather certain scraps of it. But they have failed to make it their own in any but the most superficial ways. They have acquired a smattering of ideas about physics, for example, without understanding them. They have long been half literate, and it is a popular pastime of theirs to thumb through physics texts, picking up laws of nature without learning any of the associated explanations and theories. These laws they accept on the authority of such texts. The people of this tribe all now believe on this authority that light has finite speed, and they are forever mentioning and marveling at this fact. But they have always taken it for granted that one cannot see into the past, and they have retained this assumption. Not that anyone has ever bothered to state such an obvious truth, but any suggestion that we can see anything that is past would always have been laughingly rejected by them, and still would be. They have as yet failed to notice any reason for giving up this ancient assumption. Another of their acquisitions from "science" is the notion that time can be represented by a line consisting of an infinite number of points, and they take great delight in the notion that the present is a kind of moving line of zero thickness cutting the time line and separating the past from the future. They have learned to prize the "neatness and clarity" of this conception of the present, and they always use it in visual and non-visual contexts alike.

Now comes one of these natives who has flair for philosophical skepticism; he argues as follows. "In order for someone to see an object, light must be transmitted from that object to that person's eyes. Furthermore, if we see an object, we see it in some state or states. Now, since it is a fact that light has finite speed (V is true), and since it would be absurd to suppose that we can see into the past (P is necessarily false), and since whenever we see a state of some object this necessarily is a state which that object is in at the time we see it (A is necessarily true), it follows that we cannot see objects at all." This argument seems to be deductively valid because O, when added to V, not-P, and A, does produce an inconsistent combination of statements, at least when they are taken in conjunction with this philosopher's two prefatory statements about seeing. These latter may be accepted as empirical and conceptual truths respectively. Moreover, the argument is a "sound argument" as this phrase is used in elementary logic, because each of the other premises is also either empirically true (V) or conceptually true in the sense of being a rule for the correct use of words (not-P and A). And our island philosopher is not deviating from or misusing the standard (though of course incoherent) conceptual scheme of his tribe.

His argument puzzles the other philosophers of the tribe, for they can see that it is a sound argument even though they cannot doubt that they do see objects. They worry about this for a generation or two until a visitor to their island, happening to take part in one of their seminars and hearing of their problem, undertakes to explain to them how they can solve it by exchanging their existing scheme of beliefs and linguistic conventions for a coherent one. A series of three lectures is arranged for this purpose.

In the first lecture the visitor explains to his island colleagues that the combination *A, D, E, not-H, O, not-P, T, V* is one they might adopt. That is, they *could* say that they see objects about them even while granting the finiteness of the speed of light and continuing to insist that one cannot see into the past at all. They could do this by allowing some slight duration to the present. But this would have the rather weird consequence that they could not then claim to see the sun, moon, and stars. Such a reconstruction would be logically possible but very uncomfortable for them. So in the second lecture a different line is taken. The visiting philosopher gets them to see that another consistent combination would be *E, H, O, P, not-T, V, Z*. That is, they *could* say that they see both terrestrial and astronomical objects even while granting that light has finite speed and continuing their love affair with the notion that the present is an infinitely fine line separating the past from the future. They could manage this if they would allow that they can see some things which are past. But this would have the really nauseating consequence that they could not claim to see in the present the present states of any objects, even those at their finger tips. The islanders find this ''solution'' even worse than the first one, but the visitor promises them that a satisfactory solution will finally be produced in the third lecture.

The great day arrives and he explains to them what they must do. Since they always want to pay attention to the fact that light has finite speed (*V*), the first thing they should do is admit that they can see some past states of things (they must accept *P*, thus giving up *A*). That will get rid of the worst of their trouble by allowing them to say they can see objects. Secondly, they must allow that the visual present has slight duration (they must accept *D*, thus giving up *Z*), so that they can say that they see present states and not merely past states of things. Thus the solution is *D, E, H, O, P, T, V*. This of course revises their concept of *seeing*. As I am using the term ''concept,'' our concept of something expressed by a certain word or phrase is fixed by those statements employing that word or phrase which we accept (or would accept if asked), plus our other beliefs bearing on the truth or falsity of such statements. Thus the islanders' concept of seeing was an incoherent concept in that it was determined by the inconsistent set of statements *A, E, H, O, not-P, T, V, Z.*

It may take the islanders a while to get used to the revised concept. They may find it unpalatable at first to drop such ancient restrictions as *A* and *not-P*, as well as their more recently adopted convention, *Z*. But admitting that they can see at time *t* states of objects at *t-n* in which those objects transmit light directly to their eyes at *t* should prove far less difficult for them than what they would be required to do under either of the other solutions, to say nothing of having to admit that they cannot see objects at all.

At a wine and cheese party following the third lecture, the island philosophers celebrate the solution of their problem, and the visitor then returns to his own country. A few weeks later he thinks of their problem again, sees a still more efficient revisionary solution, and cables them as follows. "You do not *have* to pay attention to *V* in your everyday thought; it is just a fad there. You can keep all the rest of your old concept of seeing if you will just drop *V* from it. If you ever really learn to do physics you will have to pay attention to *V* when doing it, but in all of your ordinary visual affairs *V* will be unnecessary even then, and a bit of a nuisance. In such affairs you can always get along better with *A, E, H, O, not-P, T, Z.*"

This is indeed the most efficient of the four revisionary solutions, at least if we may distinguish a scientific concept of seeing from the everyday concept, as suggested in the last section.

15. THE THEORY OF STAGE FOUR

There seem to be several lessons that we can learn from this story.

(1) The fact that a philosophical argument has no factual or deductive errors in it and "proves" something we all know is false does not show that the argument must distort or mismanage existing concepts. Even if all philosophical problems were generated by formally and factually impeccable arguments "proving" something we know is false, it would not

follow (as the most orthodox Wittgensteinians insist) that we are always forbidden to move from the stage of attempted dissolution to that of conceptual reform. Here it might be objected that no one ever had the problem formulated in our story, and that no group of people ever could have so transparently incoherent a scheme of beliefs and language conventions. This may be true, but it is irrelevant to the present point. We are not now arguing that anyone's concept of anything *is* incoherent, but only that *if* it is then some obviously false conclusion might be argued for in a "sound" argument employing that concept; that is, in a formally unexceptionable argument from true premises. Furthermore, even if it is a fact that no group of people could persistently adhere to so obviously defective a scheme as that of our islanders, this does not show that we never use schemes of beliefs and conventions which are incoherent in more subtle ways.

(2) Revisionary solutions to philosophical problems — if there are any problems requiring them — will not necessarily involve radical revision, i.e. conceptual change at the very core of our thinking. They need not be like the skeptic's proposal to revise the concept of numerical identity (Section 10), or like the neo-Berkeleyan's revision of the concept of a material object (Section 3). Indeed, the most economical reconstruction will no doubt leave our more basic notions relatively undisturbed. The thought is illustrated not only in the cablegram solution of merely dropping V from the islanders' everyday thought, but also in the third lecture's proposal. There, of course, the visiting philosopher never thinks of accepting a combination with *not-O* in it, and he looks for ways to save such important beliefs or structural assumptions as $H, E,$ and T: the assumptions that we can see the heavenly bodies, objects on earth, and the present states of objects on earth. He manages this by choosing D over Z and P over A. The first of these choices merely endorses what many philosophers have been in the bad habit of calling the "specious present," as though all thought had to be modeled on physics where time is expressed with the real numbers and the very notion of an experienced present is impossible. That is, it says that the islanders may properly allow the present some trifling duration, as of course we all normally do. And the second choice merely "gives our eyes access to the past," to use Sir Alfred Ayer's expression for this. It is a fittingly bland expression in the context of our imaginary problem. For while this change would

represent a fairly shocking departure from our ordinary scheme, it is not so great a revision of the incoherent physics-warped scheme which the islanders had been using.

(3) The standard for good revisionary solutions seems to be one of economizing in epistemic and linguistic change. That is, we should try to purchase the greatest coherence in our system of beliefs and language conventions for the least revision of that system. The best solution to a given problem of this nature would be that revision which removes it most economically. The extent of the revision would perhaps be indicated by the number and importance of the beliefs and conventions revised, while the measure of the gain in coherence would be the number and systematic extent of the conflicts removed. Obviously this could not be a matter for nice calculation, but there can be little doubt that some revisions would be much more radical than others, and that some achievements of systematic harmony would reach much farther than others.

Kant's "Copernican revolution," mentioned in Section 4, is the attempt by one great philosopher to solve many conceptual problems through a single, admittedly fundamental revision. Not only is Kant intentionally revisionary, but he seems to be fully aware of the need for economy. He realizes that only the achievement of great systematic harmony could justify so profound a change from the outlook of commonsense. Of course, whether his revision really is needed to save our ordinary notions of perceptual knowledge, substance, cause, self-awareness, and so on, or does succeed in saving them, are different questions from the one with which we are presently concerned. In a brief remark in the Introduction to *Individuals*, Strawson classified Kant as a predominantly descriptive metaphysician, though perhaps a revisionary one in some respects since none of the great philosophers, presumably, were exclusively one or the other. I may be saying substantially the same thing in different words when I point out that in his revision Kant strove for great systematic harmony in which *nearly* all of our most basic notions and assumptions would be preserved. The predominantly revisionary metaphysicians may be those who, in their system building, are less attracted by problem-solving economy than by novelty and daring.

(4) The same standard would seem to apply to revisionary and non-revisionary philosophy alike since a fully successful dissolution would be

a *perfectly* economical solution. That is, it would produce a reconciliation in some system of beliefs and conventions without having to change any of them. Strictly speaking it would not produce but reveal a consistent combination. It would show that the appearance of inconsistency produced by the problem-generating argument was only an appearance, and it would show this by convincingly exhibiting conceptual distortions or confusions in the argument itself. Dissolutions and revisionary solutions seem to be related to each other in the following way. First, if a philosophical problem does have a perfectly economical solution in the conceptual cards, then that is *the* solution to it, although it will not be quite clear that the problem does have such a solution until it is actually produced and worked out in detail. On the other hand, if a problem turns on an incoherent concept or scheme the only good solution it can have will be revisionary. Again it will not be clear that this is so until someone shows convincingly just what the incoherence is and how it produces the problem. But once this is shown we will know that the most economical revision is not just a second-rate thing which we have to be content with, but *the* solution to the problem.

(5) Certain obligations fall to the philosopher who goes on from stage three to stage four in his attempts to solve a philosophical problem. He must try to explain convincingly how the problem does depend on one or more inconsistencies in our existing scheme of thought, and not on difficulties which have been confusedly introduced by philosophical reflection itself. And when he gives his revisionary solution it is up to him to explain why this is probably the most economical solution open to us. These may be heavy obligations in some cases, but I see no reason why they could never be discharged if there are, indeed, conceptual problems which can only be solved at stage four. Suppose a philosopher working on a problem did manage to give convincing arguments on each of these points. Then it would only show the tenacity of our prejudice if we insisted that he had not really solved it because a way of dissolving it might still lie hidden in the cards.

PART TWO

CHAPTER 5

METAPHYSICS OUT OF LOGIC

16. INTRODUCTION TO PART TWO

In the second and third chapters we illustrated the outlook of mid-century philosophy in contrast with the older speculative philosophy. But the attitude of the post-war writers had developed from a third point of view, widely different from either of those two, which had prevailed only a generation earlier among the analytic philosophers themselves. Our illustrations in the next two chapters are intended to show the main lines of this development, thus providing that shorter and more recent perspective on the revolution in philosophy which I mentioned at the beginning of Part One. It will be well to give an advance sketch of the development, indicating how the famous arguments serving as our illustrations were a part of it. But first I must say a few words about the late 19th-century speculative philosophy against which the founders of the modern analytic school were reacting.

Moore and Russell began their adult philosophical lives with a concerted attack on the Absolute Idealism of F. H. Bradley, the most influential British philosopher at the turn of the century. In his chief metaphysical work, *Appearance and Reality* (1893), Bradley had held that common-sense and science are both inadequate vehicles for understanding reality. This is because they think "relationally." Indeed, all thought is relational, dividing the world into discrete things and relations between things, and relations between the properties of things. According to arguments developed in Book I of that work, the very notion of a relation is self-contradictory. And since nothing real can be designated by a contradictory term, all relations are ultimately unreal. Not that Bradley denied the practical usefulness of thought. He did not believe that we can dispense with common-sense, and he recognized that science improves our ability to cope with "appearances." But he severely downgraded both science and common sense as access roads to the Real. They do not merely lead us astray from time to time in our metaphysical quest; they systematically falsify the true nature of things. We could not *know* Reality unless we knew it whole, and this is humanly impossible. Even philosophy can tell us very little, for it too is relational discourse. But through this very critique of thought we can at least gain some glimpse of the Real. We get some notion of Reality from immediate experience: pure feeling or awareness before it is cast into the categories of thought. Reality is an undifferentiated spiritual whole; it is absolute or unqualified "experience." But it is not experienc*ed*, as in Berkeley's Subjective Idealism, for that would involve a *cognitive relation*. Similarly, it is not a *person* or in any way personal; the Absolute is not God.

   We shall not examine Bradley's arguments, nor shall we include an illustration from Moore's classic attack on Idealism and the Bradleyan doctrine of relations ('The Refutation of Idealism,' 1903). We have to begin at some arbitrary point in the history of philosophical discussion, and it is necessary to place some limit on the number of our illustrations. Let it suffice merely to mention in this way the type of speculative philosophy to which Moore and Russell were responding. But it should be added that while our first illustration contains no attack on Bradley's position, it does express the very opposite viewpoint. Russell is quite confident that we *can* make progress in metaphysical understanding through a process of analysis – that we do not murder Reality by intellectually dissecting it. And in our second illustration we shall see some of the details of the radically pluralist metaphysics which he developed in conscious opposition to Bradley's monism.

   Impressed by the increased scope and clarity of logic in its new mathematical dress, and by its demonstrated power to clarify the basic concepts of mathematics, Russell was eager to see whether it could be equally useful in other fields of philosophical inquiry. This hope seemed to bear fruit at once in his analysis of "descriptions," especially as it applied to certain ontological puzzles that were then under discussion (our first illustration). For it appeared that logic could uncover the "true form" of facts expressed in the misleading grammatical forms of English and other natural languages. To be sure, mathematical logic did not provide a perfect language; it lacked a vocabulary to deal with the world. But Russell came to think that its syntax already approached that of an ideally explicit and unambiguous language. Perhaps, then. we could learn from its syntactical forms what the "forms of facts" in general must be, and how facts combine to make up a world. This ambition is reflected in Russell's lectures on "Logical Atomism' (1918), which provide the subject of our second illustration. It is also seen in the linguistic and metaphysical atomism of Wittgenstein's *Tractatus Logico-Philosophicus* (1921), from which we draw our third illustration. Though presented in a highly obscure manner, Wittgenstein's version is more impressive on careful study because it avoids controversial assumptions of an epistemological kind and seems to show more directly how the meaningfulness of language demands a certain type of world structure.

Logical atomism provided the metaphysical justification for a general method of philosophizing which was then practiced by Russell and his admirers during the nineteen-twenties and thirties. According to this view, philosophy aims for exact analyses of conceptually troublesome sentences – ideally for *complete* analyses yielding full understanding of the realities dealt with in these sentences. If we could arrive at syntactically correct arrangements of the elements of sentences, and suitable semantical analyses reaching down towards the smallest elements of their meaning, we could expect to make great progress with the whole gamut of traditional problems, extending from political philosophy at one end of the analytical scale to perception and sense-data at the other. But during the middle and later thirties, many people became increasingly dubious of this ideal. Few impressive analyses were actually produced, and Wittgenstein himself became convinced that his earlier views were mistaken. In our fourth illustration we indicate some of the reasons for his change of heart, reasons which he worked hard to improve from about 1934 onward. We consider them in the form they eventually took in his *Philosophical Investigations* (1953), the work from which we drew an illustration in Chapter 2. They show why some of the main assumptions of the *Tractatus* are great oversimplifications of the nature of language, despite their initial plausibility. Thus while the *Tractatus* is a classic development of the theory of language and reality which flows from those assumptions in combination with Russell's logic, the *Investigations* is a classic dissolution of that theory.

Wittgenstein's 1933–35 criticisms of his earlier views circulated among philosophers in the form of mimeographed lecture notes, and they contributed to the general loss of faith in logical atomism. There were other important causes, several of which we shall notice in due course. By the late thirties most analytically minded philosophers had ceased to engage in metaphysical speculation of any kind, and this continued to be their attitude when discussion resumed after 1945. Those who continued to practice analysis in the style which atomism had seemed to justify were forced to look elsewhere for justification, and some found it for a time in the anti-metaphysical movement known as Logical Positivism. It was recalled that the one completely successful piece of analysis in this style, Russell's own theory of descriptions, had originally been used by him to deflate a metaphysical doctrine (someone else's, of course), not to construct one. So perhaps the syntax of logic could continue to be useful in what the Positivists saw as the two activities remaining to philosophy: prophylaxis against metaphysics and clarification of the logic of science. But in 1950 that paradigm of analysis itself came under powerful attack when P. F. Strawson showed its inadequacy as an account of the logic of descriptive phrases in natural language. We discuss this famous criticism in our fifth illustration.

Strawson's article was but one of many indications that earlier claims for the philosophical power of mathematical logic had to be considerably reduced. For about fifteen years after World War II much greater emphasis was placed on the informal elucidation of concepts through close attention to the ways in which people actually use language, and fewer attempts were made to produce exact analyses, with or without the aid of symbolic notation. Other devices of informal elucidation besides those of "ordinary language philosophy" were also usefully employed, a fact which our earlier example from Strawson can be used to illustrate.

Such, then, is our second perspective on the great change which philosophy had undergone by the nineteen-fifties. The profound respect for common-sense and natural language which is characteristic of philosophers like Moore, the later Wittgenstein, Austin, and Strawson, seemed to mark as great an improvement over earlier analytic philosophy as the latter had made over the speculative tradition.

And yet Russell's heritage — his analytical style if not his metaphysical doctrine — has refused to stay dead. Indeed it suffered no very prolonged decline on the American side of the water, where it again dominates such fields as epistemology, metaphysics, and philosophy of law, or aesthetics. Many journal articles in the former subjects use symbolic notation extensively, and Russell-like references to the "stone-age metaphysics of common sense" are not infrequently heard. Prominent philosophers again hope or yearn to discover the most general traits of reality with the aid of science and logical syntax.

Is this an unfortunate surrender of hard won ground by people who never quite saw the point and value of mid-century philosophy? Or is it perhaps a salutary counter-revolution against the looseness and impressionism found in some of Wittgenstein's admirers? A third possibility is that philosophy now builds on the strongest elements in both strands of the analytic tradition, i.e. "philosophical analysis" and "conceptual elucidation." I shall return to this question in later chapters and the Conclusion, but here it may be well to say very briefly which view I think is more likely to be correct. It seems to me that recent American thinkers in the tradition of Russell are pursuing descriptive and speculative interests which *need* not conflict with the assumptions described in Part One of this book, assumptions which still dominate various subjects in philosophy. "Scientific realism" and the "descriptive metaphysics" of common-sense may complement each other as accounts of different (though systematically related) aspects of reality. I doubt that very much sense can be made of the Russellian claim that the ancient and indispensable structures of everyday thought are somehow "real but less real" than the structures and entities of scientific theory. Furthermore, the analyst and the elucidator can each pursue his favorite method for whatever fruits of clarification or new construction it may yield. And if they are open minded they can learn from each other's accomplishments.

Let us complete our preview of Part Two by briefly describing the sequence of illustrations in our seventh and eighth chapters. Some talented philosophers who began their careers well before World War II have never been deeply impressed by "Oxbridge philosophy," as they are wont to refer to the type of thought illustrated in our second and third chapters. Perhaps this is just as well when their chief interests lie in logic itself, or in the philosophy of mathematics and science, fields in which the Oxford and Cambridge philosophers of the 1945–1960 period have had less to say, and in which Russell's contribution is permanently impressive. A case in point is W. V. Quine, the most widely known American philosopher of his generation. Our sixth illustration in this Part deals with his most influential article. An interesting feature of the article is that it reverses the "heuristic direction" between language and the world which one finds in Russell and the early Wittgenstein. While they thought that true syntax of language can help us discover how the world must be, Quine thinks that in the progress of science the world teaches us what the meaning of our words must be. And the lesson is never complete; no statement is safely and permanently "analytic," i.e. true by virtue of its meaning alone. Quine is equally well known for his project of developing "canonical notation," whether to facilitate particular scientific inquiries or to pursue the metaphysical quest for ultimate categories. While logical syntax cannot tell us how the world *must* be constructed, he thinks it can help us see more clearly how the world *is* constructed. Our seventh illustration deals with this topic.

The illustrations in Chapter 8 are drawn from two younger American thinkers whose ideas have recently been at the center of attention in philosophy of language and continue to reverberate in other areas where the theory of meaning is crucial. Keith Donnellan notices certain features of our use of descriptive phrases which were missed by Russell and Strawson alike (and for that matter by Quine), features that bring to light a certain gap between the "meaning" and the "reference" of words. Saul Kripke exploits this gap to develop a rather startling account of proper names and common nouns, especially nouns designating the "natural kinds" of things which are investigated (or can be investigated) in science. These discussions bring strong support to Quine's point of view in the article first mentioned. Kripke also thinks this new doctrine of meaning has important implications for the mind-body problem as discussed by recent philosophers. Our last illustration in this Part examines his opinion on that point.

The scheme of philosophical methods developed in Part One will continue to be useful in a number of ways. Although none of the four "stages" are in play when Russell and Wittgenstein construct their own metaphysical theories, stage three is impressively illustrated by their arguments attacking theories which they reject. One example is Russell's argument against "Meinongian" ontology (Section 17). Another is Wittgenstein's later criticism (Section 21) of his own theory in the *Tractatus*. Our stages can also throw light at times on famous arguments which do not exemplify them. We shall see, for example, how Strawson's criticism of Russell's theory of descriptions can be amplified by explaining how someone of Strawson's views might offer to dissolve the puzzle which Russell was trying to dissolve (Section 22). And we shall return to our Chapter 4 illustration of the fourth stage in order to gain a better understanding of Quine's critique of the analytic-synthetic distinction (Section 24). Stage four will also have an important role to play in the third Part of this book.

17. RUSSELL ON DESCRIPTIONS

The argument which we are about to discuss appears in several of Russell's works from 1905 onward. As I have already mentioned, it was long regarded as a model of successful analysis. It seemed to give a definitive solution to the problem to which he first applied it, and it remains a most impressive "stage three" performance. That problem has to do with so-called "Meinongian" objects: objects which do not exist but which nevertheless seem to be real in some weird sense because we are able to refer to them and say things about them. Russell thought the problem results from mistaking the grammar of certain sentences for their logical form, and that this can be seen by rewriting them in such a way as to make the surface grammar coincide with logical form. He claimed to show that the problem disappears once the true form is exhibited in this way.

Let us consider his account as a response to a specific problem-generating argument. In this case the argument is not skeptical but "hyper-realistic." It would force us to accept the reality of something which common-sense is by no means willing to accept. Let us state it in the following paragraph.

"Unicorns do not exist." "The round square does not exist." Each of these sentences says something true about something which does not exist, namely, *that* it does not exist. In order to do this, the sentences must refer to something by their subject nouns or noun phrases. They must refer, respectively, to certain things which do not happen to exist (unicorns) and to something which could not possibly exist (the round square). But how could the sentences successfully refer in this way unless there were something there for them to refer *to*? Please notice that these sentences are not about the *idea* of unicorns or about the *expression* "round square." Those kinds of things − ideas and expressions − certainly do exist, so there is no problem about admitting their reality. And the very fact that they do exist is enough to make it obvious that these true sentences denying the existence of something are not about them. No, these sentences are about horselike animals with long sharp horns growing out of their foreheads, and about the geometrical figure which is both round and square. The fact that they refer to such objects forces us to admit strange new entities to our ontology. Some of us may have thought that only particular things existing in space and time are real, such as particular men. Others may have been willing to admit the reality of "universals" such as manhood, existing over and above the manhood of particular men. But now we must also admit the reality of things which do not exist at all, such as unicorns. We must even admit the reality of things which could not possibly exist, such as the round square. And if we admit the reality of universals, we now have to admit two strange new kinds of universals, those which are never in fact exemplified, like unicornhood, and those which could not possibly be exemplified, like round squarehood.

Some such argument has frequently been attributed, though perhaps not quite accurately, to the German philosopher Alexius Meinong (1853–1920). Russell himself thought for a time that we must accept it. In the next few paragraphs I shall summarize his account of "descriptions" which seems to dissolve this problem by clearly exhibiting the underlying mistake on which the whole argument depends. I shall not allude to any of the doubts that some later philosophers have had about Russell's account; several of their criticisms are taken up in later sections. Rather, I shall present it in the original, unqualified form which two generations of philosophers found convincing, and which some still accept as sound.

First consider *indefinite* descriptions, those consisting of a noun-phrase or clause beginning with the indefinite article; for example, "a man," "a unicorn," "a man I met yesterday," "a square," "a round square." Unlike a proper name, such an expression does not pick out any particular thing even though in English grammar it often functions similarly to substantive expressions which do. Compare "I met a man" and "I met Elmer Q. Jones." The indefinite description and the proper name are the respective grammatical objects of these sentences and both may seem ot refer to a particular person I met. But a little reflection will make it clear that, unlike the name, which does pick out a certain person, and unlike the common noun "man," which denotes all particular men, the expression "a man" does not name or pick out any particular man. It is not its meaning or function to do so in the sentence "I met a man," even though someone who uses this sentence may very well have a particular man in mind. If the speaker wants to *say* which particular man he met, he will have to add something, as in "I met a man, namely Elmer Q. Jones." The difference is made clear in the language of *Principia Mathematica* (1910–1913), the classic work by Russell and A. N. Whitehead on mathematical logic and philosophy of mathematics. "I met a man" is a general statement the logical form of which is "There exists an x such that x is a man and I met x," whereas "I met Elmer Q. Jones" is a statement about two particulars, Jones and me. Its logical form contains no quantifier (no "There exists an x such that," and no "For any x"), and no propositional functions or open sentences (nothing like "x is a man" or "I met x"). Its form is simply "A met B," where the letters A and B stand for proper names.

The lesson in this so far is that an indefinite description denotes nothing and drops out in favor of one or more open sentences when we rewrite the sentence in which it occurs so that the surface grammar of the sentence comes to reflect its logical form. Thus we need not fear that the meaningfulness of "I met a unicorn" or the truth of "I did not meet a unicorn" force us to concur with the reality of unicorns on the ground that these sentences do manage to refer to them. From a correct logical point of view they do not refer to something and then say that I did or did not meet it. Rather, they respectively assert and deny that something exists (or existed) which has (or had) two characteristics: that of unicornhood and that of being met by me.

Next, let us consider *definite* descriptions, those consisting of a noun-phrase or clause beginning with the definite article; for example, "the unicorn I met yesterday," "the present King of France," "the tallest building in Chicago," "the author of *Waverley*." Because of the presence of "the," it is even easier to suppose that a definite description must function in the way a proper name usually functions, namely, to designate a real particular. But they actually have somewhat different functions, as will be apparent from the fact that we cannot substitute one for the other in a sentence without changing its meaning. For example, if we take the sentence "The author of *Waverley* is Scott" and substitute "Scott" for "The author of *Waverley*," we get the mere tautology that Scott is Scott in place of the fact of literary history with which we began.

That it is not the logical function of definite descriptions to denote something becomes clear when we analyze the logical form of the sentences in which they occur. Take "The author of *Waverley* was Scott." This sentence will be false if no one wrote *Waverley*, or if more than one person wrote it, or if the person who wrote it was not Scott. Thus the sentence means that [at least one person wrote *Waverley*, at most one person wrote it, and no one who wrote it was not Scott]. In this latter compound sentence in brackets, which is thus the logical analysis of the quoted sentence according to Russell, there is no proper name except *Waverley*, the name of a certain novel, and nothing else that we might be misled into thinking is *like* a proper name. For the definite description, "The author of *Waverley*," has dropped out. All we have now are quantifiers, open sentences, the connecting words "and" and "if ... then," and an expression for identity. Thus: "There exists an *x* such that *x* wrote *Waverley* (someone wrote *Waverley*); and for any *x* and any *y*, if *x* and *y* wrote *Waverley*, then *x* = *y* (at most one person wrote *Waverley*); and it is false that there exists an *x* such that *x* wrote *Waverley* and *x* was not Scott (no one wrote *Waverley* who was not Scott)." There is nothing left that even looks like a noun or nominative expression denoting the author of *Waverley*. Definite descriptions, in short, are no part of the logical form of the sentences in which they occur, but are only part of the surface grammar. Since they are not essential to what is being said, we need not suppose that the sentences must refer to some actual entities to which they correspond.

This is not only true of "the author of *Waverley*" and other definite descriptions having to do with something real; it is also true of "the round square," "the present King of France," and "the unicorn I met yesterday." Thus "The present King of France is wise" becomes "There is now one and only one person who is King of France, and no one who is King of France is not wise," i.e. the false assertion that there now exists just one thing which has the characteristics of being King of France and wise. Similarly, "The round square does not exist" is the true assertion that there is no geometrical figure which is both round and square, or equivalently, that roundness and squareness are never jointly exemplified. The latter two formulations give us the true logical form of the fact being stated. To be sure, a formulation like "The round square does not exist" will do very well for our usual purposes in talking Geometry, but it tends to mislead us when the purpose at hand is on-tological reflection. That is, it leads to hyper-realism when we are con-sidering what kinds of entities there are, or what kinds we are committed to by the language we use. It misleads us into saying that nonexistent things are real, at least in some watered down sense of reality, because we manage to refer to them and say something about them. But analysis reveals that the phrase "the round square" does not refer to anything, and only stands for the conjunction of two characteristics; further, that existence and nonexistence are not characteristics of things, but logical quantifiers.

If such an analysis is correct, it effectively dissolves the problem stated in the third paragraph of this Section. One way to bring this out is to ask whether the analysis proves that unicorns and the round square are *not* entities in some strange realms of watered down reality called "the non-existent but possible" and "the impossible but mentionable." The answer is that the analysis (if correct) does not prove such a thing but does destroy the only reason we had for taking the suggestion seriously. If we preserve our "feeling for reality ... even in the most abstract studies," says Russell, we will not want to take it seriously, and we will try to find a good reason not to do so. His account seems to find that reason by explaining a confusion between grammatical form and logical form on which the problem-generating argument depends throughout, and to which it owes whatever appeal it has.

I have been emphasizing the point that Russell's argument illustrates our third or "dissolution" approach to a philosophical problem. But it has more often been cited to illustrate the thesis that philosophy pro-blems arise from the logically misleading character of natural language, and that if we are to approach such problems with any hope of solving them we should consider how they might be formulated in an ideal language. The argument is thought to show how, when our work is thus well begun it may turn out to be more than half done; the solution may become patent in the "analysis": the translation into ideal language of the sentences that gave us trouble. Russell also thought that the par-ticular lesson emerging in the present case − that definite descriptions do not denote anything because they drop out in the translation — could be used in metaphysical speculation for his own account. It could be used to construct his own theory of what kinds of things are real. Let us turn to the theory of this type which appears in his lectures entitled 'The Philosophy of Logical Atomism,' 1918.

18. RUSSEL'S ATOMISM

Obviously we cannot cover all the details of Russell's lectures, but I hope we can catch the main lines of his argument by briefly discussing four pieces of apparatus that he uses. First is the syntactical structure of the new logic which he had done so much to clarify and standardize in the work co-authored with Whitehead. Second is the tradition of British empiricism in the theory of knowledge; especially the doctrine known as phenomenalism, a sample of which we have already encountered in Berkeley's philosophy (Section 3). Third is his own doctrine of incomplete symbols and logical fictions. Definite descriptions are one type of incomplete symbol. And fourth is the traditional principle of theory construction known as Occam's Razor. According to this principle, the theorist ought always to reduce the risk of error by dispensing with as many "obvious" but unproved premises as possible, and by eliminating all assumed entities that are not absolutely necessary to the theory. Let us consider these ideas in the order listed.

1. We may begin our discussion of the first idea with an allusion to the third and fourth. The theory of descriptions was impressive because it explained how to get rid of certain entities that Russell's "feeling for reality" could not tolerate. The special syntax exploited by that theory had also been put to impressive use in the attempt to reduce classical mathematics to set theory or the logic of classes, and to explain how mathematical truths can be expressed entirely in the elementary symbols of logic. It therefore seemed reasonable to hope that it would be equally useful in other philosophical projects, notably in the construction of metaphysical theories. In order to get a better idea of the latter ambition, let us first briefly add to the sketch of logical syntax given in the last section.

We saw that part of the analysis of a sentence containing a definite description is the statement that there exists an x such that x is F, where

F is such and such a characteristic. Now according to the Russell – Whitehead logic, the latter statement is in turn analyzable into a certain string of propositions stated as non-exclusive alternatives. Thus: a is F, or b is F, or c is F, or ..., etc., continuing through all the "values" of the "variable" x, i.e. all the individual things named by a, b, c, etc., which fall within the range of x. Thus one can easily see that if the foregoing "existence statement" is true, at least one named particular has characteristic F. Suppose that it is true that there exists a man who is over eight feet tall; then if we examine all men who are now alive we will find at least one (named Charlie Smith or whatever) who has attained that height.

Next, consider universal sentences of the form "For every value of x, x is F." Here the analysis is given in a conjunction (not an alternation) of singular sentences. Thus: a is F, *and* b is F, *and* c is F, and ..., etc., through all the values of the variable. The analysis will also include the statement that those *are* all the values. Suppose that the context of discourse has indicated that x ranges over human beings; and suppose that 'F' means 'is mortal' or 'dies someday.' Then the analysis is "Socrates is mortal, and Julius Caesar is mortal, and Charlie Smith is mortal, and ..., etc., listing by name every human who has lived or will live, plus the statement, "Those are all the humans."

Or consider the slightly more complex universal statement, "All crows are black." This becomes "For every value of x, if x is a crow then x is black," and that in turn is analyzable (putting 'F' for 'crow' and 'G' for 'black') as "If a if F then a is G, and if b is F then b is G, and if c is F then c is G, and ..., and so on. We go through all the values of x (all individual birds, let us say) and we form a hypothetical (if-then) sentence about each of them. Then we make a conjunction of all these hypothetical singular sentences. And once again we must add, "Those are all the values of x," if we are to express the whole meaning of the original statement that all crows are black.

More complex statements in ordinary language are analyzed into combinations of existence statements and universal statements. And the analysis may require several variables, x, y, z, ..., several predicates (including "relational" predicates, on which we will say something later), and signs for negation and identity. I shall not give examples of these more complex analyses beyond those already given in the preceding section. It will be sufficient for our purposes to mention three features of every analysis, whether it be a simple or complex one. (1) When the analysis is complete it will always include strings of singular sentences about particular entities. (2) Each of these latter sentences will contain one or more proper names and the name of a quality or relation. (3) "General" statements cannot be entirely eliminated; that is, there will always remain the statement that we have exhausted all values of the variable(s) in listing our sentences about particular entities.

What philosophical lessons do these syntactical points suggest? One obvious point is that sometimes we will not be able to know whether a statement is true, because we will not be able to examine every particular named in the analysis. That is, we will not be able to see whether it does have quality F or does stand in relation R to some other particular. And sometimes we will not even have good *evidence* that all of them *probably* have F, or that at least one of them probably has F in the case of a simple existence statement, and so on. (Contrast the case of "All men are mortal," where we do have plenty of evidence, though we cannot inspect every human.) But of course there is nothing surprising in this; we knew all along that we were not omniscient, and this syntactical analysis of the meaning of statements only makes it clearer why this is so. A less obvious lesson is that we are forced to ask whether there must actually *be* values of the variable if the sentence we are analyzing is to have meaning. Another way to put this is to ask whether certain things must *exist* (whether there must actually be real things having the names '*a*,' '*b*,' etc.) before we can say something that makes sense, even something false. This is a rather surprising question because one would have thought that we could *mean* to say whatever we wished quite independently of how the world happens to be — quite independently of what *actually* exists, or what facts actually obtain. But now it appears that the singular statements in an analysis will lack meaning unless *there are* entities named by the names, and that the ordinary sentence having that analysis will therefore lack any definite meaning unless this is so. That was the conclusion Russell came to.

2. He also thought that the entities which must exist if language is to have meaning cannot be the bearers of *ordinary* proper names like 'Ronald Reagan,' 'Man o'-War,' 'Everest,' 'Britain,' and so on. Nor can they be proper names like '*a*', '*b*', '*c*', etc., when these are allowed to

stand for individual crows or other material objects. For he held two other philosophical opinions: (1) that every proposition which we can understand must be composed wholly of constituents with which we are "acquainted," i.e. of which we have had immediate experience; and (2) that we are not "acquainted" with the objects which ordinary proper names purport to designate. Both of these opinions or these are Russellian variations on familiar themes in the tradition of British empiricism. Thesis (1) recalls the doctrine in David Hume and Bishop Berkeley (and, with qualifications, in Locke) that genuine ideas are based wholly on experience, while words or phrases which neither refer to what we have experienced nor are compounded of such references (like "the golden mountain") are really meaningless. And thesis (2) is reminiscent of Berkeley's theory of objects discussed above in Section 3, a theory which has descendants in the philosophies of Hume, J. S. Mill, and others. It will be recalled that Berkeley rejected the notion of "material substance" lying beneath or supporting the sensible qualities of an object because he thought no meaning could be attached to the phrase. And he held that a material object is nothing different from a certain *system* of actual perceptions or sense-data. These, for Berkeley, were sensations in various people's minds, plus an uninterrupted awareness of the object in God's mind. But Russell leaves God out of it and makes do with actual and possible sense-data. He says that the system of sense-data constituting the object includes those experiences someone *would* have if properly situated at a given time, even though no one *is* having any experience of the object at that time.

If the proper names appearing in the complete analysis of a sentence about ordinary objects were the names of momentary sense-data, then two problems to which I have just alluded would be solved, or so it seemed to Russell. First of all, there *would* be existing entities bearing the names, and the singular propositions would *not* lack meaning on that account. Nor would the sentence in ordinary language which is being analyzed lack definite meaning due to such a failure. There is no question that a present sense datum, for example, is real, whatever material object it may or may not help to constitute. (Hallucinatory sense-data or "phantoms" are of course real in themselves, even though they are not systematically connected to other sense-data in the ways we expect. In the case of the desert mirage, the further sense-data associated with shade

and water and drinking are not forthcoming.) Secondly, the singular
sentences in the analysis *would* be composed wholly of constituents of
which we have had immediate experience, i.e. the momentary sense data
themselves, and their qualities and relations to one another. So these
sentences would not lack meaning on *that* account, nor would the ordinary sentence which is being analyzed. Of course, language does not
contain proper names for momentary sense data but a crude approxima-
tion of a singular sentence appearing in the complete analysis might be
something like "This is red and to the right of that," where 'this' and
'that' are made to serve as proper names of sense-data. 'Red' and 'to the
right of' are names of a property and a relation of which we have had
immediate experience.

   3. Taking note of the foregoing logical and epistemological considerations, and seeing no other way to guarantee that language has meaning,
Russell thought that we are committed to recognize "atomic facts" and
their constituents as the "basic realities." An atomic fact consists of a
momentary sense datum and its qualities, or two or more momentary
sense data and their relation. Any complete account of the world would
have to contain atomic propositions corresponding to such facts. And it
would also have to contain the general propositions which cannot be
eliminated in logical analysis. In other words, the world contains some
general facts along with the atomic facts.

   What else does the world or reality contain? Here is where Russell's
doctrine of incomplete symbols and logical fictions comes into our account, although it is no clear that what he has to say on the topic is entirely consistent. He tells us that an incomplete symbol is a word or
phrase that has not meaning all by itself the way a proper name has; it
has meaning only in the context of a sentence, and it also drops out of
the analysis of any sentence in which it appears. Thus definite descriptions are incomplete symbols, as we have noted. And by a logical fiction
he seems to mean the entity which an incomplete symbols purports to
designate. Thus "the present King of France" is an incomplete symbol
and the present King of France is a logical fiction. Yet the word "fiction"
is misleading here, since Russell apparently does not wish to deny that
many definite descriptions do apply to things which exist, e.g. "the
tallest building in Chicago" or "the oldest person in this room," even
though these phrases do not stand for the tallest building or the oldest

person in the same way that proper names stand for things or persons. So I think Russell should only be taken to mean that since certain symbols like "the present King of France" and "the round square" do drop out in the course of analyzing a sentence, we are not *forced* (by their presence in a meaningful sentence) to say that they stand for something real. Thus logical fictions may or may not exist.

Now, material objects (e.g. the tallest building in Chicago) are nevertheless logical fictions in another way, according to Russell. For (A) a material object is a series of classes (a class of actual or possible sense-data at time t, another such class at time $t + 1$, another such class at $t + 2$, and so on), where the successive classes stand in certain relations required for them to constitute a "real" object rather than an "unreal" object like the mirage. And (B) Russell holds that all classes are themselves logical fictions. The whole series is, of course, a class of classes. In the course of analysis, names of classes are replaced by expressions for propositional functions or open sentences, like "x is F" and the like. A given class is nothing but the individuals that satisfy a given function, i.e. that give us true singular propositions when we substitute their names for the variable. So Russell holds that any statement about a material object can be reduced to (a vast number of) statements about particular sense-data. That is to say, it can be so reduced "in principle"; no one can *actually* give the complete analysis.

He also holds that statements about minds (even one's own mind) can similarly be reduced to statements about particular mental occurrences. For in these lectures he accepts Hume's doctrine that we have no experience of our own mind, considered as a mental "substance" or thing. (Look within yourself, says Hume, and you will only be aware of various thoughts and experiences, the so-called "contents" of your "mind." You will never encounter the mind itself.) So if the word "mind" is to have meaning it can only refer to the "bundle" of thoughts and experiences — Hume's word — which stand in certain relations, such as memory, leading you to say that they are thoughts and experiences of one and the same person, yourself. Thus a mind too is a logical fiction; it too is a series or class of classes. Here again the classes collect thoughts and experiences occurring at different points in time, and the orderliness of the series convinces one that the items they collect all "belong to the same mind."

Also to be listed among Russell's logical fictions are numbers, for he had shown in his studies of the foundations of mathematics how any cardinal number, for example, can be defined as a class of classes similar to a given class. Physical elements such as "atoms, ions, corpuscles or what not" are also logical fictions. "Your atom has got to turn out to be a construction, and your atom will in fact turn out to be a series of classes of particulars."

4. We saw that a logical fiction may or may not exist. Which of them shall we say are real and which unreal? In these lectures Russell says repeatedly that he is not *denying* that material bodies and minds and numbers exist. And more particularly, he is not denying that some definite descriptions correspond to existing things. On the other hand, he also does not wish to *assert* that bodies, minds, or numbers exist. He says that in constructing one's theory of the world there is no need for such an assertion, and we reduce the risk of error by avoiding it. For the same reason, we refuse to deny their existence. In order to account for our experience of the world and explain the fact that language has meaning, we do not have to do either one. So Occam's Razor bids us to do neither.

What sorts of entities, then, are we *forced* to list among "the furniture of the world"? According to the foregoing account we cannot do without momentary sense-data and other brief experiences. And we cannot do without brief hallucinations or illusions. They too are inescapably real. And we cannot do without atomic facts, the elementary states of affairs which make the atomic propositions true when they are true and false when they are false. I refer, of course, to the singular propositions about momentary sense-data, and so forth. And of course there are the simple qualities and relations of these momentary things. For reasons repeatedly mentioned, we must also concede the reality of certain general facts. These, in brief, are the metaphysical conclusions drawn by Russell in the last of these lectures, where we also find the following statement.

'One purpose that has run through all that I have said, has been the justification of analysis, i.e. the justification of logical atomism, of the view that you can get down in theory, if not in practice, to ultimate simples, out of which the world is built, and that those simples have a kind of reality not belonging to anything else.'

Despite his disclaimers about denying the existence of material objects and persons, and despite his wish to replace rank speculation with a logically rigorous ontology, Russell displays a kind of happy malice towards common-sense which places him closer to the older tradition of metaphysics than he may think. Having just conceded the possible "existence" of tables, he allows himself to say, "I have talked so far about the unreality of the things we think real. I want to speak with equal emphasis about the reality of things we think unreal, such as phantoms and hallucinations." These latter have "absolute and perfect reality," while tables, apparently, do not. And he goes on to relish his claim that, contrary to ordinary assumptions, the really real things are not eternal or even long-lasting, but exist for only a very short time (e.g., sense-data). Some other things *may* exist, and they may even exist for a long time; he will not deny it. But he clearly holds them to be "less real" in any event. The only "sorts of objects" that "you come across in the world," he says, are "fleeting" simples of innumerable kinds, and the atomic and general facts of which they are the constituents. So it seems that common-sense is full of illusion when it assumes that we really do encounter tables and chairs and persons! These are not experienced objects but logical constructions, logical fictions.

While Russell's pluralism, as I have said, is in some ways at the opposite pole from Bradley's monistic absolutism, they have something in common when they hold (albeit for very different reasons) that common thought is systematically mistaken in what it takes to be fully real. There is also a strong element of Idealism or mentalism which Russell shares with Bradley, whose Absolute is spiritual or experience-like, as we have seen. It is true that Russell is a bit reluctant to take such things as sense-data and other experiences for his basic realities, and he tries in the final lecture to suggest a form of "neutral monism" in which neither mind nor matter is basic. But he admits that he has not been able to work out a coherent theory to that effect while preserving the foregoing results. Finally, by even *questioning* the existence of everyday objects and minds, and by downgrading their "reality" in any case, Russell becomes an obvious candidate for the kind of criticism that was launched a few years later by his friend Moore in 'A Defense of Common Sense' (Sections 5 and 6, above). There is no doubt that Moore did aim that criticism at Russell among others.

CHAPTER 6

INSIDE THE REVOLUTION

19. SOME EARLY WITTGENSTEIN

The idea of rearing an atomic metaphysics upon the foundation of modern logic came first from Russell's friend and former student, Ludwig Wittgenstein, as Russell acknowledges in the Preface to the 1918 lectures. Wittgenstein was soon to publish his own version of logical atomism in his *Tractatus Logico-Philosophicus*, 1921, a short difficult book which is now a recognized classic of philosophy. We shall draw our next illustrative argument from this book, first because of its intrinsic importance, and second because Wittgenstein's own later criticism of the work was a major step in the development of recent thought. It sounds a bit odd to speak of "arguments" in the *Tractatus*, for the book consists of a long list of numbered assertions, sometimes rather gnomic assertions, with very little in the way of explicit argument. One has to study out the underlying system of thought in order to understand the listed statements and the author's reasons for them. This requires some familiarity with Russell and with Gottlob Frege (1848–1925), the other thinker who had the greatest influence on Wittgenstein. Even after the publication of some excellent commentaries and an improved translation of the German text, scholars continue to disagree over the precise meaning of the work. Yet, by building on what we have just been saying about Russell's philosophy, we should be able to indicate some of its principal conclusions, and we can then try to spell out Wittgenstein's reasons for at least one of those conclusions.

His logical atoms are not momentary experiences or possible experiences but simple indestructable objects which make up the substance of the world. (Unlike Russell he is not concerned with the traditional problems of epistemology.) The simple objects link together to form atomic facts or states of affairs. Corresponding to these are the atomic propositions, or rather those atomic propositions which have the same "form" as the atomic facts and therefore "picture" them exactly, all other atomic propositions being false. Atomic propositions are the theoretical end-products of analysis — "theoretical," again, because no one can actually give the complete analysis of an ordinary statement of fact. There are no qualities or relations within an atomic fact — another difference with Russell — but only the concatenated objects themselves. How these objects *can* link together is determined by their individual natures, and all these possible linkages taken together constitute "logical space" or the totality of "possible worlds." How the simple objects *are* linked up at any given time — all the atomic facts obtaining at that time — constitute the actual world, "everything that is the case." While there are general facts in the world corresponding to true general propositions, every general proposition is after all a "truth-function" of atomic propositions, which is another major difference with Russell. (A statement S is a truth-function of another statement or group of statements $T_1 \ldots T_n$ if the truth value of S — its truth or falsity — is uniquely determined by any given array of the truth values of $T_1 \ldots T_n$.) Hence, a complete description of the actual world would not have to include any general statements; it could simply be a list of all the true atomic propositions. Each atomic proposition is logically independent of all the others; correspondingly, each atomic state of affairs can occur independently of all the others.

Why must reality have such a structure? More particularly, why must there be eternal simple objects? Let us concentrate on just this one question. We shall see that Wittgenstein's answer parallels Russell's theory on several points but then takes a very different direction having nothing to do with phenomenalism of any other theory of perception or the self. I believe his reasoning can be brought out in the following sequence of points.

1. When we proceed to analyze various sentences that we understand very well, we may be surprised to notice that some of the names and other nominative expressions occurring in these sentences are actually meaningless since there is nothing in existence which they name, e.g. "the round square," "the King of France."

2. But our impression that each of these sentences has a perfectly definite meaning is preserved when we see that such expressions drop out in the course of analysis. A meaningful sentence will be either true or false, and we find that such a sentence as "The King of France is bald" becomes the false sentence, "There exists an x such that x is King of France; and such that, for any y, if y is King of France, then $y = x$; and such that x is bald."

3. But it must be noticed, further, that the meaningfulness of the latter compound sentence requires that sentences of the form "*a* is King of France," "*b* is bald," and the like, make sense. This is so even though the compound sentence does not say that any named individual *is* King of France or bald. And in order that singular sentences of that form *shall* make sense or have definite meaning, the names occurring in them, such as '*a*', '*b*', etc., must designate existing individuals.

4. Now so far this does not require that there be metaphysical simples. It only requires that there be (i) logically simple names, and (ii) some existing things which bear those names. A logically simple name is one that has no meaningful parts, though it has physical parts such as sounds or printed letters. Thus 'Carter' and 'Reagan' are simple symbols, while 'the President who succeeded Ford' and 'the President who succeeded Carter' are complex. Those two proper names are values of the variable *x*, where *x* ranges over human beings; and there *are* individuals whose names we could insert in the function "*x* is King of France" to get a singular proposition which is at least false and therefore makes sense. The name 'Socrates' is not available for this purpose, and neither is 'Louis XIV' (which also is not logically simple). But 'Carter,' 'Reagan,' and some billions of other names are available at the moment of this writing.

5. Now we must notice that the statement obtained by substituting one of these available names for *x*, e.g. "Reagan is King of France," would seem to be neither true nor false if Reagan should happen not to exist. Thus it would *appear* that whether one proposition makes sense will depend on whether some other proposition is true. In this case it will depend on whether some such proposition as the following is true: "The American politician named Reagan is still alive."

6. But such a consequence is unacceptable if language is ever to make sense. For our statements must somewhere "hook onto the world," as it were, if they are even to have meaning, and this would be impossible under the condition just described. A sentence would make sense only if another sentence were true, and the latter sentence would itself make sense only if some other sentence were true, and so on in an endless or perhaps circular chain of dependencies. The trouble is not that we would then never *know* whether the whole story was true or just an elaborate fiction. The point, rather, is that no sentence in the whole fabric would

then have definite *meaning*. For we know that logical analysis must end in a string of propositions containing proper names, and names have meaning only if there really are bearers of those names.

7. Since we know that a great many of our statements do have definite meaning, what appeared to be the case in No. 5 above must not really be so. It must be that the sentence "Reagan is King of France" does have meaning even when Reagan does not exist. The sentence must be ultimately analyzable into propositions about entities that *cannot* fail to exist, entities concerning which it would not even make *sense* to suppose they do not exist.

8. How are we to conceive that the sentence *is* so analyzable? First we notice that the ordinary proper name 'Reagan' stands for something complex, even though the name itself is logically simple in the sense given in No. 4 above. As analysis proceeds, therefore, the name must be replaced by a description of the complex thing; e.g. by the description "the former movie actor who was elected President." Next, we recall that according to the theory of descriptions a proposition containing a definite description will *not* lack sense when nothing exists corresponding to the description. Rather, it will be a *false* proposition. Now, any symbols in the description which stand for complexes (e.g. 'movie,' 'actor,' 'elected,' etc.) must themselves be replaced by descriptions until we finally reach the point (in theory) where we have nothing left but simple symbols standing for simple entities. Strictly speaking, these are the only real names, and the objects they name are metaphysically necessary and eternal. Being simple they are not destructable or decomposable, and we can infer their existence from the fact that language has definite meaning.

9. Suppose now that there never was a former movie actor who was elected President; suppose that the material of the world had not been arranged that way. Then the list of atomic propositions constituting the ultimate analysis of "There is a former movie actor who was elected President" would not be meaningless but false. For those atomic propositions represent that the simple objects in the world are connected to one another in certain ways in which (according to the supposition) they are not connected. And by the same token, "Reagan is King of France" would be meaningful but false. For it says that there is a former movie actor who was elected President, and that he is now King of France. (For convenience of exposition, and following Wittgenstein in this regard, we

take that one short description as the first analysis of 'Reagan.' Perhaps some longer and more complicated description of that particular man would actually be required.)

10. But what if we had never had occasion to invent such concepts as *movie, actor, elected,* etc.? Indeed, what if the human race had never existed? Under those conditions the sentences quoted in paragraph 9 would not be true or false because they would not exist. So is it still the case that if they are even to make sense certain other propositions which might have been false must be true? I am thinking of such propositions as that the human race did come into existence, and that it did have occasion to invent such concepts. The answer to the question is no. The atomic facts would still be whatever they are, and the string of atomic *propositions* which are the analysis of the proposition that there is a former movie actor who was elected President would either correspond to some section of the atomic facts, or they would fail to so correspond. Putting this the other way around, the elementary facts making up the actual world would either be pictured, in part, by such a string or they would not. In either event, the *proposition* which happens to be *expressed* by the *English sentence* "There is a former movie actor who was elected President" would be true or false and would therefore have meaning, because its meaning *is* that string of atomic propositions. (Under the supposition of the nonexistence of the human race, it would of course be false.)

That is the argument which appears to underlie such statements in the *Tractatus* as the following:

"2.02   Objects are simple.
"2.0201   Every statement about complexes can be resolved into a statement about their constituents and into the propositions that describe the complexes completely.
"2.021   Objects make up the substance of the world. That is why they cannot be composite.
"2.0211   If the world had no substance, then whether a proposition had sense would depend on whether another proposition was true.
"2.0212   In that case we could not sketch any picture of the world (true or false).

And a little later on in the book:

"3.23 The requirement that simple signs be possible is the requirement that sense be determinate.

"3.24 A proposition about a complex stands in an internal relation to a proposition about a constituent of the complex.

A complex can be given only by its description, which will be right or wrong. A proposition that mentions a complex will not be nonsensical, if the complex does not exist, but simply false. ...

"3.25 A proposition has one and only one complete analysis.

"3.251 What a proposition expresses it expresses in a determinate manner, which can be set out clearly: a proposition is articulate.

"3.26 A name cannot be dissected any further by means of a definition; it is a primitive sign."

It is a bold scholar or critic who would claim to explain Wittgenstein's reasoning in the *Tractatus* with any great precision. But the foregoing is at least in the near neighborhood of what various good commentators have made of these numbered statements.

Most of the *Tractatus* deals with the problems of philosophical logic, not with metaphysical conclusions extracted from Wittgenstein's answers to such problems. Those conclusions are stated at or near the beginning of the work, perhaps for greater impact on the reader. But towards the end he develops the surprising thought that metaphysical statements are, strictly speaking, nonsense. Language provides us with a scheme for talking about the world, not a scheme for talking about that very scheme. So when we attempt to say how language relates to the world, we violate its basic rules. We violate the true syntax of language which has now been revealed. To illustrate the point, consider the metaphysical statement with which we have been especially concerned, the statement that eternal simple objects necessarily exist. As we have now repeatedly seen, standard logic holds that existence is not a predicate or characteristic of anything, but a logical quantifier. It signifies that there is at least one "value" or entity which "satisfies" a certain function, i.e. yields a true statement when its name is substituted for the variable. But the phrase "necessarily exist" does not play *any such role* in this metaphysical statement. For one thing, the modal notion "necessarily" is foreign to standard logic. More importantly, there is no particular function which is here in question. It is being asserted, in effect, that *the whole apparatus of language and syntax* demands that there be eternal simple objects. Taken in context, the statement says that the names occurring in the elementary propositions are borne by objects which have the following characteristic: necessary existence.

Wittgenstein seems to offer his metaphysical conclusions as valuable insights into the connection between language and reality even though they could not be *stated* coherently. He thought they were nonsense, but important nonsense! "My propositions serve as elucidations in the following way: anyone who understands me eventually recognizes them as nonsensical, when he has used them − as steps − to climb up beyond them. (He must, so to speak, throw away the ladder after he has climed up on it.) ..." (6.54)

20. THE DECLINE OF "ANALYSIS"

During the nineteen-thirties many people began to lose faith in the whole conception of philosophy that had been instituted by Russell, the assumption that atomistic ontology and corresponding logical analysis will yield the clearest and truest picture of reality. One reason for this loss of faith was the growing suspicion that phenomenalism, crucial as it is to Russell's version of atomism, is incoherent. Not that anyone had claimed that we can actually explain in full detail how a particular object or a particular mind is constructed out of sense-data or mental occurrences. The system or structure would be too complex to work out in practice, and there would be too vast a number of particulars to fit into the system even if we could work it out. Still, the project had seemed possible "in principle." But philosophers soon came to notice the following theoretical objection. We seem to be unable to say *which* sense-data will be part of the system constituting a given material object unless we already have a well formed idea of that object. To make the point with a paradox, it is necessary that we have already constructed the object in order to identify the data out of which we are going to construct it. Which possible sense-data will constitute the old table in the attic that no one is presently experiencing? Answer: the sense-data we would experience if we went to the attic and looked into the corner where *that old table* is kept. And which thoughts and feelings belong to the bundle or system constituting Jones's mind rather than Smith's? Answer: the thoughts and feelings that *Jones* has had (or is having, will have, might have, or might have had). If there is no other way to make the required identifications, and there seems not to be, then the phenomenalist's project is logically impossible. For obviously his translations of material-objects statements into sense-data statements, and so on, are not permitted to have that circular feature.

So people became disenchanted with Russell's view "that you can get down in theory, if not in practice, to ultimate simples, out of which the world is built" – i.e. to sense-data and the like. But what about logical analysis of philosophically troublesome statements at other levels? Could some of the problems of moral or political philosophy be resolved or clarified by rewriting key statements with the aid of logical grammar? Even if we cannot carry through the mentioned analysis of bodies or persons, perhaps we can analyze larger entities, e.g. nations, into persons or functions of persons. Consider a trivial example often mentioned in this connection. We can analyze statements about "the average family" so as to relieve any puzzlement that may be felt (by a young child perhaps?) over the fact that there cannot be a family of 3.8 persons, or whatever the number is. Can we also give a perspicuous (though far more complex) analysis of apparently intelligible but puzzling assertions about nation states, e.g. the personifying and hypostatizing statement that France keeps her commitments? Can we explain how the "keeping" of a "national commitment" is some clear and correct function of the behavior of individual officials and citizens, just as "the size of the average family" is a quotient obtained by dividing the number of family members by the number of families? The answer for present purposes is that the practitioners of "philosophical analysis" (Russellian analysis) were unable to produce any such explanations, and this too was a reason why some of them lost faith in their method.

Another reason why atomism began to seem incredible to its champions after only a decade or so was the revival of opposition to metaphysics of any kind. Some "positivists" of the 18th and 19th centuries had criticized metaphysics as idle speculation because its claims cannot be empirically verified or falsified. But the new "logical" positivists who flourished in the second quarter of this century added the more radical criticism that metaphysical theses are to be rejected as *meaningless*. They held that the meaning of a statement is nothing other that "its method of verification": what would be observed to be the case if it were true. Naturally they greeted with enthusiasm that theme in the *Tractatus* according to which metaphysical utterances are nonsense, though they had little sympathy with the idea of "important nonsense." Their theory of meaning was eventually subjected to a series of damaging criticisms which forced them to quality it beyond recognition. But for a time it carried considerable weight with the many philosophers who look upon natural science as the model of genuine knowledge and rational method. The Logical Positivists themselves remained loyal to a quasi-Russellian style of logical analysis without its atomistic foundation. They held that the proper business of philosophy is (a) clarification of the logic of "science" (taken in a broad sense to include everyday knowledge claims of an empirical sort), and (b) anti-metaphysical prophylaxis (warnings against the pitfalls of metaphysical nonsense). Quite a number of other philosophers came in time to agree with them, at least for the old positivist reasons if not the new (in that case, read "idle speculation" in place of "nonsense"). This was a dispiriting come-down, however, for people who had believed in Russell's whole program. Instead of leading us to the truest and most perspicuous account of the world, philosophy tidies up after science!

There were other causes of the decline of the older analytic philosophy just before World War II and in the immediate post-war years. I shall not attempt to describe them all, but two of the most important will be illustrated in the remaining sections of this chapter. Perhaps it should be added at this point that those who have felt the spirit of the newer analytic philosophy place no such limitation on their subject as I have just mentioned, and take no such hangdog attitude. This should already be apparent from our third and fourth chapters, and the point will be borne out, I trust, by all of the remaining chapters.

21. CRITIQUE OF THE TRACTATUS

Some of the most telling criticisms of atomism and philosophical analysis were to come from Wittgenstein himself. They appear first in some rather extensive notes which he dictated to students from 1933 to 1935 (published many years later as *The Blue and Brown Books*). He worked to improve them during the following decade, and his fully developed views on the topic are found in Part I of the *Philosophical Investigations*. Our next illustration will be drawn from the latter work.

In the *Investigations* as in the *Tractatus*, Wittgenstein makes his readers work hard to discover and understand his meaning. But now our problem is not one of finding a general theory reflected in a list of highly abstract propositions; it is that of tracing many threads of argument through a long series of concrete illustrations. The full force of his new insights about language and the proper tasks of philosophy can only be appreciated through the great variety and detail of these examples. This poses a virtually unsolvable problem to anyone who would seek to provide an adequate summary of Wittgenstein's thought in limited space. But let us do the best we can by sketching out a few of the points about theses language which he uses to refute important these or assumptions of the *Tractatus*. I shall pay special attention to his attack on the tacit assumptions of the particular argument which I have set forth in Section 19 above. Incidentally, this will also illustrate the point noted earlier that even though the *Tractatus* does not exhibit any of our four "stages," Wittgenstein's later criticism of that work is a stage three operation throughout.

1. It appears to be a guiding assumption of both Russell's and Wittgenstein's atomism that language is *fundamentally* a matter of names and naming. This is even more obvious in the *Tractatus*, where the elementary propositions (the basic propositions which are said to be capable of describing the whole world) consist of nothing but names. The atomic facts are concatenations of elementary objects, and the names which constitute the atomic propositions manage somehow to picture the *way* these objects are linked together. Now the opening sections of the *Investigations* show convincingly, and rather amusingly, why a system of signs consisting wholly of names would be no more than a tiny fragment of language as we know it, and would enable us to do only a small fraction of the innumerable things we all easily do with the aid of language. The idea that learning a language consists of learning the names of things does have its appeal, as Wittgenstein shows by quoting a naive passage from St. Augustine. (1)[1] But he then goes on to imagine

simple "language games" (language-using activities) which people could successfully carry on with nothing but names, and these "games" show by the poverty of their "moves" — the distinct acts of communication and co-operation which they permit — that most of the resources of language are lacking. (2.8)

Now it might be thought that the author of the *Investigations* has failed to (forgotten how to) understand the *Tractatus* in making such a criticism. After all, the *Tractatus* does not imagine that people *operate directly* with the atomic propositions, which are the ultimate (ideal) analysis of the sentences we do operate with. But the fundamental role which names play in language, according to the author of the *Tractatus*, can nevertheless be seen from the following point. It is the *failure* of ordinary names to attach infallibly to existing things which forces him to postulate eternally existing objects to be bearers of the elementary names, so that language can have *any* definite meaning at all!

2. We have just mentioned an assumption about language which relates to the final product of the analytical process as conceived by logical atomism: the atomic propositions. Suppose we now look for assumptions operating at the beginning of the process, the first attack on sentences in ordinary language. There we find that both Russell and the *Tractatus* assume that the meaning of what is said is wholly contained within the sentence itself, as distinguished from its context of use. They assume that the meaning consists entirely in the logical syntax (which may or may not be obscured by surface grammar) and the semantic correlations between the nonlogical words and the objects, qualities, and relations they stand for. No attention is paid to the fact that the meaning of a statement will often depend very much on the activity in which the speaker is involved, beyond that of pronouncing or writing a string of words. The latter point is illustrated even in the simplest of the imaginary language-games. (There the context of action shows that "slab" means (roughly) what possessors of the English language might express (in suitable circumstances) by saying "Bring me a slab.") And Wittgenstein goes on to develop the same point with reference to a large number of

---

[1] Numbers appearing in the text will refer to sections of the *Investigations*, Part I, unless otherwise indicated.

ordinary language-using activities. Thus he reminds us how the "game" being played can divert a sentence from its most typical meaning ("Isn't the weather glorious?" becomes a statement, not a question), and how the same sentence may function either as a prophecy or as a command ("You will do this.") (22)

If we should be tempted to think that there are just three kinds of action sentences — those used to make an assertion, or to ask a question, or to issue a command — he produces a long list of language-using activities which show that there really are "countless" kinds of sentences. Consider the declarative mood alone. Sentences in this mood can be used not only to assert, but to speculate, guess, report, describe, state an hypothesis, play-act, make up a story, state the solution to a problem in arithmetic, and so on. (23) And even if we confine our attention to description, we find that many different kinds of things are called "description": "description of a body's position by means of its co-ordinates; description of a facial expression; description of a sensation of touch; of a mood." So if we recognize that the context of use contributes an important element of meaning, we should not suppose that this can easily be assimilated to the view of language found in the *Tractatus*, on the ground that the latter work is concerned wholly with description.

3. The two preceding criticisms can be further confirmed in response to an objection which Wittgenstein considers. Doesn't language at least *begin* with names and naming? Don't we first have to have names ostensively defined for us (someone points to the object and says its name) before we can understand any other linguistic form or act? Not at all. When someone points and utters a sound, we *already* have to understand the action-setting well enough to know that the "game" being played is that of ostensive definition. And then we have to have picked up further guides to know *what* sort of object or quality or relation the word being uttered is to stand for. My language teacher is pointing to someone and making a sound, but perhaps I shall take this as the name of "a color, or of a race, or even of a point of the compass" if I do not understand that we are involved (say) in the more specific game of telling a *person's* name. (28) And in order to understand *that*, I also have to know what personal names are, and some of the things people use them for. (31)

4. One of the most fateful assumptions of the *Tractatus* and of

Russell's atomism is that the *meaning* of a proper name is the bearer of that name. The assumption is not merely that the name *stands for* its bearer, as of course it does, but that the meaning *is* (identical to) the bearer. Such an assumption is made repeatedly in the ten-step argument from the *Tractatus* which I stated in Section 19 above (see steps 1, 3, 5, 6, and 8). But Wittgenstein now sees that this is a confusion. "When Mr. N. N. dies one says that the bearer of the name dies, not that the meaning dies. And it would be nonsensical to say that, for if the name ceased to have meaning it would make no sense to say 'Mr. N. N. is dead.' "

5. Another tacit and crucial assumption of the *Tractatus* is that there is such a thing as absolute complexity and simplicity. Things are simple or complex not merely in relation to our goals of understanding or action, but as *parts of the world*, as things to be named or stated in *the* world story. Thus we may be assured that there are entities which are the simplest of all, and hence indestructible, and hence guarantors that what we say has meaning (since, again, they are the bearers of the names in the elementary propositions into which our statements are analyzable). Here is how Wittgenstein objects to such a view in the *Investigations*:

'But what are the simple constituent parts of which reality is composed? – What are the simple constituent parts of a chair? – The bits of wood of which it is made? Or the molecules, or the atoms? – 'Simple' means: not composite. And here the point is: in what sense 'composite'? It makes no sense at all to speak absolutely of the 'simple parts of a chair' ... We use the word 'composite' (and therefore the word 'simple') in an enormous number of different and differently related ways. (Is the colour of a square on a chessboard simple, or does it consist of pure white and pure yellow? – Is this length of 2 cm. simple, or does it consist of two parts, each 1 cm. long? But why not of one bit 3 cm. long, and one bit 1 cm. long measured in the opposite direction.' (47)

In this section and those immediately following, Wittgenstein gives several other illustrations to show that the notion of absolute simples plays no part in ordinary thought and language use. One could add that it also plays no essential role in physical science. We can always ask whether the "atoms" (indivisibles) or "elementary particles" identified at a given period in the history of science will continue to be entitled to these labels. And physics is not even bound to continue to use the notion of smallest elements or simples.

6. The thesis of the *Tractatus* that there are and must be absolute simples depends not only on the meaning-bearer confusion mentioned above, but on the far more plausible assumption that the meaningfulness

of what we say cannot depend on what merely happens to be the case. Surely a statement *can make sense* — can at least be false — whatever the true facts may happen to be. This principle has so powerful an appeal to our logical intuition that Wittgenstein went to great lengths in the *Tractatus* to overcome all apparent exceptions to it. That is, he found a way to guarantee meaning without surrendering this intuition. But taken quite generally, the intuition is false, and we have to make a transition to the more complex and adequate view of language found in the *Investigations* before we can easily see why.

First let us briefly recall how this principle or assumption functioned in the argument of Section 19 above, before we explain how it is discredited in the *Investigations*. Unless there are certain things in the world whose nonexistence is inconceivable, things which constitute the ultimate subject-matter of our statements, the bare meaningfulness of those statements *would* depend on the truth of other statements which might have been false. What we say would not make sense unless certain facts obtained which might not have obtained. And the meaning of statements asserting those facts would be similarly dependent on the truth of still further statements, and so on without end. Thus "I saw the golden mountain" would make sense only because (among other things) a certain rare, malleable, heavy, yellow metal happens to have existed; or more minutely, because yellow objects have existed and have thus given humanity the occasion to invent the word 'yellow,' and so on for heavy, malleable, metal, and rare. In order to avoid this, the *Tractatus* adopts a view according to which language is ultimately an impersonal list of timeless propositions picturing possible states of affairs among objects which cannot not exist. And each of these propositions is guaranteed to have meaning because (i) the objects named by its names certainly exist, whether or not they are linked in the way the proposition pictures, and (ii) the proposition consists only of such names.

Now the view of language taken by the *Investigations* and stated there in explicit opposition to the *Tractatus*, is that language is part of the natural history of human beings. It is an instrument, or rather a large and diverse "family" of instruments (65) which have been developed and re-adapted to serve our needs of communication. They enable us to engage in the many language-using activities which we have found it useful (in the broadest sense of "useful") to create. People communicate about the sorts of experiences they have in common, and these depend on the way humans are constructed — on the ways in which they normally interact with their physical environment (242) — and also on the forms of social interaction which they have developed. Naturally, then, the verbal concepts which we develop will reflect such experiences and forms, and not others which we might dimly imagine, or which we could not imagine at all. It seems extremely probable that if we had had no experience of yellow objects because there were none in the world, the statement that a certain piece of metal is yellow would be one that we could not have conceived or formulated. And certainly this would be true if there were no colors at all in the world or any possible human world, but only shades of gray.

Our sentences nevertheless do have meaning, and we can understand this without appealing to the metaphysics of logical atomism. For one thing, all meaning does not rest on proper names, much less on the confused notion that the meaning of such a name is to be identified with its bearer. For another thing, "what looks as if it *had* to exist, is part of the language," to quote Wittgenstein at section 50. I take him to mean that the existence of a thing without which we would lack a certain concept in language is *presupposed* by whatever we say. Or rather, it is presupposed by whatever we say in that part of language or language-use in which the concept occurs. In that part or "game" we do not *say* that such a thing exists, for the assumption that it exists has become part of the structure and method of language itself. The situation may be compared with that of the standard metre bar formerly preserved in Paris. It is (or was) the one thing of which we cannot say that it is one metre long or that it is not one metre long. "But this is, of course, not to ascribe any extraordinary property to it, but only to mark its peculiar role in the language-game of measuring with a metre-rule." (50) And similarly with the color yellow. "... to say 'if it did not *exist*, it could have no name' is to say as much and as little as: if this thing did not exist, we could not use it in our language-game." (50)

This important truth — that language is not a kind of impersonal and timeless mirror but a complex artifact reflecting the varied contingencies of human nature and culture — is underscored by numerous illustrations throughout the *Investigations*, not merely by these explicit references to the *Tractatus* which appear near the beginning. We have already had occasion to discuss one of the most important of these other illustrations in Chapter 2, the private language problem (243-317). There we considered Wittgenstein's discussion in but one of its major aspects, that of an attempted dissolution of a particular metaphysical problem. In that aspect, he could be taken to argue, in effect, that since (i) a coherent statement of Descartes' and Berkeley's problem of perception would require the soliloquizing philosopher to use a certain kind of private language, and since (ii) private languages of that kind are impossible to construct, the alleged problem may be dismissed. But now we can understand the same discussion as part of an attempted dissolution of an entire metaphysical scheme, although one in which epistemology plays little part: that of the *Tractatus*. Language is a collection of concrete social activities, and this is what was forgotten by the author of the *Tractatus*, as well as by Descartes and others who were confident that they *could* very well invent a private language if they wished, so that it was unnecessary to do so.

I believe we can now see that Wittgenstein may have been more successful in showing the impossibility of private language than we were able to explain in Chapter 2. His case depended on the point that in such a language memory must be the final court of appeal as to the correct application of semantical rules or criteria, and memory is fallible. This was far from a knock-down argument, we saw, because uncheckable memory cannot be wholly eliminated even in the use of public language. But in light of our discussion in the present section, I think one can be more readily convinced that the creation of a private language of the kind described is surely beyond the power and resources of any solitary mind, even if the fallibility of memory in consulting one's "private dictionary" is not enough in itself to show this. For in the first place, such a language would have to be capable of describing all aspects of the material and social worlds coming within the ken of some mature mind like Descartes' or Berkeley's. And in the second place, when that mind is attempting to construct such a language it may draw *nothing* from the public language which presupposes the existence of *anything* outside that mind. We may well doubt whether there would be much if anything left in the public language with which to accomplish that stupendous task.

Such in brief is Wittgenstein's dissolution of the metaphysical theory presented at the beginning of the *Tractatus*. While the latter work does

not present a skeptical theory, and while it does not show the proud contempt for common-sense found in Russell's atomism, it does propose
some rather pretentious additions to common-sense and science alike.
The claim that what we mean to say is analyzable into elementary propositions of which we are unaware, and concerning the form of which
we are permanently ignorant except that they picture the linkages of eternal simple objects, reminds one of the worst flights of the classical
metaphysicians. Spinoza's infinite attributes of Reality, only two of
which we can know anything about, or Hegel's world-mind getting to
know itself better through human history, or Bradley's unknowable Absolute hiding behind Appearance, are hardly more extreme and unpalatable than the timeless, wordless, unformulable, and unknowable
language to which the *Tractatus* appeals. Certain preconceptions which
philosophers have had about language do apparently lead to this latter
result, this need to postulate eternal "simples" which have "form" or
"natures," and a never-never language to represent them. But the later
Wittgenstein has shown rather convincingly that these preconceptions
are avoidable and even false.

22. STRAWSON ON REFERENCE

I have mentioned repeatedly that at least one piece of analysis was
recognized on all sides as a brilliant success, the theory of descriptions
itself. Even if it ought not to be used as a building block of atomistic ontology, its effectiveness as a weapon against Meinongian objects seemed
to demonstrate the philosophical power of mathematical logic. The syntax of logic could surely be our chief tool of clarification or analysis in
dealing with philosophical problems even if there was no such parallel
between the analysis of meaning and the analysis of reality as Logical
Atomism supposed. But then the theory of descriptions itself came in for
a rather devastating criticism which seemed to show that formal syntax,
though undoubtedly of some importance in philosophy, was not the all-
sufficient device its greatest admirers had conceived it to be.

In 1950 Strawson published a widely influential article attacking
Russell's theory, and the latter has since been regarded as controversial
at best. It can no longer be considered "the whole truth," and many
would agree with Strawson that, as an account of the logic of definite

descriptions in ordinary language, it is not even correct as far as it goes. In making his case, Strawson calls attention to various points about language and the use of language which Russell's analysis seems to overlook, and to go astray by overlooking. I shall not attempt to summarize all the arguments and illustrations he uses to establish these points, but I shall state the principal ones, using italics to call attention to key words and distinctions. Then I think it may be interesting to consider how Strawson himself might respond to the metaphysical puzzle which Russell had used his theory to deflate. I refer to the problem stated in the third paragraph in Section 17, which the reader may wish to consult before continuing.

Strawson objects on two grounds to Russell's claim that the meaning of the sentence, "The King of France is wise," includes an assertion of the existence of a King of France. The first ground is that sentences (in a very familiar use of the word 'sentence') never assert anything. There is a great difference between a sentence and the various *statements* or *assertions* which that sentence can be *used*, on various occasions and by various people, to *make*. For example, the sentence just quoted may well have been *uttered* by many people during the course of two or three centuries to make many different statements, some of which may have been true while others were undoubtedly false. Having noted this distinction between sentences, utterances, and assertions, it is then easier to see that the *meaning* of a *sentence* consists of *general directions for its use*, not of what it is used on some particular occasion to assert. Nor are sentences as such ever true or false. Similarly, the *meaning* of a *noun phrase beginning with 'the'* also consists of general directions for its use, not of the particular thing which it is used on some occasion to refer to. And Strawson points out, by the way, that the use of such a phrase to refer uniquely to a particular thing is only one of its various uses. Notice the difference between "The whale struck the ship," in which "the whale" would be used that way, and "The whale is a mammal," in which it would not be used to refer to a particular animal but to a kind of animal. (In some rare contexts of communication, however, it might be used to do the former, as where the speaker and the person addressed are standing before two large aquaria, one containing a whale and one containing a shark, with appropriate name plates. But in thus qualifying Strawson's example, we do not disagree with him in spirit; we illustrate a general point which he repeatedly emphasizes, namely, that the meaning of an assertion depends on context in the broadest sense, and is affected by conventions which cannot be wholly captured by the definitions of words and the syntax of formal logic.)

The second ground on which he objects to Russell's analysis is that even when we do *use* the sentence "The King of France is wise" to say something, we do not *assert that there is* a King of France, although we imply by our action that we think there is. We are not *saying* there is, nor does what we say *entail* that there is. In view of the general directions for using such sentences to refer, and in view of the usual assumption that one is using language correctly, we are indeed signalling the fact that we think there is a King of France. But indicating that we think something is not the same as saying that thing, and it is not the same as saying something else which logically implies it. According to Strawson, Russell's mistake here results from the further mistake of thinking that a sentence has meaning *only if it is true or false* (a notable assumption of the *Tractatus* as well). This is why Russell went on to rewrite the obviously significant sentence "The King of France is wise" so that it would always be at least false; that is, by including in the translation the sentence "There is a King of France." (Of course, significant sentences really are never true or false at all according to Strawson, as already noted.)

How then would someone with Strawson's views respond to the problem-generating argument stated near the beginning of Section 17? Presumably he would respond more or less as follows. Once we realize that a sentence does not refer to something and say something about it, but that *people* often *use* declarative sentences to do such a thing, we can easily notice these points:

1. The sentence "The King of France is wise" does not refer to anything, so there is no problem of "Meinongian objects" so far.

2. Many people from the early seventeenth-century onward may have used that sentence to make various assertions, perhaps some of which were true, while others were false. These statements would have referred to various existing persons, so again there is no such problem.

3. If someone today seriously attempted to use that sentence to make an assertion, he would fail. Though he would be under the impression that he had referred to someone and had said something about him, he

would not have managed to refer to anything. So again there is no problem of "Meinongian objects" to which he supposedly had managed to refer.

4. What about the first sentence quoted at the beginning of the problem-generating argument, namely, "Unicorns do not exist"? Suppose a teacher were to use it to make an assertion; for example, to tell his first graders that unicorns do not exist. Would *he* not be referring to something and saying something about it, or rather about them, even though they do not exist? The answer − and here Strawson would be in agreement with Russell − is that the teacher would not be referring to any particular animal, but to a certain kind of animal; and the teacher would be saying that there are no animals of that kind. The same would be true if the teacher spoke slightly differently and said, "The unicorn does not exist." (Compare the above example of "The whale.") We are quite used to including *kinds* of things in our ontology, and again there is no problem of having to include "Meinongian objects."

5. What if a teacher were to say to his ninth grade Geometry class, "The round square does not exist"? It is hard to imagine why any teacher would actually want to say such a thing, but suppose one did and we asked him why. And suppose he replied, "I wanted to tell them that the plane figure described as both round and square has no instances, that there are and can be no round squares." Must we admit that he has managed to refer to an *impossible kind*, something which cannot exist, and that he has nevertheless managed to say something true about it? No, he has merely said that no figure can be both round and square, that these two unmysterious kinds have no particular figure in common − in contrast, say, to parallelograms and rectangles, or to equilateral and equiangular triangles. So again there is no problem.

In the article summarized above, Strawson does not make points 4 and 5 because he does not spell out his own solution to Russell's problem, although he states that problem, much as I have, near the beginning of his article. There is nothing wrong with this since he is mainly concerned to criticize Russell's theory of descriptions, not to solve the problem Russell had used is to solve. And anyway, it is easy to see how Strawson's own solution would go once we understand his criticism. But I think it is useful to notice that points 4 and 5 must be made if we are to dispose of the problem. This reminds us that attention to certain structural features of thought described in modern logic may be necessary for the dissolution of a metaphysical puzzle even if it is not sufficient for that purpose. The insights of "ideal language" philosophers are therefore not to be underestimated. But their tendency to rely too exclusively on such features is an important shortcoming because metaphysical problems often turn on features of languages use — features of our actual thought — which formal logic as so far developed neither describes nor corrects, but misses.

CHAPTER 7

A PASSAGE TO AMERICA

We have seen how Wittgenstein gave a destructive, and one would have thought lethal criticism of the older ideal of philosophical analysis which he had done so much to promote in his earlier work. Throughout the nineteen-fifties and early sixties, his later philosophy was at the focus of discussion and emulation, and the philosophical outlook which we described in Part One was dominant in both Britain and the United States, certainly among young philosophers alive to new movements. But the tradition of Russell soon reasserted itself, though without the metaphysical trappings of atomism. Formal logic is again held in very high regard as a tool of criticism and construction in such fields as epistemology and philosophy of language. And again there is talk of finding the one *best* way to understand the world by combining the resources of science and logical syntax.

Yet some of the most interesting and original work produced in recent American philosophy does take the form of conceptual elucidation, not strict analysis or anything posing as such. To be sure, the special "ordinary language" idioms of Wittgenstein and Austin are now seldom heard, and we find many writers using formalist techniques. But much attention is also paid to ordinary nonphilosophical uses of language that are not adequately handled by any formalism so far invented, and the result is sometimes a valuable clarification of important concepts or an improved insight into the structures of natural language itself. We shall look at some recent examples of this in Chapter 8. But first let us consider an article of the fifties which can be used as a kind of bridge between our illustrations of older analysis – Sections 17 through 19 – and that more recent American work. For in the case of a philosopher like W. V. Quine, who had published important works on logic a decade and more before the mid-century British philosophy landed on these shores, we should speak not of a revival but of a continuation of Russellian themes.

23. THE ANALYTIC-SYNTHETIC DISTINCTION

One of the "dogmas" attacked by Quine in his 'Two Dogmas of Empiricism,' 1951, is a certain distinction which philosophers of an analytical and empiricist tendency have been emphasizing at least since the time of Hume, often in opposition to the claims of metaphysics. Hume says that there are but two types of knowledge, and that metaphysics does not belong to either type. First there is knowledge of matters of fact and existence, which is gained only by observing how the world happens to be. The statements formulating such knowledge are not *necessarily* true, not true by their very meaning. Second, there is knowledge of the relations of ideas, which is gained only by analysis (including mathematical reasoning). The statements in which *it* is formulated *are* true by their very meaning, e.g. "three times five are equal to the half of thirty." Now metaphysics does not test its assertions by observing contingent matters of fact; it proceeds entirely by arm-chair reflection; and yet it claims to arrive at knowledge of how the world is, of how it *necessarily* is. This is sophistry and illusion, says Hume, because even when the metaphysician does produce correct analyses, they can tell us nothing about the world but only about the necessary relations of ideas − just as in Geometry we can prove that the sum of the internal angles is 180 degrees without assuming or showing that the world contains even one plane triangular object. Using some terminology introduced a generation later by Kant (though departing from his doctrine on the matter), we can distinguish between *analytic statements*, which can be known to be true merely by analyzing their meaning, and *synthetic statements*, which can be known to be true only through experience.

Quine attacks this distinction because he does not think the truth of *any* statement is entirely independent of experience, and because he is quite willing to blur "the supposed boundary between speculative metaphysics and natural science." He focuses his criticism upon the notion of analyticity, and he tries to show that it is unclear and unsatisfactory. He begins by pointing out two kinds of statements which are commonly said to be true by virtue of their meaning. There are statements like

(1)   No unmarried man is married

whose truth seems to be guaranteed by the logical syntax alone. We would get a true statement no matter what sense-making combination of an adjective and a noun we might insert into the form "No un-(adjective) (noun) is (adjective)." Then there are statements like

(2)   No bachelor is married

whose truth is also said to be analytic even though it is not guaranteed by logical form alone. In order to explain its analyticity one might point out that (2) can be reduced to (1) by a substitution of synonyms ('unmarried man' for 'bachelor'). But to say that these two expressions *are* synonyms is only to say that the statement

(3)   All and only bachelors are unmarried men

is *analytic*, the very notion which we were attempting to explain!

Is there any way to explain synonymy which does *not* presuppose the notion of analyticity, so that we could use the former to clarify the latter without getting caught in such a circle? One way that immediately suggests itself is to appeal to the notion of definition. Synonymous terms are those which have the same definition (or at least the same "cognitive" definition; let us ignore poetic or other overtones on the ground that we are interested in "cognitive synonymy" alone). But this quickly turns out to be a blind alley, for unless we are only talking about purely stipulative definitions (where some new verbal sign is invented to substitute for another sign, perhaps as an abbreviation), the idea that two expressions have the same definition is just as much in need of explanation as is the notion of synonymy itself; or perhaps it *is* that very notion. And the makers of dictionaries already are presupposing and using that notion when they collect information about a language and report it to us in their definitions. In short, dictionary definitions do not *explain* the notion of synonymy, and they also do not *constitute* the synonymy which obtains between a defined word and its defining word or words.

Another possibility considered by Quine is that the synonymy of words can be understood as interchangeability – interchangeability without affecting the truth of the statements in which the switch is made. Consider

(4)   Necessarily all and only bachelors are bachelors

which is evidently true. Now if we put 'unmarried male' for the second occurrence of 'bachelor' we get

(5)   Necessarily all and only bachelors are unmarried men.

And this statement, like (4), is true. But now, to say that (5) is true is to say that (3) is analytic! So our attempt to avoid using the notion of analyticity when accounting for synonymy fails again. Of course, if we could explain analyticity (the main goal) without having recourse to the notion of synonymy, that trouble would be circumvented. Rudolf Carnap had attempted something like this by invoking the notion of a "semantical rule." Semantical rules identify those sentences of (artificial) languages which are true independently of experience. But Quine explains rather convincingly that if such a language is to be usefully related to ordinary language or scientific language we must already have made use of the notion of analyticity in deciding which statements are to be placed on the list. So again, a notion which is offered to "explicate" analyticity turns out to presuppose it.

What are we to make of this so far? The points I have outlined do give us some interesting description of the notions "analytic," "synonymous," and "definition." But in showing how they interlock, and in pointing out that no one has been able to define "analytic" without using other notions in the cluster, Quine has surely not managed to establish that analyticity is a myth. On this, let me quoted a passage from an article by Hilary Putnam, who admires Quine's article but not the best-known argument in it which I have just summarized.

The only evidence that Quine produced to support this remarkable claim [that the notion of synonymy is hopelessly vague] was that he, Quine, could not clarify the notion in a few pages. Given that the even more basic linguistic notion of *grammaticality* has not been satisfactorily clarified in many pages by many authors to the present day, and that no one proposes to do linguistics without the notion, it is clear that Quine presented a bad argument against this particular notion of analyticity [i.e. the notion that it is reducibility to a logical truth through the substitution of synonyms].

But much better reasons exist for rejecting a sharp and absolute distinction between analytic and synthetic statements, reasons which are suggested by the history of science. Consider the famous "revolutions" in science which produce not merely a new list of theories or beliefs but a transformation of major concepts used in their formulation. Statements thought to be true by virtue of their meaning, and hence *knowably* true *a priori* (in advance of experience), have had to be set down as false because later experience and scientific theorizing based on that experience have *forced* a change in our very definitions. Thus space loses its "center" as we go from Ptolemy to Kepler and Newton; space and time lose their mutual independence and become variable space-time as we go from Newton to Einstein; fixed species become continuously evolving forms as we go from Aristotle to Darwin. And the same phenomenon occurs on a smaller scale in the "normal" or non-revolutionary progress of science.

Quine comes to this topic only in the sixth and last section of his article, and even there he makes the point with philosophical metaphors rather than specific illustrations.

The totality of our so-called knowledge or beliefs, from the most casual matters of geography and history to the profoundest laws of atomic physics or even of pure mathematics and logic, is a man-made fabric which impinges on experience only along the edges. Or, to change the figure, total science is like a field of force whose boundary conditions are experience. A conflict with experience at the periphery occasions readjustments in the interior of the field. Truth values have to be redistributed over some of our statements. Re-evaluation of some statements entails re-evaluation of others, because of their logical interconnections. ... But the total field is so underdetermined by its boundary conditions, experience, that there is much latitude of choice as to what statements to re-evaluate in the light of any single contrary experience. ... Furthermore it becomes folly to seek a boundary between synthetic statements, which hold contingently on experience, and analytic statements, which hold come what may. Any statement can be held true come what may, if we make drastic enough adjustments elsewhere in the system.

Sketchy as this appeal to the history of science may be, it is Quine's strongest point. Or more exactly, his most valuable contribution is to have undermined the notion that any given statement can be cleanly and permanently assigned to one of the two categories, analytic or synthetic, and in this sketch he at least points in the direction where convincing evidence will be found to support his objection. In the following section, let us attempt to spell out a bit of that evidence by returning to our illustration in Chapter 4.

24. TIME GAPS REVISITED

We shall be concerned here with the revision of the concept of seeing that actually occurred in the history of physics and astronomy, not with the problem of revising the physics-warped concept of seeing in the everyday scheme of our fictional islanders. For clarity and conciseness, we can again use the abbreviations listed above at pp. 74–75, though it will also be convenient to spell everything out in words from time to time.

First let us attempt to describe the old concept of seeing as it existed before the discovery that light has finite speed, coming as close to it as we can with the aid of our full list of beliefs and language conventions. Then let us indicate the alternative concepts of seeing that were logically available following that discovery, assuming that the experiences and theoretical conclusions constituting the discovery were to be fully accepted. Third, let us then attempt to explain which of these is (or was) the most economical and useful, thus accounting for its acceptance in pre-Einsteinian science. Fourth and finally, let us indicate at least one statement which moves out of the analytic category as we shift from the old concept through various possible revisions to the best revised concept.

I would suggest that the old scientific concept of seeing, or at least those aspects of it which are most relevant to our topic, can be represented as follows: *A, E, H, O, not-P, T, Z*. That is to say, an object must exist, and be in the state in which we see it, *when* we see it. (*A*) And of course we can see objects on earth (*E*), in their present states (*T*), as well as the heavenly bodies (*H*), and indeed material objects in general. (*O*) Not that anyone doing science would have had occasion to affirm any of these things, but we may be sure that if some whimsical person had questioned them his doubts would have been rejected as absurd. And so would any suggestion that we can see in present time some past states of objects (*P*). What we have so far – *A, E, H, O, not-P, T* – may serve to represent the *pre-scientific* concept of seeing if we then go on to add *D*, the ordinary assumption that the present has some slight duration. (Of course, this also is something which there would have been no occasion to affirm.) But with the introduction of the real number system into physics and astronomy, *D* is replaced with *Z*, the convention that the present has no duration. Now if we deal broadly in half-centuries, that change was roughly contemporaneous with the introduction of *V* (the proposition that light has finite velocity). They both occurred in the second half of the 17th century, though the correct value for that velocity was not established until much later. But for convenience of representation let us suppose that *Z* came before *V*. Altogether then, we describe the old scientific concept of seeing as first stated above: *A, E, H, O, not-P, T, Z*.

Once *V* is added to the combination just listed, we get certain contradictions or paradoxes, as explained in the opening historical (non-
fictional) section of Chapter 4. No doubt this was appreciated almost at
once by certain scientists, so that they never simply "added" *V* to the
foregoing combination but began at once to modify it in other ways —
perhaps in the back of their minds, as it were, and a bit confusedly. But
while it may be artificial psychologically, I hope it will be illuminating
historically if we do add *V* to get the whole "incoherent concept" and
then look around for ways to change it and obtain a consistent combination, a coherent concept.

Now, as it happens, when we do add *V* we get the same incoherent concept that our fictional islanders had as their everyday concept of seeing
(p. 78 above). In that story, the visiting lecturer found four consistent
combinations for the islanders to consider as replacements for that concept. We can now avail ourselves of his work for present purposes, and
consider the advantages and disadvantages of those combinations, which
were:

(1)   *A, D, E, not-H, O. not-P, T, V*;
(2)   *E, H, O, P, not-T, V, Z*;
(3)   *D, E, H, O, P, T, V*;

and

(4)   *A, E, H, O, not-P, T, Z.*

We saw that while (1) and (2) are self-consistent and manage to incorporate the new knowledge item, *V*, they are both highly "unpalatable"
or psychologically inconvenient, the latter impossibly so. (We could not
claim to see in the present the present states of any objects, even those
at our finger tips.) In the spirit of Quine's sketch, one might hazard the
guess that this psychological inconvenience could be explained, at least
in part, by showing that (1) and (2) are logically incompatible with some
of our other concepts or conceptual structures — some of our other important beliefs and language conventions — which have not come into
the present description of this one little part of the whole "fabric."

But all of that had to do with finding a consistent, usable, and
minimally revisionary *everyday* concept *for the islanders*, while our present concern is to find one that is consistent and usable in *science* with

minimum revision. With this goal in mind we can notice that (1) and (3) are unacceptable since they incorporate D rather than Z and therefore do not fit smoothly into modern physics and astronomy. And (4) is similarly unacceptable because it fails to incorporate V. Alternative (2), accordingly, is the best pre-Einsteinian physical concept of seeing, certainly of these four. True, it does have the consequence that you cannot see at t the visible states that terrestrial objects have precisely at t. But the physicist can easily live with that when doing his theoretical calculations, even though he will no doubt retain D, not Z, in his everyday notion of seeing (as well as A and not-P instead of V and P). (In fact the physicist's everyday concept will no doubt be the ancient common-sense combination noted on p. 146: A, D, E, H, O, not-P, T.)

Now consider the statement, "We can never see in present time any past state of any object." This is an analytic statement under the regime of that pre-scientific concept (A, D, E, H, O, not-P, T), and also under the scientific concept obtained by adding Z to the latter prior to the discovery of V. For the truth of the statement is guaranteed by the very meaning of "seeing" (the concept of seeing) in view of the component not-P in that meaning or concept. But it ceases to be analytic under our new scientific concept, (2). Indeed it becomes false in view of component P in (2). Thus the quoted statement has passed out of the analytic category during the course of scientific history. (It is asuming to notice that when the visiting lecturer in our story moved on from (3) to (4) with his cablegram, thus providing the islanders with the very best replacement for their everyday concept, the quoted statement moved back into that category! But of course this does not represent anything in the history of science.)

One result of representing things in this manner is that when the sample statement ceases to be analytic it does *not* became synthetic, at least not in any simple way. It becomes "analytically false," i.e. false by the very meaning of "seeing," since P is part of that meaning or concept. But of course P has *become* part of the concept only because the world has been found to have one feature, V, rather than another, the instantaneous propogation of light. We may also be rather startled to notice that V itself, which any pre-Quinean empiricist would have cited as an obviously synthetic statement, has also become part of the concept. So it too is true "by the very meaning of 'seeing' " under the new conceptual regime. But again we have to point out that *experience* has led us to make it such a part, i.e. to include it among our beliefs about seeing, and our conventions about the use of the word "seeing" and related words.

Is it a defect in the foregoing method of representing "concepts" that it should not allow statements to pass neatly and cleanly across the "analytic-synthetic divide," but should have such results as I have just mentioned? Or, on the contrary, do these results help to underscore the slipperiness of the analytic-synthetic distinction? I suspect that the latter is the case, but I shall add only a few words on the point. Since no proposition in science is absolutely secure in its truth against conceptual revisions that experience and the economy of thought may force upon us, and since new empirical knowledge-items can themselves be important factors in determining what *is* economical to think or say, philosophers might do well to recognize that such items *are* partly "constitutive of our concepts." Then they would need to develop a more complex notion of "analytic statement" and "synthetic statement" than they have had before. We shall see in Chapter 8 that there are other good reasons why philosophers should change some long-established habits concerning the use of that pair of technical terms, and two other pairs besides: "*a priori – a posteriori*" and "necessary – contingent."

Our time-gap illustration helps to make another point which several critics of Quine have emphasized, namely, that it would be quite wrong to say that there are *no* analytic statements as the term "analytic statement" was defined at the outset of Section 23 above. For there are a great many statements which are true by virtue of their meaning as long as we stay within the bounds of a given conceptual scheme. But this is not inconsistent with what Quine says, namely, that there are no "analytic statements, *which hold come what may*" (emphasis added). Granted, the point should not be left unsaid, and it may also be worth noting that some scientific conceptual schemes have continued in use for a very long time.

Finally, it very much needs to be added (and was argued for in Chapter 3) that the most fundamental *non-scientific* schemes we humans use to understand the world – schemes that scientists use and must always use to find their way to their laboratory or writing table, etc. – have remained stable since before history began. Perhaps the statement that we are often able to re-identify material objects is not quite analytic in

Quine's sense if we allow, in "come what may," that some non-human language users of the remote future may be able to get along without it. But surely *for human beings* that statement and a good many other Moore-like statements are safely and permanently analytic even in Quine's sense.

25. CANONICAL LANGUAGE

Quine seems to have at least four objectives in mind when he speaks of "regimenting" language to make it conform to the syntax of mathematical logic, and of then subjecting it to further austerities in the form of "canonical notation." One purpose is to aid in the clarification and improvement of logical theory itself. Certain formal expressions are convenient for casting ordinary sentences into explicit logical form and deductively operating on them, but theoretically suspect because of their abstractness or complexity. Suppose we find a way to replace them with longer and more cumbersome expressions which are transparently correct in elementary theory. Then we can use the latter expressions when simplified theory is our concern, and we can go on using the shorter and more easily manipulated expressions for ordinary deductive purposes. A second objective is to provide special devices of clarification, disambiguation, and intellectual economy which can be used piecemeal according to the special needs of particular scientific inquiries. Still another purpose is to provide a concise and perspicuous language for the formulation of the fundamental laws of a given branch of science. Statements of the laws of nature are (when true) permanent general truths which admit of formulation in what Quine calls "eternal sentences": sentences whose truth or falsity does not depend on the circumstances of utterance: the when, where, how, why, or by whom. Now it may be that various idioms of scientific parlance which are logically suspect or "ontologically prodigal" (i.e., which sin against Occam's Razor) can be eliminated in formulating such sentences. The result would be a sparer and more precise view of the structures of reality which the branch of science in question has so far managed to depict. Finally, there is the "metaphysical" purpose of discovering the best or truest depiction of reality in general.

Each elimination of obscure constructions or notions that we manage to achieve, by paraphrase into more lucid elements, is a clarification of the conceptual scheme of science. The same motives that impel scientists to seek ever simpler and clearer theories adequate to the subject matter of their special sciences are motives for simplification and clarification of the broader framework shared by all the sciences. The quest for a simplest, clearest overall pattern of canonical notation is not to be distinguished from a quest of ultimate categories, a limning of the most general traits of reality.

The subject of canonical notation, in service of one or more of the foregoing objectives, occupies Quine more or less continuously in the latter half of his chief philosophical treatise, *Word and Object*, 1960, from which I have just quoted. There he proposes to eliminate many features of natural language from the canon, though not from the daily usage or communications of scientists. In the case of each item, he defends his proposal with detailed theoretical arguments, and often with polemical remarks when the issue is one on which he has drawn critical fire with his earlier writings, or on which there are well known contrary views which need to be answered. Some of the features of ordinary language that fail to survive are (i) the words 'any' and 'every,' except in the sense specified in the "universal quantifier" of logic; (ii) all distinctions of tense; (iii) such singular terms as proper names and definite descriptions; (iv) indirect speech, as in "He said that so-and-so"; (v) conditional sentences in the indicative mood; (vi) conditional sentences in the subjunctive mood; (vii) "indicator" words like 'this,' 'that,' 'I,' 'you,' 'here,' 'now,' 'yesterday,' 'today,' 'tomorrow,' etc., the reference of which continually changes; (viii) the word 'because' and other causal idioms; (ix) propositions; (x) attributes and relations; (xi) propositional attitudes, as in "He believes that so-and-so" or "He fears that so-and-so." In fact, no linguistic structure remains beyond the one which is "so well understood by present-day logicians, the logic of quantification or calculus of predicates."

To understand the issues and arguments on these topics would require a systematic study of logical theory, something we obviously cannot undertake in the present book. It would not be helpful for this purpose to add more fragments of logic to those explained in Chapters 5 and 6. Still, we can provide a specific illustration if we confine ourselves to the same logical topic that came up repeatedly in those chapters, i.e. definite descriptions. As noted above, Quine proposes to eliminate them, and he uses the same device Russell used. Let us consider his reasoning in this regard by pursuing the following order of subtopics: (1) the disadvantage of definite descriptions that leads Quine to wish to eliminate them from canonical notation; (2) his reasons for accepting Russell's method of doing so; (3) his criticism of Strawson and others who reject Russell's theory of descriptions; and (4) a brief evaluation of that criticism. Perhaps we can throw a bit of light on the topic and underscore the different styles of philosophizing represented by Strawson and Quine.

1. Definite descriptions are inconvenient because they give rise to "truth-value gaps." An example is our friend from earlier chapters, "the King of France." A sentence like "The King of France is bald" is neither true nor false because there is no King of France. Often we are able to avoid such sentences because we happen to know that nothing fits the description in question uniquely, at least at the time of utterance. But the description itself gives us no warning of this, nor does the standard notation in mathematical logic, $\hat{x}(Fx)$, which may be read "the object x such that x has F. And obviously, neither the ordinary language expression nor the logic notation contains any supplementary device to guarantee truth-value when there is nothing, or more than one thing, which fits the description. But we need such a guarantee in our canonical language. For in our attempt to describe the world truly and perspicuously, we want to be able to operate with sentences that are definitely true or definitely false (and permanently one or the other).

2. Quine says that in regimenting ordinary language by making its surface grammar conform to the syntax of logic, and in eliminating some of the syntactical forms of logic from our "canonical notation," we quite properly engage in "paraphrase" or "explication," which is not the same thing as the substitution of equivalent forms. We do not claim to preserve every bit of English syntax when we take that first step; rather, we keep the main skeleton, the parts of true or deep syntax that are logically perspicuous. And in the second step (that of devising a canonical notation) we sometimes adopt structures that differ somewhat in function from the standard notations they replace. The new notation should enable us to do everything we could do with the old (or at least everything we want to do in canonical language) while eliminating the undesirable features of the old notation.

Quine accomplishes that goal in the present instance by adopting Russell's theory of descriptions. That is, he stipulates that any sentence in which the form $\hat{x}(Fx)$ occurs must be replaced with one in which it does not occur, and in which the assertion is made that one and only one thing exists which has property F. As we saw in Section 17, the long-winded semi-English for "The King of France is bald" is then "There is a value of x such that x is King of France, and for any value of y, if y is King of France then y is x, and x is bald." In logic notation, this is

$$\text{"}(\exists x) \cdot [Kx \cdot (y) (Ky \supset y = x) \cdot Bx]\text{"}$$

where '$(\exists x)$' is called the existential quantifier and means "There exists a value of x such that ...''; where '(y)' is called the universal quantifier and means "For every value of y ...''; and where 'K', 'B', '.', and ' $\supset$ ' stand respectively for the property of being King of France, the property of being bald, the conjunction 'and', and the conditional 'if ... then'. The notation for the definite description, which would here be $\hat{x}(Kx)$, has been eliminated, and since the resulting sentence asserts the existence of something which uniquely has K, it never lacks truth value. When there happens to be no King of France the sentence is false, and it is also false when there is more than one King of France (if this be possible).

3. Quine is of course well aware of Strawson's criticism of Russell's theory of descriptions, and he mentions it more than once. In a later chapter he has some interesting comments to make about people who reject Russell's theory.

According to an influential doctrine of Wittgenstein's, the task of philosophy is not to solve problems but to dissolve them by showing that there were really none there. This doctrine has its limitations, but it aptly fits explication. For when explication banishes a problem it does so by showing it to be in an important sense unreal; viz., in the sense of proceeding only from needless usages. ...

In the case of singular descriptions, the initial problems are the inconvenience of truth-value gaps and the paradoxes of talking of what does not exist; and Russell dissolves them by showing how we can dispense with singular descriptions, in any problematic sense, in favor of certain uses of identity and quantifiers. ...

It is ironical that those philosophers most influenced by Wittgenstein are largely the ones who most deplore the explications just now enumerated [that concerning descriptions, and three others]. In steadfast laymanship they deplore them as departures from ordinary usage, failing to appreciate that it is precisely by showing how to circumvent the problematic parts of ordinary usage that we show the problems to be purely verbal.

4. Since we were at pains in Section 17 to show how Russell's theory of descriptions is a stage-three device or attempted "dissolution," it is pleasant to see Quine concur in this opinion. But it seems to me that the problem which Russell was attempting to dissolve with his theory is significantly different from the one Quine uses it to dissolve. Or, perhaps more exactly, Russell's claim as to the manner in which he has dissolved it is rather different after all. When we see how this is so, I think we will also see that Quine's criticism quoted above is wide of the mark, at least as applied to the topic of descriptions.

Russell was not *attempting* to "explicate" this feature of ordinary language, i.e. to *change* it some in order to eliminate truth-value gaps and the paradoxes of seeming to refer to things which do not exist. He was trying to make explicit the logical syntax already embedded in ordinary language, and to show that when we attend to it properly we see that no such references are made. True, he was trying to eliminate the paradox of "Meinongian objects," but he claimed to do so by showing that natural language does not really commit one to recognize the reality of such objects, despite the superficial indications of English grammar (or of German grammar, etc.). In other words, he was trying to do just what Strawson said he failed to do, namely, to give an account of the logic of definite descriptions in ordinary language. Not that he had before his mind this distinction between "explicating" (Quine's sense) and rendering explicit a structure which is already there implicitly. But if we re-read his account of descriptions in the article 'On Denoting' (1905), or in Chapter 16 of his *Introduction to Mathematical Philosophy* (1919), it seems most reasonable to say that he was concerned to do the latter, not the former. In both versions he repeatedly quotes ordinary English sentences and proceeds to explain their logical form. And though he often speaks of "propositions" that contain definite descriptions, this apparently refers to the *sentences* which he cites in this connection. (In the technical sense of "proposition" often used by philosophers − that which is expressed equivalently by many different sentences in many different languages − a proposition wears its logic on its sleeve, so to speak, and thus on Russell's view would contain no descriptions.) So he seems to think that it is *already* part of the meaning of those sentences that *there exists* and *x* such that ... . This would also seem to be the only reasonable explanation of his statement, " 'the King of France is bald' ... is not nonsense, since it is *plainly* false" (my emphasis).

If I am right in saying that this is how Russell viewed the problem of truth-value gaps and Meinongian objects, then pretty clearly he failed to do what he claimed to do. The reasons that Strawson gave for such an assertion have been summarized in Section 22 above, but let us briefly mention some of them. Russell's account of descriptions is based on such assumptions as that (i) sentences [non-eternal sentences, in Quine's terminology] carry truth value; that (ii) in order for a sentence to have meaning it must be true or false; and that (iii) any sentence containing a definite description *means* (rather than merely presupposes in use) that the description uniquely applies to some existing thing. All three of these assumptions are false, and Quine himself rejects them.

Perhaps some of the philosophers referred to by Quine *were* too "steadfast in laymanship" when they refused to allow any deviation from ordinary usage. But some of them also performed the professionally valuable service of showing how other philosophers have often been led into error by *not paying sufficiently close attention* to ordinary usage and to the existing features of natural language.

RECENT PHILOSOPHY OF LANGUAGE

We can divide philosophy of language into two parts corresponding to the following distinguishable but overlapping parts of the science of linguistics: (1) syntactics or the study of grammar and word order, and (2) semantics or the study of the meaning of individual words. Both of these features of a sentence are obviously necessary to the understanding of its meaning, and so may be the linguistic and action contexts in which the sentence is used, a point we emphasized in Sections 22 and 23. On the syntactical side we just saw how one distinguished philosopher has continued Russell's method of avoiding the grammatically misleading features of ordinary language by employing the syntax of logic when discussing philosophical questions. Many examples from other recent philosophers could be given to illustrate this same tendency. Some people have also been attempting to improve standard logic in ways that will enable it to represent more of the intuitively valid forms of reasoning. Also on the syntactical side of the philosophy of language one could mention the collaboration that has gone on between formal logicians and students of "transformational grammar," the well known research program in empirical linguistics developed by Noam Chomsky and others. Chomsky's famous distinction between deep structure and surface structure has an obvious affiliation with Russell's distinction between logical form and grammatical form, and some logicians have tried to determine how the deep structure of a sentence determines its logical form, and to what extent it does.

In the present chapter let us draw our illustrations from the semantical side. Some of the most widely discussed issues in all of recent philosophy are located there, and we shall consider a consequence of arguments dealing with issues.

26. PROPER NAMES

The originality of the first argument is very striking when we consider the amount of intellectual labor that earlier philosophers had expended on the same topic without noticing the important points which the argument brings out. For once again we are concerned with descriptions and how they function in language. If the meaning of a proper name must not be identified with the bearer of the name, as we have seen in Section 22, then what is its meaning? Various philosophers have answered that the meaning of a name consists of a description of the person or object named, or perhaps a combination of such descriptions. Thus "Chicago" = "the large city at the southern end of Lake Michigan"; "Verdi" = "the composer of *Otello* and *Aida*"; "Aristotle" = "a student of Plato, teacher of Alexander the Great, and the author of the *Nicomachean Ethics*." This is plausible view, for it might well be asked how else we know to whom or to what we are referring with a proper name except through some associated description. The point is only underscored by the frequent duplication or proper names. "James Carter" may be the man next door or the peanut farmer from Plains, and there are many other "Buffalos" besides the city at the eastern end of Lake Erie. So it seems that the meaning of a proper name does consist of one or more identifying descriptions which are satisfied by just one person or thing.

Plausible as this may be at first glance, a number of writers have pointed out serious flaws in it. One trouble is that it becomes *analytically* true that Verdi wrote *Aida*, and that Jimmy Carter became a peanut farmer. It becomes a necessary truth that Aristotle wrote the *Ethics*. But surely this is wrong. That very man to whom we refer with the name "Aristotle" might have written his other works but not that one, or he *might* have died of an infection before he wrote anything. It may seem that we could avoid this trouble by stipulating that while no particular description is a necessary part of the meaning of a name, its meaning does consist in a *group* of descriptions, some minimal portion of which must be true of the bearer of the name. Such a view is characteristic of the later Wittgenstein. But Keith Donnellan has shown how proper names can be used to refer to persons or things quite independently of the associated descriptions. Indeed he has shown how descriptions can be used to refer even when the person or thing referred to does not satisfy them at all. Let us consider the latter point first.

In his article, 'Reference and Definite Descritions' (1966), Donnellan makes a distinction between the "attributive use" and the "referential use" of definite descriptions. In an attributive use of "the so and so," I assert something about *whatever* individual or thing fits the description uniquely; I may do this, for example, when I do not happen to know who or what *does* have the property "so and so." Thus, coming upon poor Smith foully murdered, and noticing the brutal manner in which this lovable person was killed, I may say "Smith's murderer [the murderer of Smith] is insane." In a referential use, on the other hand, I will employ "the so and so" to call attention to a particular individual I have in mind. Thus, when Jones has been accused of the murder and placed on trial, I may notice his erratic behavior in court and say (using the same English sentence, and prejudging the question of guilt), "Smith's murderer is insane."

As soon as we notice this distinction we become aware of certain points that loosen the alleged analytic connection between proper names and true descriptions. For example (and let us speak in this paragraph of personal names only, just to avoid extra verbiage), I may succeed in referring to a particular person and making my audience know to whom I am referring even though the description I use for this purpose is false of the person referred to, as where Jones is later proved innocent. I may succeed in my reference even when the person I am addressing knows or believes that the person referred to does not fit my description, as when he doubts very much that Jones is guilty. I may even doubt or disbelieve it myself and still manage to refer to Jones in this way, although in that case I am misrepresenting my true belief by using the description "Smith's murderer." Indeed, *no* one need fit the description; I may still use it to refer to the person I have in mind and to say something about him, as where Smith was not murdered at all but was killed in a gruesome accident. Finally, someone *else who is present* may fit the description uniquely and I still may use it to refer to a person it does not fit. Suppose I say something to you about "the man drinking champagne" when the person I have in mind is drinking a colorless sparkling soft drink from a champagne glass, while (unbeknownst to both of us) there really is just one man present in the room who is drinking champange. All this is rather surprising if the meaning of a proper name − our primary tool for referring to someone – consists in true descriptions of the person named.

It may be desirable to pursue the question more systematically, however. Perhaps anyone who uses a proper name correctly will at least *be able* to supply a set of identifying descriptions uniquely fitting the thing named. This might be so even if the description which the person may happen to use to refer to that thing on a given occasion does not truly apply to it, or does not apply uniquely. Such a "principle of identifying descriptions" is examined by Donnellan in his article, 'Proper Names and Identifying Descriptions' (1972). After pointing out certain difficulties with the claim that one who uses a proper name correctly must *always* have that ability (to supply such a set), he argues that even when the speaker has this ability it is possible that the descriptions at his command do not furnish "necessary and sufficient conditions" for what is to count as the object. And yet he may successfully use the name to refer to the object so named, and his audience may understand the reference perfectly well. Donnellan so argues with the aid of an example which is admittedly artificial, but which may nevertheless manage to enforce the theoretical point. When we see its method we may be able to supply more natural examples covering the point closely enough.

The subject of a psychological experiment is asked to give names to two colored squares that appear one above the other on a white screen which occupies his entire visual field. He names the top one Alpha and the bottom one Beta, and so informs us. Unknown to him, his eyeglasses have been replaced with a pair which invert the visual field. After a few minutes we manipulate the projector and he informs us that Alpha is now of a different color. If we ask him which square he is now referring to as Alpha, he will of course reply that it is the one on top since the relative position of the two squares has not changed. But in fact, as we know, he is referring to the square on the bottom, the square which has changed color. If this person were not a naive subject of psychological experiments, he *might* say "By 'Alpha' I mean the square that *appears* to be on top." And even the naive subject is *able* to give this description. So Donnellan adds a complicated set of further circumstances which effectively eliminate that ability. Rather than describe them here, I shall merely observe that they do seem to achieve that purpose, thus producing a pure counter-example to "the principle of identifying descriptions" stated above.

To undermine a philosophical theory with counter-examples is one thing. To supply a more adequate account of the same subject matter is another and far more difficult thing in most cases. Donnellan has been joined by Saul Kripke, Hilary Putnam, and others in the latter task. The result of their efforts has become known as the causal or historical theory of names, although Kripke prefers to call it a "better picture" rather than a "theory." (He seems to avoid the latter term because it suggests a strict analysis or statement of necessary and sufficient conditions for reference.) According to this "picture," then, proper names can refer independently of any associated descriptions because, in one important sense of 'meaning,' they have no meaning at all. They function to designate individuals, but the designating relation between a given name and a given person or thing is not fixed by descriptions essentially bound to the name but by a kind of "social baptism ceremony." And this relation is preserved causally or historically. Except in the few cases in which we ourselves might happen to be the "baptizer" or name giver, we learn from others that a certain name has been given to a certain person by his parents or contemporaries, and we pass this information along to others by the way we use the name. After each historical stage or link in this chain, users of the name continue to refer to the same person or thing originally "christened" with this name. And their references can succeed even if they are vague or misinformed about the deeds or characteristics figuring in true descriptions of the person or thing in question. Of course, there is no *actual* ceremony when most inanimate objects and animals (e.g. pets) are given proper names or receive those names. But a conventional connection between the name and the object or animal nevertheless becomes well established within the particular linguistic and cultural group, and it is transmitted to new learners of the name, to later generations of users, and often to the people of other language groups and cultures.

Such an account may seem rather obvious, even trite. But when philosophers looked carefully at its implications they were in for a number of surprises. Some of these were pointed out by Saul Kripke in an article called "Identity and Necessity," published in 1971. Our next illustration is drawn from that article.

27. NECESSARY IDENTITY STATEMENTS

Let us consider statements of identity involving two proper names. A well worn example is the statement "Phosphorus is Hesperus." ('Phosphorus' and 'Hesperus' are ancient Greek names for the Morning Star and the Evening Star, respectively, but we shall avoid the latter expressions because someone might wish to argue that they are not proper names at all but definite descriptions, despite their use of capital letters.) Now it happens that Phosphorus and Hesperus are indeed one and the same heavenly body, i.e. the planet Venus. This was an empirical discovery; the truth of our sample statement could not have been determined *a priori*, e.g. by merely analyzing its meaning. Things might have turned out otherwise; it might have turned out that the bright object seen in the evening sky is not the same bright object that we see shortly before dawn. So it seems to follow that this statement of identity is not a necessary truth but a *contingent* statement. Some other identity statements whose truth is known to us only *a posteriori* (empirically) are "Heat is the motion of molecules," "Water is H_2O," "Light is a stream of photons," and other theoretical identifications in science. These too would be contingent truths by the same reasoning: things might have turned out otherwise in the history of science. For example, the caloric theory of heat might have won out over the kinetic theory.

Before focusing our attention on identity statements involving proper names, let us mention one other type of contingent identity statement. In this type, the identity is set up with the aid of descriptions that mention "accidental" properties. For example, "The first Postmaster General was the inventor of bifocals." Obviously it could have happened that the properties mentioned by the two descriptive phrases did not belong to the same person, whether to Benjamin Franklin or to anyone else. Although the statement happens to be true, it is not a necessary truth.

So much for a brief rehearsal of more or less standard philosophical opinions before the advent of the new theory of names. Kripke's view is that identity statements of the first two types mentioned above (though not the third) are *necessary*, not contingent. More precisely, he holds that *if* they are true (as we are all firmly convinced concerning the above examples of those two types), then they are necessarily true. In order to show this he begins by making certain preliminary points. First he tells us what he means by *rigid* and *nonrigid designators*. 'Designator' is his inclusive term for proper names and definite descriptions, and a rigid designator is one that designates the same object in all possible worlds, or rather in all possible worlds in which that object exists. By a possible world he means (1) any counter-factual but possible situation, e.g. Reagan not being elected President in 1980, or this typing table now being on the opposite site of the room from where it actually is, and of course (2) any situation that actually occurs. A nonrigid designator is one that designates a particular object in some but not all possible worlds where that object exists.

As a second preliminary point Kripke draws a distinction between "a prioricity" and "necessity." *A priori* truth is a notion relating to epistemology: certain statements can be known to be true independently of experience. Necessary truth, in contrast, is a notion having to do with metaphysics: certain statements are not merely true as matters stand, but must be true under any possible circumstances. Many philosophers have been inclined to use these notions and expressions interchangeably, but they do seem to be different, as Kripke maintains. It is true that the fact that a certain statement is known *a priori* may be a sufficient *reason* to hold that it is necessary, but it is not obvious that all necessary truths are knowable *a priori*. This is something that would require considerable argument to establish, if it ever can be established. A closely related confusion is that between "a posteriority" and "contingency." That the truth of a certain statement can only be known on the basis of experience is one thing; that it can be false under certain circumstances is quite another point. Whether these two notions are co-extensive – i.e. apply to just the same statements despite their difference of meaning – is not to be taken for granted, although many philosophers *have* taken it for granted.

Let us turn, at long last, to identity statements about individual objects or persons – statements like "Phosphorus is Hesperus" or "Cicero is Tully." Kripke's strategy for showing that they are necessary if true is to consider what may have led philosophers to think otherwise. This is an appropriate strategy because the philosophers in question have insisted on the contingency of such statements even in the face of two well known points. (1) Pre-analytically or common-sensically, it would seem obvious that where two proper names '*a*' and '*b*' are names of the same object or person, the statement that *a* is *b* does not just *happen* to be true but is guaranteed to be true. (2) A clear and seemingly valid argument can be given to that effect using the notation and inference patterns of standard logic. (Kripke states such an argument at the beginning of his article.) So if it turns out that people have refused to be convinced by these two plausible points while basing their own opinion on fallacies, there may not be much left to say for the contingency of this type of identity statement. Let us briefly indicate three (not all) of Kripke's criticisms and illustrations to this effect.

(A) One thing that has probably led people to feel that identity statements about individuals are contingent is the tendency to confuse necessity with *a priority* and contingency with *a posteriority*, as already mentioned. Philosophers assume that because the truth of "Phosphorus is Hesperus" is only known *a posteriori* it must be a contingent truth.

(B) Some philosophers have misread "Phosphorus is Hesperus" as the statement that the *word* 'Phosphorus' and the *word* 'Hesperus' are names of the same heavenly body. This latter statement, of course, is only contingently true. People might have used those names to designate objects which were in fact numerically different. But this is irrelevant to the question at hand. "Two plus two are four" might also have been false in that uninteresting way. But as its component words are *actually* used, it expresses a necessary truth.

(C) People take the *name* to be synonymous with some *description used to fix its reference*. But they are not synonymous, and the following is one way to make Kripke's point. Suppose some high school Latin student has fixed the reference of the name 'Cicero' with the description 'the author of [such and such] works.' By 'Cicero' he means to refer to the man who wrote those works. The name then designates *that man*, not whoever else might have written them if Cicero had not. And let us suppose that the student also learns that an ancient orator named Tully is famous for having denounced Cataline, so that he fixes the reference of the name 'Tully' with the description 'the orator who denounced Cataline.' As we know and as the student eventually learns, Tully is Cicero. Now, the orator in question (that very man) might not have gone on to write those works. In other words, the statement "Tully is the author of those works" is true but contingent. If we then falsely suppose that 'Cicero' and 'the author of those works' are synonymous expressions, we may mistakenly substitute the latter for the former (in the back of our mind perhaps), thus deriving the supposedly equivalent contingent statement: "Tully is Cicero."

Actually Kripke thinks that the reference of a name is seldom fixed by a description. It is usually fixed by the kind of social baptism that we referred to earlier. Yet even if the reference of names *were* fixed by descriptions, as many theorists have supposed, it would still be wrong to think that the name and the description are synonymous. That mistake is made often enough, and it is a prime reason why the theorists in question have then gone on to deny that identity statements about named individuals can be necessary statements.

So much for identities involving proper names. What about general identifications like "Heat is the motion of molecules"? As noted earlier, Kripke maintains that they too are necessary statements, and this result is even more surprising if correct. To back it up he begins by considering the circumstances which people have had in mind when they have supposed that heat might have turned out *not* to be the motion of molecules. Here are two of such circumstances:

(i)   The sensation which we call "the sensation of heat" might not have been caused by the motion of molecules but by something else. Suppose that this is how we had happened to be constructed. Then it looks as though heat would not have been the motion of molecules.

(ii)   Or suppose our neural construction had been such that the increasing average speed of the molecules caused us to have the sensation of *increasing cold* rather than heat. Then cold, it seems, would have been the motion of molecules.

Thus it would appear that while the statement "Heat is the motion of molecules" is true, it is not necessary. It holds good in the actual world but not in all possible worlds.

Kripke argues as follows that such a conclusion is wrong. Imagine a situation in which there are no organisms on earth sensitive to heat. (Probably this situation once obtained, but never mind.) There would still be heat, e.g. from fires heating up the air. This is our normal way of describing such a situation, and it shows that we use 'heat' as a rigid designator for a certain external phenomenon. That is, we use it as our name for that phenomenon in every possible world in which it occurs at all. To be sure, we use the description 'that which causes us to have [such and such] a sensation' to fix the reference of the word 'heat.' And to be sure, it is only a contingent property of heat that it does cause that sensation, just as writing certain works was a contingent property of Cicero. But heat would be heat even if it did not cause these sensations in us or in other creatures, just as Cicero (speaking quite literally) would have been Cicero even if he had never written those works. And scientific investigation of that external phenomenon has shown it to be molecular motion. The phrase 'molecular motion' is also a rigid designator, so the statement "Heat is molecular motion" is true in all possible worlds where heat occurs at all.

28. MIND-BRAIN IDENTITY

In the article we have just been discussing and also in his longer work, *Naming and Necessity* (1972, 1980), Kripke considers what bearing these last points may have on a widely discussed theory in contemporary metaphysics. Reflecting on the perennial problem of the relation of the mind to the body (see Section 1, above), some recent philosophers have taken the radical line that sensations (and perhaps more complex mental events) are not *caused* by certain states of the brain but are *identical* to those states. Perhaps pain, for example, is identical to the stimulation of what brain physiologists call the C-fibers. (There is an observed correlation between the two.) This theory is more jarring to common-sense than older forms of materialism. Instead of saying vaguely that mind is somehow reducible to matter, it offers the specific claim that pain is *nothing different* from certain bio-physical happenings. This is strongly counter-intuitive because we seem to *mean* such vastly different things by "pain," a word which names a kind of human *experience*, and "bio-physical event in brain tissues," a phrase which has to do not with direct experience but with the theoretical concepts of physics and physiology.

The champions of the Identity Theory, as it is called, seemed to achieve an important break-through when they explained how words can designate one and the same thing even when they differ so widely in meaning. This is true not merely in cases like "the Morning Star" and "the Evening Star," where both phrases designate a physical object, but also in theoretical identifications in which one word or phrase names a certain kind of experience while the other is drawn from physical science. For example, "Lightning is a discharge of atmospheric electricity." If certain bright flashes in the sky can be literally identical to (not merely caused by) electrical discharges – and they not only can be but are thus identical – then why cannot pains be identical to certain electrical events or states in the brain? This rhetorical question obviously did not prove that the Identity Theory is true, but it seemed to show that the theory must be taken very seriously. And it was often accompanied by the following explanation. A statement like "Pain P = brain state S" is indeed a *contingent* statement; it shares this property with statements like "Heat is molecular motion," "Water is H_2O," and "Lightning is an electrical discharge." In each of these four identities, the terms on either side of the copula or identity sign are quite different in *meaning*, and this accounts for the fact that we can quite easily *imagine and feel convinced* that pain, for example, is not a brain state. That it should *not* be is *possible*; yet it may still be so in fact, just as these other contingent statements have been found to be true in fact.

At first glance, Kripke's surprising but well-argued conclusion – that many theoretical identity statements in science are necessary if true – would seem to lend some support to the Identity Theory in metaphysics, even though it conflicts with the point just made. For surely the words "pain" and "brain state" are rigid designators, and thus we see that the identity of pains and brain states might not only be true but necessarily true. Kripke, however, thinks his result is an embarrassment to the Identity Theory. Let us consider his reasoning in this regard, and then let us ask whether the Identity Theorist can make any good reply to it. I shall present this as a dialogue of two speeches.

Kripke: Mr. Identity Theorist, you have made the philosophical claim that the statement "pains are brain states" ("P = S" hereafter) is a contingent truth. You have said that people can imagine P existing without S because that is at least a possible situation. "P = S" is not an analytic truth, hence not *a priori* or necessary. This is your explanation of how people are able to imagine the false state of affairs in which P is not S. But "P" and "S" are rigid designators, and I believe I have shown that if P is identical to S then they are necessarily identical. By the same token, the statement "It is false that P = S" is impossible. So if you accept my account of meaning, you are committed to hold that people are under some illusion when they *think* they can imagine that P is not S. We can very well imagine a contingently true proposition being false, but we can hardly imagine impossible propositions being true. In particular, we cannot imagine that one and the same thing should both exist and not exist at one and the same time. But if my account of meaning is correct *and* your theory that pains are brain states is correct, that is just what people are attempting to do when they imagine that P could exist without S.

Now how are you going to explain the illusion that people have when they think they can imagine such a thing? The only model I can think of for what the illusion might be, or at least the model given by the analogy you yourself suggest, namely, heat and molecular motion, simply does not work in this case. In *that* case, the illusion was created by the mistake of taking a contingent property of heat (that it causes us to have such and such a sensation) to be an essential or defining property. We can of course imagine that whatever it is that causes us to have that sensation is not molecular motion but something else. But you, Mr. Identity Theorist, cannot similarly explain and so dispel the supposed illusion that pain could be something different from a brain state. For it is not a contingent property of pain that it causes the experience of pain. The experience of pain is nothing but pain itself.

So you need some very different philosophical argument from the sort which has been given in the case of heat and molecular motion. And it would have to be a deeper and subtler argument than I can fathom and subtler than has ever been given in any of your literature that I have read. [This paragraph and the preceding one closely paraphrase and quote from the latter part of Kripke's article.]

Identity Theorist: For the purposes of this reply I shall assume that your theory of meaning is correct. Thus if P = S, as I maintain, people are indeed imagining an impossible situation when they imagine P existing without S, or vice versa. Nevertheless they can and do imagine these things. For of course *they* do not hold that P = S, and neither have I managed to prove convincingly that P = S. If I had done so, everyone could see (having the benefit of your linguistic points) that they would only be contradicting themselves if they then said "It seems to me that

P might very well not be S." That would be tantamount to saying "It seems to me that P might very well not be P."

Clearly, there is some sense in which we *can* imagine an impossible situation holding good, as long as we do not know that it is impossible. And of course one instance of this is imagining that something X is not Y when (unknown to us) X is identical to Y. Consider the case of heat again. Clearly it was possible for the scientists of two and a quarter centuries ago to imagine that heat was "caloric fluid" and not molecular motion. It would be possible for uninstructed people today to imagine such a thing. *I* cannot imagine it because, knowing that heat *is* molecular motion and accepting your theory of meaning, I literally cannot conceive of its being anything else. (For reasons that you have pointed out, I might be able at some future time to conceive of this, and then to imagine it, and then to believe it. For, scientists in the future may discover that they have been the victims of massively misleading evidence, and that heat — that which actually causes us to have the sensation of heat — is not molecular motion but something else. In that case, having learned of such a discovery, I should *no longer* know that heat is molecular motion, for I should no longer be even justified in believing it.)

To return then to pain and brain states. Since I *hold* that P = S, I am also committed to hold (in light of your points about meaning) that it is impossible for P not to be S. Furthermore, I am *committed not to imagine* that P is not S, if it makes sense to say this. I think it does make sense, for it is psychologically possible for me to feel, in some weakened mental state, that P *could* possibly not be S. To be sure, I would be contradicting myself in feeling this way or being struck this way. I would be denying what I had clearly recognized before: that "P = S" is necessary. But while it scarcely makes sense to say that I am committed not to do the impossible, it is all too possible to contradict oneself.

What then must I say to *other* people, who *are* logically entitled to imagine that P is not S? And how does your account weaken the Identity Theory by depriving it of some apparently powerful argument? The first question can be answered quite briefly, but the second will require a little more space.

(i) I can still admit to people, as I did before, that they can very well imagine and be intuitively convinced that P is not S. And I can still tell them, as I did before, that if I am right they are imagining and believing something which is false. Only now I must add, "and necessarily false."

(ii) I have to admit that I have lost what seemed to be a handy auxiliary argument. I used to explain to people that their imagining that P is not S (and their intuitive conviction that P is not S) is aided by the contingency of theoretical identifications. They *could* imagine and believe it, I said, because the thing is possible after all, even if not actually the case. I see now why that was all a mistake. Nevertheless, I can still make the *main* point that I made before. The fact that people can imagine P not being S, and can feel ever so strongly that it is not S, is no evidence that it is not S. For one thing, there is no inconsistency between P being S − even necessarily S − and their believing that it is not S. Furthermore, I can still undercut the strong intuition that pains just cannot be brain states in view of the great dissimilarity in meaning between "pain" and "brain state." For just as before, I can point to the extreme difference in meaning (or in apparent meaning, if you insist) between "water" and "H_2O," between "lightning" and "electrical discharge," and so on. Indeed, your theory of meaning gives me new assistance in this connection. It helps me explain more accurately than I could before how words that have very different "apparent meaning" or "surface meaning" can designate one and the same natural phenomenon. Granted, I must not try to explain this by saying that the experience of pain is only contingently related to pain. But I am really under no temptation to say this, or to give any other explanation of the alleged illusion that people can imagine P not being S. For as I have explained, there is no such illusion in the case. People really can and do imagine it, although *I* cannot imagine it when I combine your doctrines with my own and accept their joint consequences in a clear-minded way.

So ends the dialogue. I believe our Identity Theorist wins this particular debate. Let us attempt to pinpoint Kripke's mistake a little more precisely. Here, I think, is a fair reconstruction of his reasoning:

(1)   The Identity Theorist said we can imagine that P is not S because at least that is a possible state of affairs, though not an actual one.

(2)   But it is *not* a possible one given the truth of the identity theory (P = S) and the soundness of my doctrine of meaning. For in that case "P = S" is necessary and "P is not S" is impossible.

(3)   So we *cannot* imagine that P is not S. One cannot imagine something which is impossible.

(4)   So the Identity Theorist has to explain how the illusion arises that we *can* imagine such a thing.

(5)   Now I, Kripke, cannot think of any other way in which he might attempt to explain that illusion except by saying that we take as an essential property of pain something which is merely an accidental property, viz., that it causes the sensation of pain. But that will not work (etc., as above).

The mistake is in the second sentence of (3): "One cannot imagine something which is impossible." This is something Kripke does not explicitly say in the article we have been discussing, but it is clearly a tacit premise of his argument having to do with the identity theory. The correct premise would be, "One cannot imagine something which one understands to be impossible."

In a "brief restatement" of this argument in footnote 18 of the article, Kripke says the Identity Theorist must explain how the necessity of "P = S" can be reconciled "with the apparent fact that C-fiber stimulation might have turned out not to be correlated with pain at all." But the Identity Theorist can simply reply, "Well, that apparent fact is no fact − not even an apparent one any more − if (i) pain *is* C-fiber stimulation, and (ii) 'pain' and 'C-fiber stimulation' are rigid designators. All you have done, Mr. Kripke, is force me to choose between that apparent fact and the conjunction of (i) and (ii). I choose the latter, since I am assuming for the sake of the argument that your theory of meaning is correct."

Of course, none of this proves the truth of the mind-brain identity theory or even renders it more probable. And Kripke does deprive that theory of one auxiliary argument, as noted above, if we accept his impressive account of meaning.

29. RETROSPECT

Before turning to the ethical and social side of recent analytic philosophy, it may be useful to look back over Part Two and see whether these illustrations can be combined with those of Part One to produce a more unified view of the side of philosophy with which we have been concerned so far. We particularly need to ask what all the illustrations taken together can tell us about how the Russell and "Oxbridge" traditions relate to one another, and to the speculative tradition of earlier centuries. Not that we can hope to arrive at any definitive answer to so broad a question. It would require a whole book even to make the attempt, and a book rather different from the present one. Still, it may be helpful to offer some tentative conclusions, and I hope those which I am going to suggest will be supported well enough by the preceding twenty-eight sections to be worth serious consideration. I shall arrange them under two topics: metaphysical theory and analytical method.

Our "four stage" apparatus developed in Part One brings out a major difference between the metaphysical theories of the early 20th-century analysts and the theories of former centuries, or many of the latter. Instead of attacking common-sense as incoherent, and then offering an allegedly coherent reconstruction of it (the traditional "TWO and FOUR" pattern), Russell and the early Wittgenstein construct a world scheme out of clues supplied by a particular discipline with which they happen to be much occupied and profoundly impressed, mathematical logic. The resulting picture of the world does not really involve any attack on common-sense, or any claim to correct it. Rather, it claims to go deeper and reveal structures of the world undreamt of in everyday thought. Russell does retain the anti-common-sense animus of much classical philosophy, but this is not really demanded by his theory, which pointedly refrains from rejecting the entities of everyday experience. In the *Tractatus* there is no disparagement of common-sense at all. We noted briefly in the Introduction to Part Two that the "ONE and THREE" pattern − we could call it the "defense-of-common-sense pattern" − is also not in play in these metaphysical speculations. But perhaps it is worth noting that Russell does use a *remnant* of older philosophizing in that pattern, namely, phenomenalism. We saw in Chapter 1 how, for Berkeley at least, a phenomenalist theory of objects is an attempted dissolution of the problem of perception.

In Quine's scientific realism we are confronted by a third type of metaphysical theory. Here one describes the world by extracting more general structures or traits from the results of all the physical sciences. This project will probably strike present-day readers as less dubiously speculative than Logical Atomism, to say nothing of the reconstructionist theories of former centuries. No doubt it is a very difficult and still rather vague project, and Quine's contribution thus far takes the form of preparing a linguistic vehicle suitable for stating that general picture as it emerges from the separate disciplines, i.e. as it is extracted and built up from them by philosophers of science turned metaphysician. We saw that his work in that linguistic vein sometimes takes the form of explicative dissolutions. Problems are "banished" by showing that they arise from "needless usages" – needless for the purpose of describing a world, though not for the purposes of everyday communication, even between scientists at work. But here, as in Russell and the early Wittgenstein, neither the "ONE and THREE" pattern nor the "TWO and FOUR" pattern of reasoning is the *main* road leading to one's picture of the world.

Still a fourth type of theory is found in the "descriptive metaphysics" of Strawson. To contrast it with all the others, we may notice that it does not attempt to discover *how the world must be* (as the early analysts and the traditional metaphysicians do), nor does it attempt to show *how the world is* (as Quine would do). Rather, it tries to describe how our *basic everyday scheme* for dealing with the world *is and must be*. We observed how Strawson makes extensive use of the "ONE and THREE" pattern as an implement of such description. By seeing how philosophers have often concocted problems and theories out of their own misconceptions or violations of that scheme, we come to see its structure more clearly.

Are Quine's project and Strawson's project mutually inconsistent? We should not hastily conclude that they are. In the first place, they have rather different goals: to describe the most general traits of the world, and to describe the basic structures of our everyday scheme for dealing with the world. In the second place, it is far from obvious that the results of the former project will have *any* implications for the latter. There is no reason at all to think they will alter our *description* of the most fundamental structures of common-sense. And it seems very unlikely that they will entail that we either should or could deliberately alter those structures themselves. Theories drawn from the separate sciences do not seem to say anything *contrary* to what is said or assumed in the basic common-sense scheme. This was well explained a good while ago by Susan Stebbing and others in their criticisms of scientific popularizers` who carelessly or confusedly tell us that the chair we are sitting on is not really solid but mostly empty space. Why will the highly general theories of nature built up in the Quinean project be any different in this respect?

Let us turn to our other announced topic: the present status of, and relationship between, the analytical methods of the "Oxbridge" and Russell traditions. We saw in Strawson's criticism of Russell's theory of descriptions how the syntax of logic has its limitations as a device of philosophical description, notwithstanding its advantages (emphasized by Quine) as a device of explication. But there can hardly be any doubt that the Russell tradition has made a permanently valuable and even great contribution to the methods of philosophy. This is especially clear in areas where it is plausible to think that problems may admit of exact descriptive analysis using tools originally developed to investigate the foundations of mathematics. And the techniques of formal logic will undoubtedly continue to be *one* of our most valuable resources in other fields as well. Some very brief illustration of this point was also attempted in our discussion of Strawson's criticism.

Now that Russell's analytical style again enjoys high prestige on the metaphysical and linguistic side of philosophy, it would be a great pity, in my opinion, if the best insights and high sophistication of the mid-century British philosophers (including those who are still among us) should fall into neglect or disrespect among the younger American thinkers. But there are hopeful signs that the Oxbridge tradition has found its way into the thinking of our more talented people despite all party affiliations concerning method. To illustrate the point, here are a few items that can be gleaned just from the illustrations in the present chapter.

(1) In making his new points about descriptions, Donnellan uses a method which is highly reminiscent of J. L. Austin and the later Wittgenstein. "Don't just *think* about these expressions and how they relate to preconceived logical forms. *Look* at the way they are actually *used*." In following this advice, Donnellan takes several steps beyond Strawson's results in his ordinary-language classic, 'On Referring.' To mention just one of those steps again, he notices that people can and often do manage to refer to something by using a definite description which does not truly apply to anything. Strawson had looked more carefully at usage than Russell had, but not as carefully as he might have, and not with as wide a lens as Donnellan uses.

(2) Kripke shows his awareness of the point (and illustrates it most impressively) that valuable insights are possible in philosophy without achieving or claiming anything like a strict analysis or Russellian "theory" of the problem under discussion. And yet he seems to accept the Russellian ideal as normal, for otherwise there would be no need for the disclaimer: his statement that he is not presenting a "theory" but only a "better picture."

(3) In giving his better picture of common nouns that stand for natural kinds, he sometimes resorts to "ordinary language" arguments or something rather similar to them; and rightly so. What better way to begin to show that 'heat' is a rigid designator than to ask "what we would say" — what we would say (for example) about the presence or absence of heat in a world without sensitive organisms but with air and fires. Admittedly there is some variation here from Austin's classic injunction to ask "what we should say" in such and such a situation (I mean a variation other than the shift from the standard English 'should' to the American 'would'). Kripke's question, in effect, is "What *do* we *now* say" about an imagined situation in which we could never find ourselves. That is Putnam's question too in various science fiction examples which he contrives to support the same account of natural-kind terms.

A closing caveat may be in order. Logical analysis and conceptual elucidation in the Oxford – Cambridge style are not the only important methods of analytic philosophy. Witness the historical method which establishes Quine's important insight about analytic truth, an insight which his "failed analyses" of 'analytic' and 'synonymy' do not establish. Attention to the history of science has also been important in the development of the new semantics discussed in the present chapter.

PART THREE

CHAPTER 9

VALUES IN GENERAL

30. INTRODUCTION TO PART THREE

The purpose of this last Part is to present some illustrations from recent moral and political philosophy, and to show how one ·of the methodological themes developed in Part One has special significance for that whole area of philosophy. In the present section, I shall first give a brief preview of the illustrations and then comment on how they relate to that theme.

The central problem of moral philosophy, in modern times at least, has been the nature of moral judgment and the grounds of moral truth. It is a skeptical problem *par excellence*, for while all normal people conduct their daily lives on the assumption that there are moral truths (even people who decide to be moral only when it pays), no philosopher has been able to give a satisfactory account of moral truth. Forceful arguments of a radically skeptical kind are easy to construct "proving" that moral judgment is at bottom a nonrational affair: − that there are no moral truths or falsehoods, and that the reasons people give for their moral judgments are inevitably specious or inconclusive. Before confronting the problem head-on, we begin with a kind of preparatory skirmish. Our first illustration summarizes R. M. Hare's descriptive account of value standards in *The Language of Morals*, the most widely discussed ethical treatise of the nineteent-fifties and early sixties. With the aid of Hare's description, we show that many *non-moral* evaluations, at least, are quite definitely true or false, and provably so. The point is an easy one, but this explanation gives us the opportunity to clarify a certain conceptual structure which will be useful in discussing the problem of moral truth, though it will not be sufficient for solving it.

A skeptical argument presenting the problem is then given at the beginning of Chapter 10. We go on to sketch out an ethical theory which adds certain other structures to the one just mentioned, and proposes a solu-

145

tion. This theory belongs to a type of ethical theory which has had many prominent representatives during the nineteen-sixties and seventies. Works by Kurt Baier, Marcus Singer, R. M. Hare (his second book), John Rawls, and William Frankena (especially the 2nd edition of his well known textbook) might be cited in this connection. They all take "the moral point of view" as the overarching principle of morality, though they do not all call it by that name. It is a *procedural* principle laying down requirements as to the *manner* in which we are to go about forming and defending our moral opinions. It seems to be a true principle in the sense that it helps to "constitute" or "define" critical moral thought as we know it. But whether it can yield a doctrine of *substantive* moral truth − truth in the moral evaluations we arrive at when taking the moral point of view − is the principal topic explored in the chapter. In the course of the discussion we comment in some detail on three other types of ethical theory which have been prominent during the last half-century and are still very important in the on-going debate: Utilitarianism, the Emotive Theory, and Intuitionism.

Chapter 11 turns to a problem of applied ethics which has been discussed by many politicians, lawyers, journalists, and scholars during the last decade or two. It is the problem of privacy, and it includes the question, much discussed by philosophers, whether people have a moral and political *right* to privacy. We shall briefly review the contributions of several recent writers on the latter question, and we shall add some constructive criticisms. One purpose of this illustration is to sample the impressive literature of *practical* philosophy which has been developing in recent years.

Moral thought and political thought surely belong to those "suburbs" of the mind referred to at the beginning of Chapter 4, not to the "old city" which seems to be unchangeable for creatures built as human beings are built. Indeed the kind of moral and political criticism that aspires to be well informed, impartial, and fully rational must surely be placed in the very newest suburbs. Even as an ideal that we usually fall short of satisfying, it seems to be recognized in the modern world by only a small minority of people, and there are long stretches of history and culture in which we find hardly a trace of it. Thus it would not be subject to those strictures on conceptual reform which we emphasized in Chapter 3 and again at the end of Section 24. Granted, one should not be quick to find conceptual incoherence in any field of thought which people have been cultivating for practical ends over long periods of time. But when we are dealing with thought habits and conceptual structures that have only been haltingly developed by a small segment of humanity during the past few centuries, we should not be surprised to find that they have yet to work themselves into a fully consistent set of basic assumptions.

The ethical theory outlined in Chapter 10 takes note of this point, and the solution it proposes is frankly revisionary. In the course of the argument we shall attempt to identify the inconsistent assumptions of moral thought as it is presently understood and practiced by critically reflective people. We shall look for the most economical way of adjusting those assumptions to produce a consistent pattern or combination, and we shall also point out how three of the four major types of ethical theory discussed in the chapter are themselves revisionary, whether wittingly so or not. The notorious obscurity as well as the powerful appeal of the fourth type − Intuitionism − will be explained by the fact that it attempts to retain *all* of the assumptions that give structure to critical morality as we have known it.

The theme that moral and political philosophy is quite properly reconstructionist or conceptually radical is continued in the final chapter. There we shall argue that the existing conceptual apparatus concerning rights is inadequate to permit rational disposition of the more controversial claims of political right. But philosophers can describe the specific shortcomings of this apparatus and make useful suggestions for repairing or supplementing it. We shall attempt to illustrate the point in connection with the right to privacy.

31. STANDARDS

In order to appreciate R. M. Hare's account of value standards, let us begin by considering some homely examples in which there is no doubt at all that we can tell the good from the bad, and no serious question as to what the proper criteria of goodness and badness might be. We can then inquire after the origin and justification of these criteria. A good carving knife will be distinguished from a mediocre one or a poor one by the fact that it holds a sharp edge and is long and flexible enough to make thin slices if we wish. A good watch is one that keeps accurate time for years of normal use, and seldom needs adjustment or repair. A good chronometer, on the other hand, is one that measures time with great accuracy and precision, and is highly reliable. In most cases, something may be relatively good of its kind without satisfying *all* the relevant criteria in high degree. Thus, some good cars are very comfortable, reliable, easy to operate, safe, and smart looking, although they consume more than the average amount of gasoline. But other cars which are equally comfortable, reliable, easy to operate, safe, and smart, but more economical in gas consumption, will be even better. Obviously one could go on listing many other *kinds* of things in which we distinguish between good, bad, and indifferent members of the kind. And one could go on listing the familiar sets of criteria on the basis of which we make such distinctions − a somewhat different set of criteria for each kind.

Is it just an arbitrary convention that we have the criteria of value we do have, so that anyone would be free to question or reject them if he wished? Or, on the contrary, do value criteria have an objective basis in fact and reason? In all the examples mentioned in the preceding paragraph, it is easy to see that there is an objective basis. Each thing mentioned is an artificial object which is intended to do something, to function in a certain way. The name of the thing calls attention to this function. A relatively *good* thing of one of these kinds, then, is a thing which performs its function (or enables us to perform it) relatively well, or better than most things of the same kind. And a thing will perform or enable us to perform that function well if it has certain characteristics and lacks certain others which would interfere with that function. Accordingly, the former characteristics and the absence of the latter are the criteria of a good object of the kind in question. This is no matter of opinion but a demonstrable fact. You could not rationally say that a dull, rigid carving knife is better because you have decided to take dullness and rigidity as *your* criteria of goodness in this case; that would be excluded by the very nature and purpose of carving knives. Of course, if you found that a certain dull, rigid knife sold as a carving knife was actually very good for slicing large cheeses, then you might rationally and truly say that it is a good cheese knife.

These results can be readily extended to kinds of things which are not artificial objects or do not have functional names. For in referring to the function of an object (which may or may not be spelled out in its name) we only call attention to the purpose or interest we normally have in choosing among objects of the kind. It is this purpose or interest which determines what the criteria shall be. And it is perfectly possible to ascertain what our normal purpose or interest in choosing is, and hence what the correct criteria are, even in the case of many things which have no "function," at least in any narrow sense of the word. A thing may not be designed to *do* anything because it is not *designed* at all. And yet there may be a certain interest we normally seek to further in choosing among items of that kind, an interest which will be furthered more or less efficiently by the object chosen if it has certain characteristics, and otherwise much less efficiently or not at all. For example, in choosing players for an athletic team the interest we have in mind, or ought to have in mind in so far as it is an athletic team we are building, is winning games. The candidates most likely to help us do that are those who have the physical characteristics, skills, and aptitudes appropriate to the sport in question. Thus the criteria of a good basketball player are somewhat different from those of a good baseball player or a good football player. And the criteria of a good professional basketball player are somewhat different from, though in many ways similar to, the criteria of a good high school basketball player, and so on.

Now in a great many cases it is an ascertainable fact whether a certain item of a certain kind satisfies the criteria of a good thing of that kind, or whether it satisfies them better than some other item does. To be sure, there will be doubtful cases, as where one candidate for the team has certain desirable traits but lacks others, while his rival has the ones he lacks but lacks the ones he has. We may not be sure which criteria ought to be given greater weight, which sort of player is more likely to help us win. But there are many cases which are not doubtful or borderline, cases where it is obvious that one player is very good indeed, or clearly better than another.

In the preceding paragraphs we have often spoken of the "normal" purpose or interest in choice. But cannot these purposes or interests change? Even while most people continue to further certain interests when choosing among items of a certain kind, what is to prevent other people from taking an eccentric line and favoring different interests? How can the majority dictate to the minority? Or how can the last generation dictate to the present one in this regard? Since the new generation, or the minority, may have different purposes or interests, they must use criteria suitable to them. How then can it be a *fact* that a certain item of a certain kind is good when some of these interests and resulting criteria (those of the majority, let us say) tell us to choose that item, while the minority's interests and resulting criteria tell us not to choose it?

Hare was himself concerned to emphasize that our interests can and do change, so that our standards (sets of criteria) must also change if they are to continue to be intelligent or valid. For this reason, I believe, he did not consider or answer the foregoing objection in *The Language of Morals*. Indeed, he apparently agreed with the objection at least as far as moral criteria are concerned. He thought that everyone must choose his own ultimate criteria of value, his own basic principles according to which some actions and character traits are good (to be done or emulated) while others are bad and to be avoided. This choice of basic principles could be rationally made, he said, by informing ourselves about different *ways of life* and deciding which one we prefer among those actually available to us. The right principles would then be those which are most compatible with that way of life. But other people could prefer different ways of life, so they might easily embrace very different principles with equal justification. There could be no question of one person showing the *truth* of an evaluative statement depending on such principles, for there is no reason why someone else should not reject it on the basis of his own principles.

32. TRUE VALUE

In the foregoing analysis, Hare does not draw any major distiction between moral standards and other value standards.He points out that both kinds have a basis in fact: they are *necessary* if we are to realize our purposes in choice. But he also *seems* to allow that both may be freely rejected by someone whose purposes in choice are different. If this were really the case, his analysis would not enable us to show how certain value statements are definitely true and others definitely false. But there is an important respect in which it is not the case, at least for a great many (not all) *non-moral* standards. In the remainder of this chapter we shall attempt to explain this as briefly as possible before going on to consider moral standards in the following chapter.

To make the point abstractly before illustrating it, we often are not free to reject the usual or normal criteria of value because we are not free *while evaluating items of a certain kind* to replace the normal purpose in choice with one of our own. When I say we are not free, I mean we are not logically free. It would not *make sense* thus to embrace a different purpose and the resulting criteria. This is because we would then no longer be evaluating items of the kind in question. Of course we are free to stop evaluating them, to give up that sort of evaluation. But we cannot consistently claim to continue to make and defend evaluations of that sort while rejecting the purpose and criteria proper to it. As long as we assert that something is a good so-and-so, we are logically obliged to observe the criteria which flow from the purpose that defines so-and-so as a certain class of things to choose among.

To turn to an illustration, what would it mean to say that I am free to adopt my own eccentric purpose or interest in choosing among carving knives, so that *for me* a good carving knife is a dull, thick, rigid one? If it meant anything intelligible it would only be a misleading way of indicating that I am not interested in choosing among carving knives as such, but that I have some other purpose in mind besides that of carving roasts, or carving them well. Perhaps I only want to cut thick slices of meat. Or perhaps I want to practice knife throwing with a fairly large knife, and I have no such knives to choose from except the family carving knives. Then I will look for a rigid, pointed knife which will stick in the side of the barn, but which has a very dull edge that will not cut me as I grasp the blade and throw. This all makes good sense, but the criteria thus rationally identified are not the criteria of a "good carving knife" but of a "good throwing knife chosen from among the available carving knives." If I told someone without further explanation that the pointed, dull, rigid knife which I had thus chosen was a good carving knife, I would be saying something false. And if he then examined it and pronounced it a poor carving knife, he would be saying something true. Furthermore, if I then explained to him the purpose I had in mind in choosing among my carving knives, this would not show that I had not *said* something false. It would only show that I had *meant* to say something which happens to be true, but had failed to do so. And he could then tell *what* I had tried and failed to say, namely, that this is a good throwing knife chosen from among the available carving knives.

To vary the illustration and make two related points, suppose some primitive people unacquainted with knives of any kind, whether for scaling, skinning, fighting, throwing, carving meat, or any other purpose, were to find a collection of what we call carving knives. They might come to prefer some of these knives to others for aesthetic or magical or other reasons which could be spelled out. But obviously it would be false to say that these reasons would indicate their criteria of a good carving knife. For they would not even have the concept of a carving knife, or of a knife, as long as it never occurred to them to do with these objects any of the things people do with knives. Somewhat similarly, it would be possible for a person who does know about knives to choose among such objects on some occasion for a purpose totally unrelated to their purposes as knives: and he, no more than our primitives, would be choosing among knives as such. We could not say that he was entitled to have his own criteria of a good *knife* based on that purpose. It would also be possible for a highly eccentric person who knows about knives to decide that he will have no use for knives ever, so that he will never have occasion to choose among knives as such, or to use the criteria of a good knife in selecting one. But such a person could not thereby abolish or change the criteria of a good knife, or of a good carving knife, or of a good throwing knife, and so on. These criteria would still be what they are; he simply would have no use for them in his tool using life, although even he might still have a use for them in his linguistic life, as when he managed to understand someone who spoke or wrote about good knives.

Finally, imagine that knives were done away with altogether because people had come to hate them and would not even pronounce the word "knife," while the phrase "a good knife" had become an abomination to them. Still, for a time at least, they would retain the concept of a knife, and even of a good knife. In an unguarded moment they might recall the difference between a good knife in general and a poor one, or between a good hunting knife and a poor one. And the statement − made by a naughty child perhaps − that a dull, rigid knife cannot be a good carving knife, or that a bayonet with a broken point cannot be a good bayonet, would still be true. The moral of this fantasy is that even though one might object to the normal criteria of a good thing of a certain kind because one objects to that *kind* of thing and its uses, one cannot rationally escape from, or change, those criteria *as long as one is evaluating things of that kind.*

To say this is not to deny that criteria can change. The criteria of a good family car have changed somewhat since the days of the Model T Ford because (among other reasons) there has been a change in the state of the engineering arts by which people seek to further the purposes they have in choosing among family cars. That is, we still look for safety and reliability and economy rather than high speed and great maneuverability, but the family cars of today (let us hope) are on the average safer and more reliable than those of fifty years ago. If so, the *degree* of safety or reliability in a *relatively good one* is now higher. Nor does this account deny that *commonly recognized* criteria can properly be criticized and reformed to bring them into *better* agreement with the normal purpose in choice. For example, if good medical practice (practice according to the standard in use by most reputable doctors) were to lag ten years behind new physiological knowledge and therapeutic techniques, any doctor who relies upon it might be properly corrected. For "good medical practice" (using ironic quotation marks now) would not really be good medical practice any more.

Obviously we could make the same sorts of points about *many* kinds of things people evaluate, although this description will not easily apply to some other kinds. (There seems to be no indisputable purpose in choice determining the criteria of a good painting, for example, or of a good Christian.) Clearly then, many value statements or claims are true and can be shown to be true by sound deductive reasoning. And of course it is then obvious that many other value assertions are false and can be shown to be false in the same way. The reasoning is sound because it validly deduces the statement to be proved from a non-evaluative premise which is known to be true (a description of the item being evaluated) and an evaluative premise (a statement of the standard) which is known to be valid in light of an indisputable purpose in choice. This is the simplest type of case, where the standard consists of a single criterion. In the more usual case, the evaluative premise will include an "other things being equal" clause because there are multiple criteria, and then we shall need a third premise to the effect that other things *are* equal. This third premise can sometimes be shown to be true beyond question, as where the criteria form a finite checkable list and the thing being evaluated either satisfies them all in high degree, or satisfies hardly any of them. Here too then, the reasoning is sound. In the case of many standards, to be sure, a complete list of criteria cannot be given. But even in this type of case, it can often be *known* that one is *justified in asserting* that other things are equal. Consider the following example:

Premise 1: A wrist watch that keeps accurate time for years and seldom needs any adjustment or repair is, other things being equal, a good one.

Premise 2: My wrist watch has been keeping accurate time for ten years since I bought it, never gaining or losing as much as half a minute over the course of a month, and I have never had to have it adjusted or repaired during that time.

Premise 3: Other things are equal. [I am justified in saying so because my watch appears to have no other features which would interfere with its function; e.g. it does not cause normally sensitive skin to break out in a rash, it does not easily become disconnected from the band, etc.]

Conclusion: My wrist watch is (or at least has been) a good one.

Beginners in moral philosophy sometimes argue that the statement of a standard − be it a moral or a non-moral standard − can never be shown to be true or valid because that would require an endless recitation of further descriptive facts and evaluative premises. This is contrary to our actual scheme for rational evaluation, a scheme according to which many standards can be finally and conclusively validated by reference to an existing, unchallengeable purpose in choice. It is at least arguable, however, that we can never establish the truth or validity of our ultimate moral premises. By setting moral evaluation to one side I hope we have gained a better understanding of at least one of our conceptual schemes for evaluation, and an important one, even if we still do not know what to do with moral evaluation.

CHAPTER 10

ETHICAL THEORY

33. THE PROBLEM OF MORAL TRUTH

In light of our results in Chapter 9, let us now formulate a skeptical argument to present the problem of moral truth. The argument will occupy all of this brief section.

(1) It is entirely permissible to challenge common moral principles or criteria in the course of moral debate. That is to say, we may do this even while choosing which actions to approve or disapprove for stated reasons. To illustrate the point one need only mention some principle like "contraception is wrong," a principle which may be widely accepted in the group to which the debating parties belong. While it would be pointless to challenge the accepted criteria of a good football player in the course of choosing players, the questioning of accepted moral criteria is by no means uncommon even if we do not find it in the discussions of highly conventional people.

(2) With an eye to the outcome of Section 32, someone may wish to reply that while the purpose of winning games played according to present-day rules pretty obviously requires the criteria of a good player recognized by present-day coaches, moral criteria tend to get out of date. No one is hired to keep them current; few people would lose their jobs because of bad judgments made in reliance on obsolescent moral standards. Yet under new conditions of life moral standards may no longer serve the fundamental purpose of moral choice, which is to promote the welfare of the human group. For example, a high death rate, especially among infants, and a corresponding need for a high birth rate to maintain a scanty population once demanded the rule against contraception if that purpose was to be served. But under the present conditions of much lower infant mortality and a continuing high birth rate in most of the world, such a rule is no longer required and is even harmful. Therefore (the reply concludes) we *can* show the truth of probable truth

155

of some moral judgments, and the falsity or probable falsity of others, by applying standards that have been *brought into line* with the underlying purpose of moral choice.

(3) But such a reply actually helps us see more clearly why there probably is no such thing as truth in moral evaluation. It shows how moral truth would have to rest on a purpose in choice which is itself unchallengeable, and there seems to be no such purpose. Morality and moral criticism do not seem to make up that kind of institution; they do not seem to have that sort of conceptual structure. Surely we all have the intellectual right to challenge a purpose in moral choice which we sincerely find objectionable or questionable. Consider even the highly respectable purpose that was taken for granted in step 2 above, namely, to promote the welfare of the group. If we found, or had good reason to suspect, that the most efficient pursuit of that purpose would have results which strike us as grossly unfair, we might wish to reject it as the all-controlling purpose of moral choice. Suppose it turned out that a certain society could only attain the highest per capita welfare achievable by that society if the majority kept slaves (the "illfare" of the enslaved minority being taken into account in calculating this result). Some members of the society might then take exception to that goal and the moral criteria endorsing slavery which it requires. Surely they could do so without violating the rules of moral thought.

(4) Our concern for justice or fairness is not the only reason we might have for sincerely rejecting a fundamental purpose in moral choice which some philosopher had claimed to identify. There are notions of sacred duty and intrinsic decency which we might also refuse to surrender to the purpose of maximizing welfare, or to any other purpose philosophers might propose. Even if the vast majority of the people of our society voted to accept a certain all-governing purpose for moral preference, we would be intellectually entitled to reject it (and suffer the consequences no doubt) if it violated our own deepest ideals. This seems to be a well recognized feature of moral reflection and debate. We do not think that a prophet without honor in his own country is making any *logical* mistake when he questions its principles and basic goals. He is simply carrying moral thought to a deeper level of criticism.

(5) It is thus apparent that the relatively clear model of evaluative reasoning and truth explained in Sections 31 and 32 is not available for understanding moral reasoning and truth.

(6) No other clear model seems to be available. To be sure, the moral philosophers known as Intuitionists have proposed other ways to understand moral truth, saying that we can recognize certain principles as self-evident, at least if we have been brought up properly. But this is not a clear account, and it has usually been supported by the question-begging claim that moral values (for example, rightness in actions) are "non-natural properties" which we simply "intuit" with a special "moral sense" or "faculty of moral reason" once we are well acquainted with the natural characteristics of the action being judged. These values are said to be "facts in the world" existing independently of human convention. But there is no way to tell which of our alleged intuitions of these facts are objectively true, and which are subjective illusions.

(7) Since no intelligible account of moral truth exists in spite of all the effort philosophers have devoted to the question, there probably is no such thing as moral truth. Although we have seen that a skeptical view of *all* evaluative statements and arguments cannot be supported, we ought to be skeptics as far as moral evaluations are concerned. There is good reason to suspect that the giving of moral "reasons" is not a form of rational argument at all, but a type of discourse in which people attempt to *persuade* one another, by more or less subtle *emotional* appeals, to accept a certain attitude or principle, and hence to embrace the particular judgment it requires for the case at hand.

34. TWO TYPES OF MORAL THOUGHT

The problem just stated can be usefully approached by distinguishing two broad types of moral thought and showing that it properly applies to only one of them.

In the first type we make and defend moral judgments simply by invoking traditional "self-evident" rules of right conduct. Suppose a man has bullied another person for no reason but personal amusement, or has robbed and killed someone merely to enrich himself, or has raped someone, or has lied and cheated others for personal gain. Such actions break rules which are obviously not based on merely personal preferences but are the ancient standards of communal life. Neither are these rules independent of all human convention, "existing in the world absolutely." At least there is no need to indulge in such dubious speculation in order to account for their existence and authority. Each person is bound by them because the community recognizes them and, in one way or another, enforces them. Indeed, the overwhelming majority of people recognize them as valid even when they break them, as their feelings of guilt attest. It is not as though the rules against murder, mayhem, rape, theft, and so on, had been laid down by some deliberate legislative act which might have created different rules. On the contrary, such rules are part of the immemorial "definition" of right and wrong in the community, in practically any community. Within moral thought of the type we are presently describing, it would not even be conceivable that these should not be the rules. Any legislative deviation from them would simply be wrong. Their palpable self-evidence, which many philosophers have interpreted in terms of a "moral sense" intuiting those "absolute values existing in the world," should probably be understood in terms of semantical rules. We not only learn at an early age to condemn stealing, lying, cheating, robbing, killing, and so on; we also learn at the same time that stealing, lying, etc., are the criteria for correctly using the word "wrong." Accordingly, the very notion that we could have rules permitting, say, robbery for personal enrichment will seem impossible because self-contradictory: they would be rules saying that a certain kind of wrong action is not wrong. With respect to a particular society, these same things can also be said about certain of its rules which are not found in all societies; for example, its specialized incest rules, or its rules demanding certain religious observances.

This first type of moral judgment — judgment purely according to traditional community norms — can be relatively simple or complex according to the nature of the case being considered, and it has its own phase of criticism. For example, a particular action by someone may be a breach of one rule but required by another: the Good Samaritan must break his promises to Jones in order to assist Smith who is in dire distress. So judgments of casuistry, in an innocent sense of the word, must be made concerning the relative importance of the two rules in the special circumstances of the case. And this will no doubt involve some consideration of the "point" of the respective rules. Thus the advantage of co-operative effort is one point of the rule that we ought to keep promises; health and survival are the point of the rule that we ought to help people in serious danger. Other rules serve other values sacred and profane.

A second and more deeply critical type of morality makes its appearance when people begin to form the idea that it is possible for some of the principles of their community, even rather fundamental ones, to be wrong. Obvious examples are principles endorsing slavery and the subjection of women. This may come about through new acquaintance with the principles of other societies, through agitation by certain groups complaining of their condition, through an appeal to ideals of the society which certain of its principles no longer serve, and in other ways. The idea develops that moral right and wrong is something different from the traditional norms of one's society, or at least from some of them. Morality is assumed to have some broader basis, and moral judgments are accordingly made not only of persons and their actions, intentions, character traits, etc., but of the traditional norms themselves.

When people make moral judgments of this second type they usually regard them as objectively correct, not as mere expressions of personal preference, e.g. distaste for slavery and the subjection of women. They think these practices "really are wrong," as they put it. It is true that at this juncture of cultural history some people turn to skepticism and give up the idea of moral (as distinguished from legal) right and wrong. At least they profess to give it up; their skepticism is often shallow and academic; their true feeling is likely to be that (for example) it really was wrong of the Nazis to kill ethnic minorities. In any case the latter opinion would be held by the overwhelming majority of people who make judgments of the second type. But what is it that makes this opinion true, if it is true? Certainly not the fact that we in *our* society condemn genocide, nor even the fact that most Germans do and did think it wrong.

The Intuitionist moral philosopher will say that this judgment owes its truth to those absolute moral values which exist in the world independently of our moral attitudes and conventions. And perhaps there will now be a note of triumph in his voice as he explains to us that it is precisely this second type of moral judgment, coupled with our conviction that judgments of this type are indeed true or false, which forces us to concede that there are such absolute values. Indeed, he will add, the second type is really the only type of moral judgment, properly speaking. A judgment of the first type merely applies the traditional norms of a society, and it will be true (*as* a judgment of that type) if it applies them correctly, whether or not they are valid with respect to absolute morality. Of course, people who make only judgments of the first type seldom are aware of this distinction of types, and yet they do mean to make moral judgments. So (the Intuitionist adds) we can say that their judgments *are* morally true *when* they correctly apply the communal principles which happen to reflect absolute moral values, as many of them do.

Such is the Intuitionist's theory in briefest outline. Whether or not we can accept his mysterious ontology of values, we must admit that people's common insistence that there is truth and falsity in moral assertions of the second type does seem to drive us in that direction, at least until we can think of something better.

Another kind of moral philosopher, called the Utilitarian, claims to give a clearer and truer account. We have already sketched his views in step (2) of the problem-generating argument given in Section 33, but let us now state them a little more fully. Certainly what he has to say is a good deal less mystifying than the Intuitionist's theory. He claims, in effect, that moral evaluation fits the logical form of rational evaluation explained in Sections 31 and 32. He thinks he is able to identify the point of all moral value judgments, *the* purpose or interest which people normally have in all moral choice. He believes there is but *one* ultimate goal which we are normally attempting to achieve when we adopt a certain course of action as morally right while avoiding others as wrong, or when we hold that certain habits or character traits in children are to be praised and encouraged morally while others are to be discouraged, or when we denounce a certain piece of legislation in moral terms while finding another one morally acceptable, and so on through all the other kinds of things which we evaluate in moral judgments of the second type. The *valid* principles of moral conduct, therefore, are those which are required for the attainment of that goal. They are the criteria of right and wrong which, if respected in our conduct and moral teaching, would best serve to achieve it. And for reasons similar to those given in Section 32, the Utilitarian holds that it would be inconsistent for anyone to refuse to recognize those criteria or principles while purporting to evaluate something *morally*. Utilitarian theorists are not all agreed on precisely how this goal should be expressed, but for present purposes we may say (with convenient vagueness) that it is "the maximum happiness or welfare" among those whose interests are being considered, whether these be the members of a given society, or all human beings, or all sentient beings, as various theorists have proposed.

Most Utilitarians seem to think that the traditional norms of a given society were developed historically for the attainment of communal happiness or welfare — not in any deliberate or calculating way, to be sure, but nevertheless in rough appreciation of the economic and other conditions of life facing the community, and of the ways of regulating behavior which would tend to promote the general welfare under these conditions. Some of these regulations — including the paradigmatic principles of right and wrong listed above as common to almost all groups of people — are demanded by that goal under almost any conditions. But some of the rules of life demanded in one set of circumstances will be inappropriate in others. Not only will different societies need to have somewhat different moral principles, but new generations within the same society will sometimes need to change the inherited principles in order to adjust to new economic and other conditions, most notably to new conditions of knowledge and useful technique. This is how the Utilitarian accounts for the common assumption, in moral thought of the second type, that the traditional norms of one's society are themselves subject to moral evaluation. And this is how he attempts to justify our conviction that judgments of this type admit of truth and falsity. To repeat the example in step (2) of Section 33, if I live in a society whose moral norms still condemn contraception, I can truly judge that these norms are to that extent wrong because the wellbeing of present and future generations, both in this society and in the world at large, demands that the growth of population be reduced or stopped.

Such is the Utilitarian's theory in brief. Unfortunately, its relative clarity in comparison with Intuitionism does not seem to be matched by accuracy in its description of moral judgment. Steps (3), (4), and (5) of Section 33 seem far more accurate. There is every reason to doubt that *all* moral preferences or choices have the "purpose" or function of promoting the general welfare. While it is certainly true that many commonly recognized moral principles do seem to have this function, many others apparently do not. Some of the latter are very old principles which may always have served other values than that of maximal happiness or welfare, and they have often been given precedence over the latter value when in conflict with it. The most famous examples are the principles of justice and equality mentioned in Step (3).

Faced with this objection, various Utilitarian theorists have attempted to show that justice itself is derivable from the greatest happiness principle. But these attempts have not been convincing. A favorite argument is that while the most efficient welfare-producing *act* open to a person on a particular occasion may be unjust, the *rule* of acting justly will be more efficient than any rival rule, so that the problem is solved by distinguishing "act Utilitarianism" from "rule Utilitarianism" and choosing the latter as one's moral theory. An act is right if and only if it conforms to the rule or set of rules which is most efficient in producing welfare. But several forms of rule Utilitarianism are in turn distinguishable within that broad formula, and on closer inspection (the details of which cannot be given here) it is far from clear that they would preclude all seriously unjust rules under all possible conditions of society, or even under the present conditions of our own society.

It would also be noted that Utilitarian writers have sometimes spoken as if their theory is not a mere description of moral thought but a *recommendation* of the structure we must give to moral thought if it is to be rational and admit of true and false judgments. Whether such a stage-four proposal would be economical is a question to which we shall return in the last section of this chapter.

There is another important feature of the second type of moral thought which seems to eliminate all possibility of interpreting it along the lines of Sections 31 and 32. This is the fact that people who engage in this more deeply critical reflection reserve the right to *choose their own basic principles*. If there were some all-controlling, indisputable purpose in moral choice – whether the one proposed by Utilitarians or some other – then certain moral criteria or principles would be demanded for its attainment, and we would not have the intellectual right, when judging something morally, to deviate from them. But morally autonomous people claim the right to modify or reject any principle which strikes them on due reflection as improper. This is why they feel to criticize and reform the tradition principles of the societies in which they were born and in which they continue to live. It would not be correct to say that their criticisms are all made in furtherance of some one purpose or interest in moral choice which they regard as binding. The problem-generating argument of Section 33 also appears to be correct when it points out that people could not effectively *agree* that such and such a purpose in choice shall be *the* point of morality hereafter. They could not do so, that is to say, without changing the second type of moral thought into something rather different from what it is now. They would be destroying its feature of autonomy in judgment whereby each person is the guardian of his own principles and, in Kant's famous phrase, gives the moral law to himself.

We can sum up our results in this section by pointing out, first, that most moral thought in which people have ever engaged has undoubtedly been of the first type, and here there is no question that many judgments can be true or false. There may be some concrete moral problems as to which traditional norms are either silent or in hopeless conflict, but in a great many easy cases neither of these conditions obtains. But secondly, there is little satisfaction in this result because, having once clearly distinguished between the two types, we begin to wonder whether judgments of the second type really *can* be true of false. It is not easily seen how they can be.

35. REFORMING THE CONCEPT OF MORAL TRUTH

In this section I shall sketch a solution to this problem which I have proposed elsewhere in a book-length study. It would be impossible to present the argument in full detail, but I hope this section and the next will at least show that stage FOUR is probably the best approach to the problem, and that the solution offered here is well worth considering in our search for the most economical one.

The proposed solution has two parts. First it claims that there is an objective standard of good *moral reasoning* on the logical modal of Sections 31 and 32 even if there is none for *substantive moral evaluations*. Second, it holds that a substantive moral evaluation of the second type discussed above is true if (and only if) it would be accepted by everyone or practically everyone who satisfied the standard of good moral reasoning when making up his or her mind on the moral question concerned, or when arguing for his or her position on that question. I believe the first of these two propositions is descriptively true of our existing conceptual scheme for critical morality. The second is a proposal for adjusting that scheme to make it fully coherent. Let us discuss them in that order.

To show the truth of the first proposition, one needs to identity an existing standard of good moral reasoning; that is, a standard which is commonly recognized by those who engage in moral reflection and discourse of our second type. And one also needs to show that it is an objectively valid standard, i.e. that the criteria of good reasoning which constitute that standard are demanded by a purpose-in-choice which is definitive for this activity, i.e. the activity of choosing which reasons to accept and which to reject when thinking critically about a moral question. Now there is a well known and commonly recognized standard of good moral reasoning *performances*, and I would suggest that good moral *reasons* are those which a person accepts when reflecting or arguing well, i.e. in accordance with that standard. The standard is as follows. When considering a moral question we must not judge hastily, without fully informing ourselves of the relevant nonmoral facts; we must attend carefully and imaginatively to those facts; we must judge in a disinterested way, i.e. without giving special weight to our own interests or those of our family, friends, race, etc., and without playing favorites among individual people; and we must form our opinion when we are calm and have our wits about us, not when we are angry, grief-stricken, intoxicated, or in some other condition which interferes with good judgment. Even though we are entitled to choose our own principles, and to make up our own minds on more particular questions, we are required to do so from the moral point of view, to use a phrase which philosophers have often used to sum up these requirements. Hereafter let us write MPV whenever these is occasion to refer to them. Now just as we should be convinced only by those nonmoral facts and moral principles which appeal to us as relevant and important when considering a moral question in that way, so also we should offer *those* reaons, and only those reasons, when defending our moral view on that question. When I say that this is part of our conceptual scheme for the second type of moral thought distinguished in the preceding section, I mean that people who engage in that type of thought (and they are a significant if small minority in modern culture) typically do recognize that MPV is binding upon them. Not, of course, that they always manage to live up to it. Indeed, it may be true that no one is ever perfectly impartial on a moral issue involving his or her own important interests.

But how are we to show that this *is* a valid or binding standard? How are we to answer the Emotivist, the philosopher who takes the position stated at the very end of the problem-generating argument in Section 33? He will say that in asserting the validity of this standard we merely express another moral attitude, and that its proof is subject to all the obstacles stated in that argument. The answer, I believe, is that we can show the validity of MPV by identifying the definitive purpose or interest which is served by choosing among moral reasoning performances. In other words, we look for a purpose or interest that people normally have in preferring some such performances to others; an interest, moreover, which demands the criteria constituting MPV. This purpose or interest, I suggest, is to promote as much moral agreement as possible among morally autonomous people, and as much mutual respect as possible when they disagree.

There is not much question that such a purpose or interest *would* demand MPV as the standard for preferring some moral reasoning performances to others, and for picking out some of them as unqualifiably good. For in what better way could we increase our chances of reaching agreement on a debatable moral question, and of maintaining mutual respect when we disagree, than by discussing it in a calm, well-informed, carefully imaginative, and impartial way? The problem is rather one of showing that such is indeed the "immanent purpose" or "institutional point" of this choosing activity as people actually engage in it. The main difficulty here seems to be as follows. Many people who engage in this activity probably do have such a purpose in mind; they would say, if asked, that it is one of the things they are trying to achieve in this activity. But many and perhaps most morally reflective people would no doubt say that their *chief* purpose is to *establish the truth*, to arrive at the correct answer to the moral question being discussed. I shall not present the rather long and complex argument by which I think this difficulty can be overcome. Suffice it to say here that the goal of truth (supposing there really is such a thing as truth in moral evaluation of the second type) is surely *compatible* with the goal of moral consensus and mutual respect. And whatever other method there may be for properly determining the truth of critical moral evaluations, it surely is compatible with our satisfying MPV.

If it be granted, then, that MPV is an objectively valid standard, we may say that anyone who has satisfied this standard while defending his actions morally, or while explaining his moral opinion about something, has *justified* his actions or opinion in the sense that he has *given demonstrably good reasons* for them. This is a different and apparently more appropriate sense of "to justify" than the sense which would be suitable when referring to judgments of the first type, namely "to show the truth or probable truth of a judgment." It is not to be assumed, of course, that people who satisfy MPV will *always* arrive at the *same* judgment on a given moral question. It is more likely that while they will *widely* agree on a good *many* questions, they will also disagree on certain others, whether because of differences in temperament, moral training, or some other cause. Nor is it to be assumed that they will always have the *same* good reasons to offer – the same principles and facts, taken in the same order of importance – when they defend their judgments, even when they agree in those judgments. The point is simply that a person who has satisfied MPV when selecting and offering his reasons will have given reasons that are demonstrably good ones *for him* to give.

I have just said that this is an appropriate sense of justification when we are speaking of justifying moral judgments of the second type. But I must hasten to admit that it will seem a very odd sense to anyone who remains wedded to the notion of objective truth in critical morality, a notion which people who think critically in morals do normally cling to, as I have acknowledged. This leads to the second part of my suggestion for solving the problem, the part according to which we must make some adjustment of our existing concepts or structural assumptions in this type of moral thought. We have seen, I hope, that critical moral judgments cannot be true or false on the ordinary model for rational evaluation explained in Sections 31 and 32. And of course they cannot be true or false on the model of communal morality referred to in Section 34. The only other relevant notion of evaluative truth and falsity that I know of is the one offered by Intuitionist moral philosophers, i.e. agreement or disagreement of our judgments with those "absolute values in the world" to which the Intuitionist appeals. Should we accept this notion, or should we conclude that the urge to insist that our autonomous moral judgments are objectively true is a hangover from moral thought of the first type, a hangover which is to be explained by the fact that even people who engage in the second type of thought have often not clearly distinguished between the two, or have not accepted all the consequences of the distinction?

My own opinion is that we should accept the latter alternative. The In-tuitionist's ontology has very little to recommend it. Our only inkling as to the nature of those absolute values-in-the-world comes from theological ethics, and even that light blinks out when we try to fix our gaze upon it. For people who believe in God cannot hold, on reflection, that the rightness of an action consists in the fact that God wills it. They must hold, rather, that God wills it *because* it is right – because there is this independent absolute value-in-the-world, the nature of which thus remains unexplained. (Not only is it true that God *would not* make purely sadistic murder morally right. Even the pious must admit on second thought that he *could not* do so.) We can also take a cue from Strawson (see Section 9 above) and ask how we are to *identify* items of this kind which we are being asked to include in our ontology. The answer cannot be that we identify them in our well considered moral judgments. For people sometimes disagree in these judgments, and many people would sincerely doubt whether such entities exist. There must be some way to conceive of them and identify them apart from those judgments if we are to accept them as the realities which make the judgments true or false. But no other way is known, and why then should we admit them to our ontology? We are told nothing about them *except* that they are the objec-tive basis for our urge to say that our critical moral judgments are valid or true.

We are not at a loss, on the other hand, to explain how that feeling or urge might occur without any objective basis. Part of this explanation is already implicit in our description of moral thought; such a feeling is entirely in order with respect to judgments of the first type, and few besides moral philosophers will have had occasion to distinguish between these two types in any careful way. One reason why we might not naturally make the distinction is that many judgments which are true in thought of the first type correspond in concent to judgments which prac-tically anyone who tries to satisfy MPV (and perhaps everyone) would make in thought of the second type. Again I refer to judgments applying principles found in practically all societies, when the case being con-sidered is an easy one. Perhaps another reason why we do not make the distinction readily is that MPV is recognized as binding not only in the more fully critical type of moral thought but in communal morality as well. There it seems to play the following supporting role. When we apply

moral principles we sometimes encounted borderline cases, and we also
have to deal with cases in which the accepted principles conflict, with no
established priority to resolve the difficulty. Then, even if we are thinking purely in traditional or communal terms, we will be forced to judge
for ourselves how best to interpret and shape the traditional principles.
And it seems a fair statement that we are commonly expected to be well
informed and impartial when doing so.

Let us therefore propose a conception of evaluative truth which differs
from all three conceptions mentioned above. Let us say that a moral
evaluation of the second type will be true just in case it would be the consensus of people who form justified judgments on the moral question
concerned. Now there are many principles that everyone or practically
everyone who tries to satisfy MPV will choose, including the principles
repeatedly mentioned as common to all or practically all societies. These,
and judgments applying them to easy cases, will be consentiently true,
and any principles or judgments contrary to the consentient principles
will be false. There is no reason to expect a consensus on the relative importance or priority of the consentient principles whenever they conflict,
but it is important to notice that even then there will *often* be a consensus.
To illustrate the point with a trite example, everyone satisfying MPV will
agree that we ought to break our promise to play golf with Jones when
this is necessary if we are to save Smith from bleeding to death and there
is no one else to help him.

Some of one's principles may thus be neither true nor false even
though justifiably chosen. And a good many particular judgments will
be neither true nor false though justifiably made. It should be noted, by
the way, that even truth in the first type of moral thought is based
ultimately on a consensus: that of the people in an historical community,
including the present generation who have been reared in its morality and
have learned to approve and condemn certain kinds of behavior impar-
tially, and to use standard language to express such approval and disap-
proval. It should also be mentioned that the very principles and
judgments one would cite to illustrate the common-sense conviction that
there obviously is truth in morals are just those principles and judgments
which would qualify as true under this conception.

Here then is how we might attempt to solve the problem stated in Section 33. We could leave everything as we found it in moral thought of

the first type, which has been by far the more important of the two types in the whole history of culture and is still dominant for most human beings. We could also leave everything as we found it in the more critical type of moral thought *except* the assumption that evaluations made there can be true in some objective but unspecified sense. There we could substitute the critically inter-subjective sense of truth which I have just described.

36. THE ECONOMY OF THIS REFORM

In the last paragraph of Chapter 4, we saw that two obligations are incurred by anyone who proposes a stage-four solution: (1) to explain how the problem arises from specific inconsistencies in our existing conceptual scheme, not from difficulties produced by philosophical misunderstanding or misuse of that scheme, and (2) to explain how the proposed solution would correct the existing scheme more economically than would other revisionary solutions. In order to discharge the first obligation, we must explain how the common belief that the principles of one's autonomous, critical morality are (or can be) objectively true is inconsistent with certain other structural beliefs.

For a start, let us notice that all the assertions of the problem-generating argument of Section 33 have been found to be substantially correct except the seventh, the skeptical conclusion. The first step is true because we surely *are* permitted to challenge many commonly accepted moral principles. Steps three and four give an apparently true answer to the objection raised by step two when they maintain that there is no indisputable purpose governing all moral choice. Thus the model for objective standards explained in Sections 31 and 32 would be inappropriate for morals, just as step five maintains. Step six correctly points out that the value objectivism of Intuitionist ethics is highly obscure and implausible. And while the same step is incorrect in its opening suggestion that there is no other clear model of evaluative truth, the only other model which we have been able to identify (rather than invent) is the model of communal authority, and it must be excluded from morality of the second type where our problem is located. So even on this point step six may be accepted as true for present purposes.

As we pointed out in Chapters 3 and 4, however, a problem-generating argument might still be guilty of some underlying distortion or violation of existing concepts even if all its explicit steps seem to be acceptable. So let us attempt to list the major assumptions about morality on which the argument relies, and then let us ask whether they depart in any way from the existing scheme.

1.   A moral principle cannot be true merely by custom or convention.
2.   A moral principle cannot be true merely by divine fiat.
3.   Each person must finally judge for himself or herself which moral principles are to be embraced and which ultimate purposes in moral choice may be accepted.
4.   Some moral principles are true or valid, and not merely in the sense of being required by, or consistent with, more fundamental principles.

It seems rather clear that all of these assumptions are commonly made by people who engage in the more fully critical type of moral thought. And it would appear that if we accept the first two we cannot consistently accept the fourth. This is because statements 1 and 2 seem to refer to the only two ways in which moral truth is conceivable in existing schemes of thought, and these ways only apply to morality of the first type. To be sure, Intuitionists try to identify another way:

5.   Moral principles are true in virtue of their agreement with absolute moral values existing in the world independently of human choice or convention.

And, of course, Utilitarians and other "teleological" moral theorists try to identify still another way:

6.   Moral principles are true when required by the indisputable purpose in moral choice.

But we have seen, I hope, that neither of these suggestions is tenable. And this can only strengthen our belief that statements 1 and 2 refer to the only ways in which moral truth has been conceivable heretofore. Accordingly, given statements 1 and 2, statement 4 must be false unless we introduce some new meaning of "true or valid." This is our explanation of how the existing conceptual scheme for moral thought of the second type is inconsistent, so that it requires conceptual reform if the problem of moral truth is to be resolved.

Let us turn then to the relative economy of our proposed solution. I have often referred to three ethical theories or types of theory that have spoken to this problem: Utilitarianism, Intuitionism, and Emotivism. Each has its variations, but I think we can single out their principal contentions in order to estimate their relative economy. We shall then enter our own proposed solution in the same competition.

Since assumptions 1 through 4, above, represent elements of existing thought figuring in the problem, a perfectly economical solution – a dissolution – would save all of them. This is precisely what the Intuitionist attempts to do, and some Intuitionist writers have indeed said that, unlike their Utilitarian and Emotivist rivals, they do not wish to change anything in the way people now think. It might be questioned whether the Intuitionist really does attempt to save assumption 3, that pertaining to autonomy in moral judgment. After all, we would not be free to deviate from principles corresponding to the "objective values in the world." But it can be seen as follows that the Intuitionist's doctrine really is consistent with 3. He holds that each person must judge for himself which principles are valid and what their relative importance or stringency is for answering a given moral question, without being bound by any allegedly universal purpose in moral choice. And since moral judgment is commonly conceived, and conceived by the Intuitionist, as judgment *concerning the truth*, it would be no infringement of a person's intellectual right to judge for himself that he should be obliged to conform to the truth once he has seen it.

The Intuitionist's attempt to save everything, however, seems to prevent him from saving anything. For he would reconcile assumption 4 with the other three in a way that is so obscure and incredible as to be virtually empty. At first we may have the impression that the Intuitionist's ontology of values is at least an intelligible suggestion even if a dubious one to modern secular ears. The true values would be those which are constituted as such by God. But the suggestion loses most of its content once we are free of this view which even thoughtful believers must repudiate. In saying that the Intuitionist's ontology loses its content, I refer again to the impossibility of independently identifying those entities to which he appeals as the ground of moral truth, the entities which supposedly constrain even God's moral judgment. So Intuitionism would seem to have a very high price tag: it depends essentially on a factual claim which is both obscure and incredible. It attempts to render our scheme of thought consistent by introducing a new structural belief which is hardly understandable, and for the support of which there is no independent evidence but only the remnants of a myth which itself conflicts with powerful "intuitions." I refer to convictions like the one mentioned above concerning God's will and sadistic murder.

Let us move on, then, to Utilitarianism. I have already suggested that some Utilitarian writers do not make it very clear whether they merely intend to describe and clarify ordinary thought, or to recommend a change in it. (The same is true of some Emotivists.) Considered as a purely descriptive theory, Utilitarianism tries to produce a dissolution by using the kind of logical model explained in Sections 31 and 32. But if what I have said before on the point is correct, this would be a very bad stage-three solution because it is based on a serious misdescription of existing thought. The Utilitarian retains assumptions 1 and 2, above, but he introduces statement 6 in order to save assumption 4. Unfortunately, statement 6 conflicts with existing assumptions in the type of moral thought with which the problem is concerned; most notably it conflicts with assumption 3, which is thus unwittingly sacrificed.

Considered as an intentionally revisionary theory, Utilitarianism has precisely that high price: the elimination of personal autonomy in the choice and modification of our basic principles and purposes. At best it leaves us a weak kind of autonomy in which we are free to do our own casuistry and make our own mistakes in devising principles to suit *the* indisputable purpose which the Utilitarian prescribes to us. If we found that certain principles required by that purpose were obnoxious to us even when we had satisfied MPV, we would nevertheless have to accept them. And this is what many people might very well find in unfair principles of distribution required by the purpose of maximizing welfare or happiness. They would also find that rules of obligation defining the institution of promising, as well as other institutions which they believe are "morally valid," must be overriden for the least interference with that purpose.

It is true that in exchange for these great deviations from existing thought and practice, Uitlitarianism is said to give us a common decision procedure for answering moral questions. But it seems very doubtful that we could reach any more consensus in that way than we could by collectively satisfying MPV. This is because the short-term and long-term effects of our actions and institutions on the happiness or welfare of the population are often very complex and difficult to estimate, even apart from the great and perhaps fatal difficulty of finding a noncontroversial meaning for "happiness" or "welfare." But there is no doubt at all that in eliminating strong personal autonomy we would be cutting out a major component of modern critical morality. Indeed, it would seem that strong *substantive* autonomy, subject to the *procedural* controls of MPV, is the heart of a fully critical morality.

Turning then to Emotivism, we find that it retains assumptions 1, 2, and 3 but sacrifices 4 outright, whether we interpret the Emotive Theory as an intentional revision of existing thought or as a misdescription of it. Thus it too is a very costly solution at stage four. Indeed it is only a special version of skepticism itself (see p. 157 above).

Our own solution retains assumptions 1, 2, and 3. It also adds to 3, not in order to change or qualify it but merely to call attention to the fact that it must be supplemented by another existing assumption, namely, that in judging for oneself one ought to satisfy MPV. We also retain assumption 4, but with the significant qualification that moral principles are true only when, and in the novel sense that, they would represent the consensus of people who reflect properly, i.e. in substantial compliance with MPV. This is of course a rather weak sense of truth. As I have said, it allows the possibility and indeed likelihood that some principles are neither true nor false. We can make the further point, however, that there is one *procedural* principle of fully critical morality which is objectively true, namely, again, that one should reflect and argue in compliance with MPV.

This method of estimating the relative economy of proposed revisionary solutions – merely counting the structural assumptions they save or sacrifice – is of course rather crude. But I think it does at least qualify our solution as one of the two finalists in the present competition, the other being revisionary Utilitarianism. In order to choose between them, we must now look more closely at the extent to which they would change existing moral thought in order to achieve a consistent scheme.

First of all, by substituting consentient truth for objective truth in the second type of thought, we make no change at all in existing beliefs as to how one ought to reflect and argue in critical morality. That is, one may still attempt to do so in compliance with MPV; more precisely, one may continue to recognize PMV as a valid standard for moral thought and discourse. No new restrictions or other changes are imposed. Under the Utilitarian solution, on the other hand, all critical moral thought would henceforth be channeled into a single pattern which has heretofore been only part of it. *Some* principles have no doubt been justified by their tendency to further happiness or welfare as *one* of the major purposes of moral choice. But not all important principles have been so justified; nor have the dominantly utilitarian principles of morality received *absolute* justification in this way, as though morality had no other purpose. Rather, they have had to be balanced against principles serving other purposes, and they have often been considered to be outweighed by those principles in particular cases, as I have repeatedly mentioned and briefly illustrated. This more subtle and many-sided mode of reflection and argument would be swept aside, so that only principles serving *the* goal (Utility) would be accepted as valid. And this would be more than a change in patterns of reflection and argumentation. One can hardly overemphasize the point that if we were all to reform moral thought along the lines proposed by revisionary Utilitarianism, we would suffer a loss of autonomy which would be extremely painful to everyone who believes that there are moral principles which must not be sacrificed to utility. To say this is not merely to insist on abstract individualism; it is to underscore the importance of justice and the principles which give it effect, as well as various other principles which we embrace after proper moral reflection.

Our solution does cost something, of course, and many will even say that it is no solution at all because "the very problem" was to explain how *objective* truth is possible in critical morality. But such an objection actually provides some confirming evidence for our description, which holds that insistence on objective truth even in fully critical, autonomous morality, is itself one of the existing conceptual elements giving rise to the problem. *Of course* many moralists will be disappointed by this solution; it could not be a plausible solution unless they were. But such moralists should be referred back to Chapter 4, where we attempted to explain that while it is always initially desirable to aim for perfect economy and hence total victory over the skeptic, this goal may be theoretically impossible in some problems. And then such moralists should be asked to explain how we have failed to show that the present problem is of that kind. Perhaps they will be able to do so, but it is no answer merely to insist that a revisionary solution is no solution.

How much then does our solution costs? Obviously there can be no absolute measure, but I would suggest two reasons why it probably costs a good deal less than may appear at first glance. The first reason is that we have seen how genuine rationality is possible in autonomous moral thought, even in the choice of basic substantive principles. To admit that autonomously chosen principles are not "objectively" true is very far from admitting that one moral opinion is as good as another, or that moral reasoning is a useless pretense. If MPV is an objective standard, as we have briefly attempted to show, then there can be plenty of good reasoning in morals, and this reasoning can be the basis of a growing critical consensus even if there are no "moral values existing in the world absolutely," whatever that might mean. Secondly, the conceptual element thus partly sacrificed should begin to shrink in emotional importance once we have clarified out thought along the lines of the foregoing descriptions and recommended solution. By this I mean that the urge to say that our moral principles are true by reference to "objective moral facts" should begin to subside. For we should then see more clearly that there is no rational or institutional basis for it, while there is a basis for rational community without it. This, I suggest, is how philosophy can help us reshape our thought towards greater integrity and coherence.

CHAPTER 11

APPLIED ETHICS

Philosophers have recently been giving more attention to specific moral problems and contemporary issues of public policy than they ever have before. While they have always discussed such large political topics as justice and the legitimate functions of the state, they have seldom addressed themselves to so many issues under current public debate, and they have seldom gone into such issues in the detail which is now becoming commonplace. After being concerned with more general studies in the middle third of the century, many moral philosophers have turned to practical problems, sometimes in collaboration with lawyers, economists, and other social scientists.

A list of topics on which many useful articles by analytically oriented philosophers have appeared during the last decade would include war crimes, civil disobedience, conscientious objection to military service, freedom of expression, justice in international relations, imperialism, racism, school desegregation, sexism and women's liberation, affirmative action for minorities and women (including the issue of reverse discrimination, so called), the I.Q. controversy, abortion, rape, violence in general, suicide, famine and affluence, revolution, capital punishment, the "enforcement of morals" (focusing on the issue of decriminalizing homosexual behavior), sexual perversion, problems of medical ethics (especially those raised by the new medical and surgical techniques), paternalistic laws, and "animal rights." In addition to these more specialized discussions, we also find broader treatments of the perennial problem of distributive justice. Quite often the two types of discussion are intertwined, as in the topic of resource management and our duties to future generations, for example. A good *many* articles have appeared in philosophy journals on almost every one of these topics.

But do philosophers have anything unique to contribute to public debate on such matters? Good social scientists and legal scholars are themselves "analytical," after all, and they usually possess more information on the topics under discussion. Have the philosophers in question merely grown tired of more abstract topics? Are they merely a group of intelligent amateurs, thoughtful moralists whose opinions may be welcome, but who have no special knowledge or skill to offer in the field of public affairs? By drawing our final illustration from this new literature, I hope to show that analytic philosophers can indeed contribute valuably toward the solution of moral and political problems, just as they can help to clarify and improve the most general assumptions of moral thought, as seen in the last chapter. In one sense, to be sure, all professionals are amateurs in the sphere of politics; yet they often have something special to add to public debate, and this is true of the philosophers as well.

A second goal of this chapter is to illustrate an aspect of philosophical method which has not been emphasized in any of our previous examples, although it pertains to stage four and was touched upon in Quine's references to "explication." According to our definition in Section 2, above, a stage four solution is required by problems which exploit a "real inconsistency or other inadequacy" in our concepts, and the sort of trouble to which I now draw attention must be resolved not through reconstruction of an inconsistent concept (as in Chapters 4 and 10) but through new construction to improve some notion which is still inadequately developed, however important it may be in discourse. In our example, which will be drawn from recent discussions of the right to privacy, the problem is again produced by a skeptical argument – one claiming that there is no such thing as a right to privacy as such. And as usual, any serious attempt at a solution of the problem must depend on careful descriptive study of how the notion which gave us trouble functions in nonphilosophical thought. But instead of showing how the problem-generating argument is based on a misunderstanding or abuse of existing concepts (stage three), or how it exploits the inconsistency of existing concepts (the type of stage four solution previously illustrated), the description reveals that the notion in question is still inchoate – not sufficiently well formed to do the jobs we ordinarily attempt to do with it. In order to present the problem and sample some of the descriptive studies which have been made, I shall first briefly review a number of relevant articles. I shall then argue that certain claims and distinctions unknown to ordinary political thought must be added to it if we are to have a useful conception of the right to privacy and a more adequate basis for claiming such right.

37. A PROBLEM OF PRIVACY

The question of the existence and extent of a moral right to privacy has
loomed in the background of public debates concerning the new techniques of electronic surveillance and data processing, techniques which
have vastly increased the ability of government and private agencies to
keep people under observation, and to gather, store, and quickly retrieve
great quantities of information and misinformation about them. Not
that the journalists and politicians taking part in these discussions have
attempted to clarify the very concept of privacy; nor have they often
given reasons why people do or do not have a pre-legal right to privacy.
But the crucial importance of such topics for the merits of their debate
is not hard to see. First of all, if privacy is not a "right" but only an "interest," it will have considerably less weight when it conflicts with other
values, e.g. the public interest in more efficient law enforcement, to cite
only one. A personal right seems to be a private interest which *ought not*
to be overridden by countervailing public interests unless the latter are
of great urgency, which a marginal increase of efficiency would not be.
Secondly, if we are to consider whether there is a moral right to privacy,
we need to become clearer on what we mean or ought to mean by privacy,
and the reasons why privacy is or is not important enough to enjoy that
privileged status in policy making.

In several discussions of contemporary moral problems, Judith Thomson has identified key issues and taken controversial stands which have
stimulated other philosophers to reply. Her article 'The Right to Privacy'
(1975) began such an exchange by arguing for the following skeptical
position. There is no such thing as a general right to privacy which is the
basis of our entitlement to privacy in our persons, homes, papers, and
so on. Such protections derive from our right to control our persons and
property. For example, our right that others shall not observe certain
parts of our bodies without our consent is just one right in the cluster of
rights comprising "the right over the person." And our right that no one
shall look through our personal letters or effects without our consent is
just one right in our cluster of property rights. There are no rights in the
privacy cluster which are not to be found in one of these other clusters.
"It is possible to explain in the case of each right in the [privacy] cluster
how come we have it without ever once mentioning the right to privacy."

She thinks this explains the difficulty philosophers have had in their attempts to clarify *the* right to privacy by explaining what the various specific rights to privacy have in common. She believes there is nothing there to be found. There is no general justifying ground, and hence no right to privacy as such.

It seems to me that some of the reasons she gives when claiming to fit specific, traditionally recognized "privacy" rights into one of the other clusters are rather strained. But I shall not pursue this question. For even if she were entirely successful in that project, there would still be an excellent reason to continue the search for a general right to privacy. Suppose the government began to use computer data banks in ways that violate no traditionally recognized privacy rights and no right in any other cluster, but ways that nevertheless offend our sense of privacy and our desire for privacy. This could easily happen; indeed it probably has happened a great many times, even though the proposal for a "National Data Bank" in the federal government was defeated some years ago. Reliable scholars assure us that there is a lively exchange of information between the computerized files of various government agencies. Much of this information may have been freely given to the separate agencies, and to private agencies that pass it along to them. And much information about a person that is otherwise available to them may not be considered sensitive when considered item by item. But when all this data (including false data) can be quickly gathered from many sources to construct a mosaic or profile of the person, this will be considered objectionable by many. And all the more so when done under informal administrative arrangements rather than specific statutory authority. But there is as yet no clear and well recognized right to privacy against the new methods of processing and distributing information. If Thomson's view is correct, it would appear that those who object to such uses of data banks cannot properly claim an infringement of their moral or political rights, at least not their right to privacy. In debating whether legal restrictions should be placed upon such uses, they could not correctly claim the superior weight or priority mentioned above. So if we think privacy is a crucially important interest which is likely to become even more vulnerable to technical changes, we should continue our efforts to explain its general nature so that we might plausibly make such a claim.

38. SOME DESCRIPTIVE INQUIRIES

In a published comment entitled 'Thomson on Privacy' (1975), Thomas Scanlon agrees that the various recognized privacy rights "do not derive from any single overarching right to privacy." But he suggests that they do find a "common foundation in the special interests that we have in being able to be free from certain kinds of intrusions," and in our interest "in having a well-defined zone within which we need not be on the alert against possible observations." This zone is marked out by the various existing conventions in the privacy cluster, and of course it is not defined purely in spatial terms. He believes that it is less important what the conventions and zone precisely are than that there be a definite zone to which we can repair. Would the existing conventions and zone tell us how to redefine it in light of the new electronic techniques for which there are no settled privacy conventions? Certainly not directly or easily. We would need to give "a general account of these interests [and] an account of the structures and foundations of those conventional norms specifying when, where, and in what ways we may and may not be observed [and] kept track of. ... To make these decisions [redefining the zone in light of new technology] we need to know what we are changing, what its justification is, and what the relevant grounds are for judging alternatives."

But perhaps there is a *general* interest in privacy, the nature and importance of which is sufficient to give rise to that "overarching right." This is the direction taken by James Rachels in his comment on Thomson and Scanlon entitled 'Why Privacy is Important,' 1975. He adopts and extends an idea found in Charles Fried's *An Anatomy of Values*, 1970. Fried had argued that privacy is important because it "creates the moral capital which we spend in friendship and love." If we do not close off certain aspects of ourselves from public knowledge, we have nothing left with which to sustain these essential relationships through disclosures to, and sharings with, our friends and lovers. Rachels adds the thought that personal relations of many kinds not only those between friends or between lovers, but also those between parent and child, businessman and employee, doctor and patient, and so on – depend in a similar way on privacy. "In such cases, the sort of relationship that people have to one another involves a conception of how it is appropriate for them to behave with each other, and what is more, a conception of the kind and degree of knowledge concerning one another which it is appropriate for them to have.'' He illustrates in several ways how we probably could not maintain our system of associations without variable restrictions on such knowledge, restrictions which privacy is needed to secure. For example, if friends had to speak *as* friends in the presence of a casual acquaintance, they would be forced to say things inappropriate for him or her to hear. Or if they refused to speak as friends do speak because some such outsider was *always* present, they would probably cease to be friends after a time.

A year or so after the appearance of those pieces, Jeffrey Reiman published an article called 'Privacy, Intimacy, and Personhood' in which he criticized the Fried – Rachels account of the importance of privacy, and offered one of his own. Focusing on friendship and love relations, he first concedes that the quasi-economic or scarcity conception of privacy favored by those writers has certain strong points. It makes jealousy more understandable, and it also explains the fact that we have an interest in restricting information about ourselves even apart from any fear that it will be used to harm us. (Some writers on privacy overlook this.) But he thinks this conception gives a misleading account of friendship and love, relations which he considers to be much more dependent on a "reciprocal desire to share present and future intense and important experiences together'' than they are on the mentioned restriction of information to outsiders. It is true that friends and lovers do normally reveal aspects of themselves to one another which they do not reveal to the public at large, and it is also true that this may facilitate their sharing of experience. But it is not always necessary, and it does not go to the essence of the relation. Imagine two psycho-analysts who decide (whether wisely or not) to analyze one another, or two urologists who decide to examine one another. They might well exchange information not revealed to anyone else and still not become friends, because they do not care for one another or desire to "share important experiences.'' This latter conception of the intimacy of friends and lovers not only avoids the unsavoriness of the market interpretation but also makes it at least logically possible to have *many* intimate relationships, however difficult this may be psychologically for people of our culture (or just possibly, for humans generally). Reiman also points out another good reason to doubt the Fried – Rachels explanation of the importance of privacy. It seems obvious that people who have little capacity or opportunity for intimate relationships have just as much right to privacy as anyone else.

What then *is* the fundamental interest which gives rise to the right to privacy on the ground that privacy is necessary to secure it? Reiman moves toward his own explanation by examining the views of S. I. Benn, which he thinks are a step in the right direction. Benn had suggested – in his article, 'Privacy, Freedom, and Respect for Persons,' 1971 – that privacy is necessary if we are to respect persons as persons, and especially if we are to respect them as choosers. "Covert observation – spying – is objectionable because it deliberately deceives a person about his world, thwarting, for reasons that *cannot* be his reasons, his attempts to make a rational choice." That is, the person thinks his situation is one in which he is unobserved, and the spy changes that situation without his knowledge or consent.

But while Reiman agrees that the right to privacy is indeed connected to "personhood," he thinks there is a flaw in Benn's account. As it has just been too briefly stated, that account would obviously give us a much greater right to privacy than anyone thinks we really have; for example, it would give me the right not to be observed by someone from his window as I absent-mindedly stroll by. To prevent this sort of result, Benn had said that one only has a right to be free from unknown or unwanted observations of things that are considered part of one's identity by the conventions of one's culture, e.g. one's body and certain possessions. But *why* is it morally wrong that *such* things be observed without my knowledge or consent? Apparently because I have a right to privacy, a right which would thus seem to be presupposed in the attempt to explain its foundation.

How then *is* the right to privacy connected to personhood? Reiman's answer is that

Privacy is a social ritual by means of which an individual's moral title to his existence is conferred. Privacy is an essential part of the complex of social practice by means of which the social group recognizes – and communicates to the individual – that his existence is his own. And this is a precondition of personhood. To be a person, an individual must recognize not just his actual capacity to shape his destiny by his own choices. He must also recognize that he has an exclusive moral right to shape his destiny. And this in turn presupposes that he believes that the concrete reality which he is, and through which his destiny is realized, belongs to him in a moral sense.

Reiman illustrates this thesis (without claiming to prove it) by referring to Erving Goffman's study of "total institutions" (most prisons and mental hospitals) where, according to Goffman, essential "territories of the self" are violated in many ways through the destruction of privacy. Reiman also speculates that in order to gain a sense that the body which is causally connected to certain thoughts is *my* body, or that those thoughts constitute *my* consciousness, it is necessary that a social institution or complex of social practice exist in which we refrain from controlling one another's actions, and from observing one another too closely.

This suggests that there are two essential conditions of moral ownership of one's body. The right to do with my body what I wish, and the right to control when and by whom my body is experienced. This in turn reflects the fact that things can be appreciated in two ways: roughly speaking, actively and cognitively. That is, something is "mine" to the extent that I know it. What I know is "my" knowledge; what I experience. Thus, it follows that if an individual were granted the right to control his bodily movements although always under observation, he might develop some sense of moral ownership of his physical existence. However, that ownership would surely be an impoverished and partial one compared to what we take to be contained in an individual's title to his existence.

Let us briefly criticize this suggestion before continuing. The criticism may seem rather captious at first, but its purpose should soon be apparent. One must admit that "moral ownership of one's existence" is a fitting expression in this context, though a necessarily figurative one; and one must also admit that such "ownership" would be "impoverished" if one had active control of one's body only under constant observation. Yet why exactly is this so? By mentioning "two dimensions of appropriation" and citing the notion of "my" knowledge of my activities, Reiman does not really give an explanation. The phrase "dimensions of appropriation" only continues the figure of speech, and my knowledge of myself and my activities is literally and truly mine whether or not other people share this knowledge. Of course, it may be that there is some secondary use of "mine" according to which something is not really mine (not even knowledge) unless I have it all to myself. But invoking this secondary sense would not explain the importance of privacy; it would only restate it. We are not told *just how or why* it is that we lack the sense of self-ownership unless social recognition of that ownership takes the form of a right to privacy.

The point can be brought out in another way. When Reiman says that the two essential conditions of moral ownership of my body are "the right to do with my body what I wish, and the right to control when and by whom my body is experienced," the careful reader naturally asks, "*Anything* I wish? Is it the right to act in any way I see fit? And is it the right of *total* control over such experiences of myself by others?" The latter question is the one that Benn had not answered to Reiman's satisfaction. But Reiman addresses it only at the very end of his article, and all he says on the point is that "It is sufficient that I can control whether and by whom my body is experienced in some significant places and that I have the real possibility of repairing to those places." But what places *are* significant in this connection, and what makes them so? Why is it necessary to my sense of personhood that I be able to repair to *those* sorts of places, whatever they are? To ask a possibly equivalent question, why is it necessary that I be able to restrict others from having *those* sorts of experiences of me?

39. CONSTRUCTING THE RIGHT

Perhaps it is a bit unfair to badger a philosopher for these further psychological details. Having given a somewhat plausible sketch of an explanation, Reiman may be entitled to sit back and wait to see whether psychologists and sociologists will be able to complete it by identifying those "places" and "experiences" more specifically, and by trying them causally to the sense of self-ownership as he has sketched it. But it is important to emphasize that these further details do need to be filled in by someone if the explanation is to be complete. For then it becomes apparent that they will have to be filled in somewhat differently in different circumstances.

To see this, notice first that the kinds and numbers of "places" to which someone will need to be able to retire will vary somewhat from those required by another person of markedly different temperament. We have all known people who seem to require more privacy than their neighbors, or different kinds of privacy. But if we are to have a *right* to privacy, it is apparent that there will have to be some way of "averaging" these requirements, some "social estimate" of *common minimal* or *optimal* restrictions on experience by others. For rights need to be knowable, and at least in principle, socially enforceable. It is entirely possible that we should sometimes lack the right to things which we seriously but too eccentrically need. (This is not to deny that we may be morally entitled to take special steps to get such things for ourselves, within limits; it is only to deny that we are always entitled to the existence of social practices regularly according them to us.)

The next thing to notice is that the amount and type of privacy which people *typically* or *minimally* require for the sense of self-ownership (assuming they do require some) will vary from culture to culture. The Bedouin and certain other nomadic peoples, for example, stand near the extreme where little or no privacy is enjoyed or, apparently, needed. If this is so, it follows from Reiman's explanation that the moral right to privacy has no absolute content, since this "averaging" or "minimalizing" or "optimizing" would have different results from culture to culture, at least when there is a marked difference with respect to such psychological facts. Indeed, not only the content but the very existence of the right to privacy may be culturally contingent if we may judge from the apparent example of the Bedouin. Of course, that example and others would have to be carefully investigated before we could be confident that some groups of humans need no privacy at all in order to retain the sense of self-ownership and personhood. It might be found that individuals in privacy-bereft cultures entirely lack the important condition thus vaguely identified. But my immediate point is that *if* there are people with no such typical need, or *if* people in general have the (to us dismal) potential of retaining that sense with little or no privacy (say by learning to live without privacy when they have been deprived of it over long periods in a totalitarian society), then it follows from Reiman's account that the right to privacy could literally cease to exist.

In any event it is a consequence of his suggestion that the right to privacy is *importantly* dependent on culturally variable conditions. And to point this out is much in the spirit of his article (recall his remark on the culturally variable capacity for intimate personal relations).

Notice too that his suggestion depends on the assumption that there exists a certain right which is more fundamental and more general than the right to privacy. Let us call it the human right to the existence of

social practices under which we are able (if we are not *too* eccentric) to
feel that we own our own lives. The purpose of the discussion, after all,
was not merely to explain why we need privacy but to show that we have
a right to it.

For the sake of our illustration, let us now assume that Reiman's suggestion is generally on the right lines. Then, in light of the last half-dozen
paragraphs, I think we can identify at least three conceptual elements
which have to be added if we are to move ahead toward a solution of the
problem. All three are required if we are to obtain a less vague and controversial conception of the right to privacy than we now have, so that
the claim to this right can function more rationally in political debate.
And I believe all three of these elements are presently missing from ordinary political thought.

1. If the right to privacy is indeed based on our need to feel that we
"own our existence," we still have to make some more specific and
justified claims about the nature of that connection, particularly as it occurs in our own psycho-social tradition. We have to show more particularly what kinds and occasions of privacy are crucial to that human
need for people of our culture, and what sorts of incursions are specially
inimical to it. Otherwise we will be less able to invoke this right convincingly against specific privacy-invading activities that serve some useful
purpose, while we exempt certain other useful activities. We shall be
especially embarrassed in fields where there are no firm privacy conventions already in place because the activities in question make use of new
technical devices. Now, I think it is safe to say that any idea of these more
specific factual claims, or of the empirical inquiries that would be needed
to confirm them, is absent from our prephilosophical and prescientific
thought about the right to privacy.

2. For reasons already indicated, the formulation and investigation of
these more specific claims (when and if it occurs) will have depended on
the recognition that political rights — or at least this right — may be of
variable content from one society to another, and that it may not even
exist in some societies. Such an idea seems quite foreign to ordinary
political thought. Important political rights, in contrast with most if not
all legal rights, are popularly supposed to be the uniform and inalienable
possessions of all human beings, or of all adult human beings. So we
were taught in school, and so we have read in the Declaration of In-

dependence. Surely the right not to have our privacy invaded by the government in certain offensive and dispensable ways is to be numbered among those important political rights. But if Reiman's suggestion is generally correct, we have now discovered that some humans may lack this right entirely, while others who have it may still be entitled to much less privacy than you and I are entitled to have. It is true that philosophers have previsouly had occasion to develop the notion to which this recognition is tied − the notion of derivative moral rights, rights which depend for their existence and content on more general rights in the light of variable circumstances. But this apparatus is probably not found in the plain man's thought about rights, and surely he has not applied it to his cherished political rights.

3. Finally, the assumption that we all have the *more general* right here referred to cannot be left as a mere assumption. For if the right to privacy is to be fully useful in rational criticism, it obviously is not *sufficient* that it be conceptually "developed" in the way indicated above. It must also be shown, in some sense, to *exist*. And since we are supposing, with Reiman, that its existence depends on the right to social practices under which we are able to feel that we own our lives, the *latter* right must therefore be shown to exist. This is necessary in principle even if not required for practical debate, and it may be necessary in practice also. By this I mean that the existence of the latter right would need to be shown in order to "solve the philosophical problem" even if practically everyone who engages in political discourse could be expected to concede that we all do have such a right. Actually, a good many people seem to deny it both in their settled habits of exploiting others and in their concerted political actions. A few even deny it in words, e.g. those who say there are natural slaves. Now once again it seems obvious that in our pre-philosophical thought about rights we are entirely unaware that there is a need to formulate such a right as this, and to show that it exists.

But how could one possibly show that people have that more general right? In order to give an example of such an argument, though certainly not to claim a solution to this problem, let me point out that Reiman's suggestion can be adopted as a special application of the ethical theory outlined in the preceding chapter. While his own brand of moral secularism does not commit him to that particular view of moral truth, the two viewpoints would seem to be entirely compatible. And the bridge

between them would be the more general right to which I have been referring. For surely there would be a consensus, among people who substantially satisfy MPV on the question, that everyone has *this* right. These
autonomous and definitively rational moral judges would surely agree
that each person's need to feel that he owns his existence must be secured
by appropriate social practices, and that the individual must not be
deprived of the protection and nurture of those practices – at least short
of a grave emergency confronting all, and with due exceptions for extremely costly or harmful manifestations of such need.

What shall we say about societies in which this more fundamental right
is systematically violated? Would it eventually lapse there, perhaps as
people gradually came to accept their unfortunate condition? Not according to the theory of the preceding chapter. Even in a society based on
slavery, to take the most extreme case, this right would not be diminished
at all in the relevant literal sense, but simply violated. Of course, the non-
slaves in such a society seldom take the moral point of view towards
slaves, either in thought or in action. But anyone who does take it
towards systematically exploited persons or groups must hold that the
society in question (perhaps his own) is morally corrupt and violates fundamental rights.

Let us sum up the methodological points of our illustration. One cannot say (as in a stage three argument) that Judith Thomson is guilty of
distorting or misusing existing concepts when she holds that there is no
general justifying ground for the right to privacy, for it is not at all clear
at present what that ground might be. And this deficiency in ordinary
thought about our supposed right to privacy does not seem to arise from
a conflict between definite assumptions structuring such thought (as one
would say in a stage four argument of the sort previously illustrated). On
the contrary, existing assumptions are apparently too vague and unstruc-
tured to provide such ground. Amplifying Jeffrey Reiman's suggestion
(though without necessarily accepting it), we have sketched a different
kind of stage four argument proposing the following definite structure
to make good the noted deficiency.

A.   Humans need to have the benefit of social practices which
         enable them to feel that they own their lives: – rule-governed
         patterns of group behavior under which they are able to feel
         that they control their own destiny.

B.   Social practices according the right to privacy are among those which are so required, at least in many cultures.

C.   How much privacy and what kinds of privacy are required for that purpose by people of our culture — and hence what more specific form the right to privacy takes among us — is something that needs empirical investigation. Of course, this presupposes that the foregoing assumptions, A and B, will also have been empirically confirmed.

D.   Some convincing support must be provided for the claim that everyone has a right to the satisfaction of the need referred to in A. The ethical theory described in Chapter 10 might be considered for this purpose.

As we have already explained, three elements of this structure do not seem to exist in popular political thought, and one might add that they are also probably absent from the thought of rather sophisticated people who do not make a special study of morals or politics. They are: (1) the factual claims and need for inquiry referred to in C (covering A and B as well); (2) the notion of derivative political rights, a notion that figures in the whole sequence A through D; and (3) the notion that we need to claim and prove the existence or validity of the more general right referred to in D.

40. THE METAPHYSICS OF POLITICS

Along with the methodological point just noted, the foregoing illustration was offered to show that philosophers can do certain things with public policy issues that social scientists and lawyers *cannot* do equally well through their own analytical devices. Has it really shown this, and if so precisely how? To answer the question, let me first try to locate in very general terms the special interests and skills which I believe philosophers can bring to such issues. I shall then briefly illustrate this general statement with reference to the foregoing discussion.

Moral and political issues may involve conceptual problems as well as straightforward questions of fact and value. In attempting to cope with them we may need to clarify, reform, or add to the very tools of thought with which we are accustomed to formulate and debate such issues. Now philosophers have no general patent on conceptual elucidation, but some of these problems are of a type that social scientists and lawyers are often ill-equipped to handle, problems which they sometimes even pride themselves on rejecting as unscientific or metaphysical. And metaphysical they are, in a sense of the word often used in this book, especially in Part One. That is to say, they are problems which involve everyday nonscientific notions of an extremely general and fundamental sort. In the broad field of thought from which we have drawn our illustrations in these last three chapters, they are ideas like value, responsibility, justice, and right; in the illustrations used in our first four chapters, they are ideas like space, time, mind, matter, seeing, knowing. As we have often noted, the problems to which these structural notions give rise have sometimes led philosophers to propound dubious cosmic speculations like Berkeley's subjective Idealism, or radical reconstructions of common-sense like hard determinism, the theory that no one is ever responsible for his actions. Scientists and secular scholars outside philosophy have regularly turned their backs on such speculation, and one can only applaud their good sense. But this does not solve the conceptual difficulties that *give rise* to those problems and theories, difficulties which remain to infect moral and political debate. In refusing to discuss *them*, or in remaining half oblivious of them, many a social scientist or legal scholar has become a bad metaphysician all unknowingly, and his bad metaphysics has made his empirical and conceptual work less relevant than it might otherwise be for the solution of political problems. It seems to me that analytic philosohers of the present generation are probably better equipped to remedy this situation than any other group. For the philosopher's concern has always been to clarify such ideas for the relief of those difficulties, and recent philosophers have remained loyal to this calling while improving its standards and rejecting that kind of speculation for their own part.

So much for the general statement, and now for the illustrations. In our discussion of privacy we saw at the very outset that it is necessary to ask whether people have *a right* to privacy, and by this we meant a moral and political right. Existing legal rights may be inadequate, and they are vulnerable to repeal and judicial erosion. There is also no assurance that new legal protections will be added to meet the danger posed by the new technical devices. Indeed, one of the questions at issue is whether they ought to be added, and if so where and how. Various groups of people have a special interest in electronic spying and dossier building, and the majority can hardly be trusted to remain alert on this question or on any other question. People who are worried by these new and highly efficient ways of invading our privacy would therefore like to be able to make a valid claim of right to be free of such invasions. They do not wish to leave the question to pressure-group politicis, or to a majority decision conceded to be morally acceptable whichever way it goes.

But many social scientists and lawyers are frankly mystified by all talk of moral and political rights. Their mystification is often the result of a moral skepticism which takes hold of their professional thought even if not of their day-to-day conduct as moral persons. A typical reaction, not unlike that of many a beginner in moral philosophy, might be sketched out as follows:

"Ah, but people make conflicting claims about rights, don't you see? Civil liberatarians and police officials, for example, are likely to disagree about the moral right to privacy. How then are we to determine who is right about rights? Surely not by taking a poll. Rights are said to have some firmer basis than popular agreement. But what firmer basis can there be, if we are not willing (as we are not in law and social science) to ground claims of right on religious belief? The claim that someone has a moral or political right to something should probably be understood as a confused emotional appeal of a rather subtle kind, an attempt to dress up one's special interests or needs in language that invokes a kind of imaginary authority. It is a misleading analogy to the real authority standing behind legal rights. Surely the only real rights *are* legal rights."

In a word, many social scientists and lawyers hold a position rather similar to that of Emotivism in ethical theory, whether or not they have thought much about ethics or heard of that label. They assume, in many books and articles and conversations, that this is the properly scientific view, the only alternatives to naive traditionalism and theological ethics. They have not had occasion to see, as I hope we have seen in Chapter 10, that such a position is only the beginning of ethical reflection. It is at best a skeptical springboard to propel us toward a more careful description of moral thought and talk, including talk about rights.

The doctrine that there are no moral or political rights — because talk of rights is emotively confused, or whatever reason may be given — is itself a metaphysical theory, again in a sense of that expression which I have often used in this book. It departs far too radically from ordinary assumptions of a structural or fundamental kind, and it is induced by conceptual puzzlement. People have no right, then not to be tortured by governments which legally decree that they shall be tortured. And ethnic minorities legally excluded from the protection of the state have no right not to be put to death if the state's legal rules and forms are properly followed in killing them. Any social scientist or lawyer who adhered consistently to a position having these consequences would not be likely to advance our understanding in a field of thought and practice that is full of talk about non-legal rights, the field of public policy debate and legislative decision. Nor will it be sufficient for a social scientist, a legal scholar, or anyone else, merely to assert that there *are* moral and political rights. For some people who agree with this assertion may still disagree about a certain right currently invoked on a given side of a given policy issue, e.g. the general right to privacy. And some of them, like Judith Thomson, may even have respectable arguments to offer in denying that there is such a right.

If we are ever to resolve such a disagreement by rational means, there apparently is no way to avoid asking such broader questions as "What *is* a moral or political right anyway?" and "How in general does one justify a claim of moral or political rights?" Or more perspicuously, "What sorts of reasons count as good reasons or adequate reasons with people who seriously debate claims of that kind?" In other words, we need to do some descriptive metaphysics of morals and politics. And of course it is not excluded at this level of conceptual elucidation that we may be forced at some point to accept an economical revision of ordinary notions, or to supplement them with new notions.

If we should make any progress with those broad questions, we may then be in a position to ask and propose tentative answers to more specific questions like "What might be a sufficient justifying basis for the claim that we all have a general right to privacy?" In attempting to answer this question, philosophers will naturally avail themselves of existing psychological and sociological opinions, as the people discussed in this chapter have done. And they may also manage to suggest some new questions for empirical inquiry which psychologists and other social-scientists may wish to follow up in determining the general nature of our need for privacy, and how that need may be adversely affected by various types of privacy invasions. Finally, philosophers may be able to suggest a broader ethical basis for the claim that we all do have a right to the satisfaction of that need.

CONCLUSION

My purpose has been to explain recent professional philosophy in its dominant "analytic" style by exhibiting some of its principal methods and concerns in a number of substantial illustrations. There is no need to dwell once again on those aspects of the subject which these illustrations were individually offered to document. Instead I should like to end by calling attention to four other important features of recent philosophy which they collectively illustrate. Such an explanation will also serve to recall the main contents and themes of the book.

1

It is an old complaint against philosophy that unlike the various sciences it never makes progress. Its problems are never solved but only discussed again and again; its theories are never refuted or definitely improved upon but only ignored after a time as attention shifts to new theories. Now, taken quite literally and universally, this complaint has never been justified. If we go back to the beginning of Western philosophy, we find that Aristotle's logic, for example, is immeasurably advanced over that of his great teacher, if Plato could even be said to have "a logic," while Plato's own discussions of certain logical topics (in particular negation) are unquestionably superior to those of his Eleatic predecessors. And it would not be hard to cite cases where later philosophers have made such progress in their empirical and formal researches as to lay the foundations of new sciences and mathematical disciplines. Yet this complaint has long been true of traditional philosophy in certain famous topic areas that were not taken over by the new disciplines. For example, there is no agreed criterion by which we can attempt to estimate the relative truth of the metaphysical systems of Descartes, Spinoza, or Hegel, if only because these systems legislate their own fundamental criteria and are traditionally accorded the right to do so. Or again, the moral and political discussions of Kant and Mill are not superior in content or quality to those found in Aristotle's *Nicomachean Ethics* and *Politics*; they merely develop quite different assumptions.

In this respect, however, recent analytic philosophy is markedly advanced over earlier thought, whether analytic or speculative. Not that it accumulates firm results to any extent comparable to what occurs in the more developed of the sciences; but it does sometimes solve its problems, and if often achieves clarifications that can be confidently built upon. Like many other intellectuals, recent philosophers are a contentious lot who are often too partial to their own brain children; yet they often do build on each other's results. This has become possible because of their tendency to concentrate on narrower topics, and to develop standards of clarity and thoroughness more demanding than those of their predecessors. Furthermore, many of them do agree that certain criteria *are* fundamental for our most direct commerce with the world, namely, those which function in the most basic structure of common-sense. And paradoxical as it may sound, philosophers have good reasons for accepting these fundamental criteria, a point which I attempted to develop in the first three chapters.

The modestly accumulative nature of analytic philosophy is reflected in most of the illustrations of our opening chapters, where we repeatedly were able to develop for our own purposes some argument or elucidation given by one of the leaders of recent thought. Thus in Chapter 2, and in the last section of Chapter 3, we presented an interpretation and defense of the crucial point which G. E. Moore had put to great use without himself defending it against certain objections. I refer to the fact (using our terminology, not his) that a stage one response to skepticism is really unanswerable in the old city of the mind. In Chapter 3 we developed Strawson's stage three solution to the re-identification problem by presenting and answering a series of objections that can be brought against his solution.

The fact that philosophy now accumulates results and makes steady if slow progress was also illustrated in later chapters. Thus we traced a four-part development of the "theory of descriptions" in Chapters 5, 6 and 7. And in Chapter 7 we also saw how Quine's critique of the analytic-synthetic distinction can be clarified by attending to certain well known criticisms, criticisms that we were able to illustrate with material drawn from our fourth chapter. In Chapter 8 we saw how the theory of meaning developed by Kripke and Putnam builds on certain points brought out by Donnellan. Chapter 9 added a point to Hare's elucidation of standards in order to show more plainly how true evaluations are possible. Then we built on that result in Chapter 10 when we used it to identify an objective standard of good reasoning in critical morality. The theory of good revisionary solutions which we also invoked in that chapter had itself been worked out in Chapter 4 by reflecting on the solution to the time-gap problem favored by various philosophers. Finally, we saw in Chapter 11 how several thinkers dealing with the concept of privacy have criticized and built on each other's work in order to develop an increasingly adequate account.

2

Present-day philosophy is also "relevant." Contrary to the common accusation that it is a merely technical and conservative game, useless to outsiders, it can and does make valuable contributions to other areas of intellectual and practical life. We saw in Chapter 10 how conceptual description and elucidation can enlarge our understanding of whole departments of thought and action, in this case moral reasoning and its major subspecies. That it has this capacity should be reasonably clear from that discussion even if the particular view of moral truth which I advocated should turn out to be mistaken. Illustrations of the same general point could have been included from Philosophy of Mathematics, Philosophy of Science, and Philosophy of Law if it were not necessary to place some reasonable limit on the length of this book. In each case we could have shown that in clarifying key concepts philosophers have gained a better understanding of the first-order discipline in question, a better grasp of the nature of its subject matter and of the forms of reasoning that are appropriate there. We did take some side glances at Philosophy of Science, and throughout Part Two we saw how Philosophy of Language can deepen our understanding of the most important of all tools, language itself. In Chapter 11, finally, we listed a great many issues of practical policy on which analytic philosophers have recently contributed to public enlightenment, and we then discussed one of them in considerable detail.

So much for the charge of irrelevance. While the charge of conservatism is also inaccurate, one can readily understand why people have sometimes thought it appropriate, especially as applied to recent British philosophy. For we saw in Chapters 2 and 3 why many philosophers have held that the basic structures of common-sense need not be changed, and indeed cannot be changed as long as humans are constructed as they are. Since traditional philosophers fought some of their most famous battles over those very structures, and sometimes offered radical reconstructions of them, it is not too surprising that such a point of view should be thought conservative in every way. But we saw in Chapters 4 and 10 that philosophy can now also play the role of liberal reformer. Our descriptions in the latter chapter claimed to reveal that the structural assumptions of one of the newer and more important suburbs of the mind – critical morality – are not yet fully coherent, so that conceptual change is needed. And however economical our proposed reform may be, it definitely alters one's view of social reality if accepted. Finally, it should be clear from Chapter 11 that the new philosophy can also have a radical function, that of formulating and explaining political rights more convincingly in order to undermine laws and social practices which appear to violate them. This is conceptual creativity as well as political radicalism since there presumably is no Platonic storehouse of absolute rights, each with its eternally correct analysis awaiting discovery. Political morality, like language itself, is part of that natural history of humanity emphasized by the later Wittgenstein, and of course it is still developing. Anyone who strives for greater clarity about fundamental rights is perforce an innovator, at least if he carries the discussion very far beyond platitudes. In sum, contemporary philosophy is conservative *and* liberal *and* radical, depending on the level and type of thought which it is attempting to clarify or improve.

3

A complaint frequently made against recent philosophy by more traditionally minded thinkers is that it lacks historical perspective, and that it usually underestimates the contributions of earlier philosophers. The charge is no doubt justified as applied to some analytic philosophers. (It is equally clear that *some* historians of philosophy have not spent enough time with present-day work to understand it or see what the study of classical writers might contribute to it.) On the other hand, some outstanding analytic philosophers have been very acute students of the classics, and many a contemporary article or book begins with a careful discussion of what Aristotle, Leibniz, or Mill, etc., had to say on the topic at hand.

Recent philosophy not only profits from the study of intellectual history; it can also help us improve our historical understanding. I believe the illustrations in this book lend support to this claim with respect to two related strands of the history of ideas. I refer to the tradition of metaphysical theorizing itself, and to the attempts by various writers during the last two and a half centuries to discredit that whole tradition. The most widely accepted of these attacks was the one formulated by Hume and summarized at the beginning of Section 23, although equally famous criticisms were launched by Kant and the positivists. (On the latter, see Section 20 for a brief discussion.) Hume's criticism, it will be recalled, is that metaphysics confusedly attempts to straddle the analytic-synthetic divide; this is what he was saying in effect, though the "analytic-synthetic" terminology had not yet been coined. Any true statements that metaphysical speculation arrives at with its purely *a priori* methods will *not* disclose features of reality (much less necessary features), because these statements will be analytic truths merely, i.e. statements about "the relations of ideas." But in summarizing and illustrating Quine's criticisms of the analytic-synthetic distinction, we saw that a given statement may not be exclusively synthetic or exclusively analytic in all conceptual schemes in which that statement (or something extremely close to it) may be used.

It is a consequence of the latter insight that the critical analysis of concepts is *not* an impossible way to gain a *better* knowledge of matter of fact and existence. This is true if only because we must take into account the empirical support which various statements already have if we are to work out a coherent and usable scheme. So if some revision of one of our basic common-sense schemes *were actually needed* because the scheme *really was incoherent*, and if it were psychologically possible for humans to accept and use the proposed revision, this *would* be a vastly important result and not mere "news from nowhere." We would have found a better way to look at the world and manage our everyday experience. It would be a truer way in the sense of being more coherent and adequate for our needs. And in this new way some statements formerly held to be necessarily true might not be true at all, while some others formerly held to be impossible might be plainly true.

The lesson in this, I believe, is that the age-old attempt to reach a better understanding of reality through reconstruction of defective common-sense concepts has only been carried on *in the wrong parts* of common-sense. For the question still remains: Which of our conceptual schemes really are incoherent and changeable, and which of them have only been made to appear so by the philosophers' misunderstanding and abuse of them? The underlying claim of much recent philosophy which I attempted to spell out and defend in the first three chapters is that there is no good reason to think that the oldest and most elementary schemes of common-sense are incoherent or changeable, and that *this* is why the great revisionary systems of Western metaphysics were radically misguided. On the other hand, I suggested in Chapter 4 and argued in Chapter 10 that there is every reason to think that some other schemes of common-sense are incoherent and in need of reform. Still others need to be refined and supplemented, as I attempted to illustrate in Chapter 11.

What about the non-speculative types of metaphysical philosophy reflected in our illustrations: Description of common sense à la Strawson, and description of the most general structures of reality implicit in the theories of science à la Quine? And what about the other brand of 20th-century metaphysics which we have had occasion to discuss: the atomistic speculations of Russell and the early Wittgenstein? For reasons explained in Section 21, I agree with the older Wittgenstein that these latter are sufficiently misguided and obscure to be bracketed with the tradition of earlier centuries and downgraded accordingly, though only Russell goes out of his way to disparage common sense. Both are of great interest for understanding later developments, but one would hardly build on them today in a serious inquiry into truth. I shall touch on the Strawson and Quine projects in the next and final section.

4

It is sometimes put forward nowadays that philosophy is really dead or dying as the result of its revolution. So the last "feature" I wish to emphasize is that, on the contrary, it is very much alive and thriving. I hope that anyone who has carefully read through our illustrations will find it so obvious that philosophy is in a lively state that he will wonder how any informed critic could possibly doubt it. But some people seem to manage this by paying attention to one very important development while ignoring another which is equally important. Both developments are reflected in our illustrations, and it may be instructive to notice how these pessimists arrive at their position before we point out their oversight or blind spot.

Suppose one begins (as I would myself) by being highly impressed with mid-century British philosophy, and especially with Wittgenstein's and Austin's attacks on traditional epistemology and metaphysics. These twin subjects have as good a claim as any others to have been the core of philosophy for almost all of the modern period, i.e. from the early 1600's to the middle of our century; and now they are thoroughly discredited. The problem of perceptual knowledge which descends from Descartes and Berkeley through Kant to such late writers in the tradition as C. I. Lewis and A. J. Ayer is no longer worth our serious attention if Wittgenstein, Austin, and a good many others are to be believed. And neither is the closely-related project of finding the absolute structure of the world, unfiltered by the human senses and understanding. That goal is hopeless when pursued in the deeply confused ways of traditional metaphysics, and neither can it be reached through "scientific realism," the program espoused by Quine and his followers. We cannot hope to gain *metaphysical* knowledge by generalizing the results of science, because there is no ultimate, permanently best and necessary scheme for science. Quine's own attack on analytic truth has made us realize this. Not only is there no hope that we shall soon discover that absolute scheme, but in the nature of the case there is no reason to think it is there "waiting to be found." The very notion way be as confused and empty as that of "how the world would appear to beings with 'perfect' senses and understandings."

It may be true that philosophers can occasionally be of help in the lesser Quinean project of clarifying the conceptual schemes of science. But that is a far cry from the traditional ambitions of metaphysics, and it is not really to be distinguished from the more theoretical part of science itself. All honor to anyone who actually achieves a simplification or unification of theory, but he earns his laurels as a scientist, not as a philosopher. And it may also be true that some few philosophers interested in questions too poorly organized as yet for empirical inquiry will be able to make useful suggestions to clarify relevant concepts, thus aiding in the foundation of new disciplines. But while these proto-scientists also deserve all praise and encouragement, their activity has little to do with the traditional ambition of philosophy, that of discovering *ultimate* truths, the most general traits and structures of reality.

And what about philosophy's traditional pretension to be the judge of other disciplines, evaluating their rational status and tracing their inter-relations? This claim was based in part on the notion that philosophy pursues the most radically critical method of all in epistemology, where it scrutinizes the possibility, nature, and warrants of knowledge in general. And it was also based on the notion that philosophy alone seeks to discover *the* most generally adequate scheme for understanding reality, a scheme capable of organizing and criticizing the results of the sciences, along with other major activities like art and religion. Obviously such a claim or ambition must also be given up now that the traditional projects of epistemology and metaphysics are discredited. So another major role of philosophy drops away. No doubt the people who still occupy academic departments of "Philosophy" can go on collaborating with historians, literary scholars, and other humanists to help bring the several arts and sciences into some more intelligible relationship, and to do whatever *can* be done to bridge the gaps of understanding between different cultures and historical periods. But any thought of relating them all to *the* true scheme for understanding reality, and then evaluating or interpreting them in terms of it, must now be abandoned. Philosophy thus comes to an end in everything but name, to be replaced by the more urbane form of humanistic scholarship which recent European writers have been calling "hermeneutics."

It is obvious that the point of view which I have just sketched can draw support from *some* of the materials in our illustrations, and especially from the way I have interpreted and appreciated those materials. But I hope it will be equally clear to readers of this book how, in adopting such an outlook and attitude, one ignores the fact that post-Wittgensteinian philosophy has already entered upon a brilliant new career which it has been pursuing with impressive success for thirty years. This is the career of conceptual description and clarification in which we attempt to gain a better understanding of human thought itself, and to suggest needed improvements in the structure of thought, rather than spinning out theories of the universe or looking for absolute conceptual schemes. And in this project we find that *many* of the traditional problems still lack definitive solutions, though descriptive philosophy by no means limits its attention to them. It is not entirely clear how anyone familiar with contemporary philosophy could fail to appreciate the high quality and excitement of much of the work produced in recent decades. One guess would be that it is due to lingering regret over the lost glamour of speculative metaphysics, plus failure to immerse oneself deeply in one or two special areas of current discussion. Only in the latter way can one hope to measure up to the high level of competence now common among the better writers in philosophy of language, say, or in philosophical logic, philosophy of science, philosophy of law, etc. Among those who *are* in thorough command of some of the best recent work, such a blind spot might still result from concentrating too exclusively on the destructive claims of philosophy in relation to its past, paying too little attention to its affirmative achievements – descriptive achievements which sometimes lead us, by the way, to reject popular dissolutions as facile and specious.

While much good work in descriptive philosophy tends to be narrowly focused, and the present standards of competence are partly the result of this, there is no reason why larger structures of thought should not also be investigated, as in the projects partly carried out in Strawson's *Individuals* and brilliantly envisaged in Quine's *Word and Object*. Descriptive metaphysics of common sense and clarification of the conceptual schemes of science are both of high interest as humanistic and scientific studies. And so, perhaps, is the attempt to "limn the most general traits of reality," *provided* we take this as a kind of Kantian regulatory Idea directing an unending search for greater generality in science with the aid of simplified syntax, rather than as an article of literal faith that there is one best scheme for depicting reality if we could only find it.

At the close of Part Two I briefly discussed the relation between Strawsonian and Quinean description, and I expressed the opinion that they are compatible, i.e. that the conceptual schemes of science require no change in the core of common sense. But I did not consider the further question whether common sense is "less fundamental" for understanding reality and even "reducible" to science, so that in principle if not in practice our everyday thinking could be replaced without loss by thought using only the conceptual schemes of science — say those of microphysics. This obviously is not the case at present, even in principle, but is there good reason to think that it might become so at some future point in the development of science? Or, on the contrary, must the explanatory categories of science inevitably fall short of describing such things as a person, reasoned belief, deliberate action, moral blameworthiness? It is in connection with these most confusing and tantalizing questions that many of the traditional problems of philosophy come crowding back to plague and bemuse us, and in several cases they have received more patient and fruitful investigation during these last three decades than ever before. To document this claim we need only direct our attention to the several impressive literatures which have grown up on the topics of personal identity, causation, action, reasons as causes, the mind-brain identity theory, moral and criminal responsibility. Other recent discussions which connect with the traditional problems, helping to illuminate them while also uncovering new conceptual issues, are (1) the recent literature on "possible worlds," which not only impacts upon older theories of meaning and the mind-body problem, as seen in Chapter 8, but aids in the interpretation of modal logic and has implications for the ancient problem of evil in philosophical theology; (2) modern theory of rational decision-making, which throws important new lights on the problems of ethics and political philosophy; (3) the recent lively debates over the nature of legal reasoning in difficult cases, debates which have improved our understanding of the classic problem of "natural law": How does legal validity relate to moral validity? The list could easily be extended, and it will be in the Bibliography following the Notes.

Perhaps we can organize our thoughts on this topic — the present tasks and prospects of philosophy — with one last glance at our scheme of "stages." I shall only invoke the third and fourth stages, stage two being a will-o'-the-wisp and stage one being only a preamble to philosophical work, though sometimes a most salutary one.

Contrary to what is suggested by the pessimistic point of view sketched above, stage three work is far from complete on those traditional problems where it seems most appropriate and likely to succeed in the long run: those arising from plausible but presumably specious attacks on the most fundamental concepts of common sense. Furthermore, there seems to be no reason why a good Wittgensteinian must hold that stage three work in philosophy will *ever* be complete. One can hardly suppose that the classic problems of philosophy exhaust the ways in which people can misunderstand and mismanage coherent schemes of thought, including those not yet invented. And even if all stage three work were not complete, there would still remain those problems which arise in whole or in part from the incoherence or other inadequacy of some of our less fundamental schemes. This is particularly common, it would seem, in philosophical puzzlement connected with morals, politics, law, religion, and art – that great hemisphere of philosophy which is virtually ignored in the point of view sketched above.

A most important point is that even stages three and four taken together are only *part* of philosophical work as we must now understand it. We have learned to see that while both of them are aids to, and are aided by, conceptual description, the latter is not confined to problem-solving (much less to the solving of traditional problems) but can be intrinsically interesting and valuable when carried on for its own sake. Some of the most ingenious conceptual mapmaking, issuing in new understanding of familiar tools of thought, has come from people like Frege who have a flair for asking odd questions (What is a number? What does the symbol 1 mean?) where *no* puzzlement was felt by most philosophers.

In order to gain a better appreciation of descriptive philosophy after Wittgenstein, the admirers of that great thinker would do well to recall a well known tension in his later work which he never satisfactorily resolved. I refer to the partial opposition between (i) his need to *relieve* puzzlement through many reminders of how we normally think and talk when we are not occupied with philosophy, (ii) his recognition that mere cessation of puzzlement is intellectually worthless if it is not accompanied by understanding of the relevant structures of such thought and talk (otherwise an anti-philosophy pill would serve his purpose as well), and (iii) his rejection of all "theorizing" in philosophy, by which he appears to mean not only speculative metaphysics growing out of unrelieved puzzlement but systematic analysis and description of existing conceptual structures. The tension arises from the undeniable fact that understanding can often be improved and made more secure by systematic work. (Indeed, abstract reflection can show that some of our "reminders" were themselves misleading; witness the case of the manometer in Section 8.) No doubt, understanding can also be clouded when systematic thought passes from description into scholastic constructions too far removed from the needs of ordinary life and practical communication. But while there is always ground for the Wittgensteinian fear that this will occur when people philosophize, we are fortunate that the best thinkers of the last three decades did not give way to that fear so far as to abstain from systematically describing and clarifying the structures of thought.

NOTES

Nothing in these notes is needed in order to follow what is said in the text, but they often provide additional explanation. After completing each section of the text the reader should consult the corresponding section of the notes.

CHAPTER ONE

Section 2. The Four Stages Described

Page 8. *Donne's famous phrase.* From his Devotion XVII. John Donne, *Complete Poetry and Selected Prose*, John Hayward, ed.; London, 1962.

Section 3. The Four Stages Illustrated

Page 12. *Three Dialogues between Hylas and Philonous.* For a definitive edition of this work, which also appears in various inexpensive college editions, see *The Works of George Berkeley, Bishop of Cloyne*, 9 vols., A. A. Luce and T. E. Jessop, eds.; London and New York, 1948–1957. Some general works on Berkeley are: G. Dawes Hicks, *Berkeley*, London, 1932; G. J. Warnock, *Berkeley*, London, 1953; A.-L. Leroy, *George Berkeley*, Paris, 1959; G. Pitcher, *Berkeley*, London, 1977. For a thorough summary of Berkeley's philosophy, see Frederick C. Copleston, *A History of Philosophy*, London, 1946, Part II of Vol. 5, at pp. 9 – 62. Also see the article on Berkeley by H. B. Acton in *The Encyclopedia of Philosophy*, Paul Edwards, ed., New York and London, 1967, at vol. 1, pp. 295 – 304. Copleston's history and Edwards's encyclopedia may also be consulted for reliable summaries and discussions of the classical philosophers who are to be mentioned more briefly in the next section: Bradley, Descartes, Hegel, Hume, Kant, Lewis, and Malebranche.

Section 4. A Change of Emphasis

Page 17. *Descartes on the problem of perception and the physical world.* See especially his *Meditations on First Philosophy*, which appears in many inexpensive editions. A frequently cited translation appears in E. S. Haldane and G. R. T. Ross, *The Philosophical Works of Descartes*, Cambridge, Eng., 1911–12; 1967.

Page 17. *C. I. Lewis on the problem of perception and the physical world.* See his *An Analysis of Knowledge and Valuation*, LaSalle, Ill., 1946, Book II.

205

Page 18. *Kant's "Copernican revolution" as a stage four theory*. In this connection his principal works are the *Critique of Pure Reason*, translated by Norman Kemp Smith, London and New York, 1929, 1933; and *Prolegomena to any Future Metaphysics*, with a revised translation by Lewis White Beck, New York, 1950.

Page 18. *Metaphysical problems (in our sense) formulated by David Hume*. Most of them are found in Book I of his *Treatise of Human Nature*, and (sometimes only sketchily) in his briefer and less demanding work, *Enquiry concerning Human Understanding*. In the latter work see Sec. IV, Parts I and II (induction); Sec. VII, esp. Part II (cause and effect); Sec. XII, Part I (perception and the external world): Sec. XII, Part II (space and time). On the problem of personal identity, see *Treatise*, Book I, Part IV, Sec. 6, and the Appendix.

CHAPTER TWO

Page 21. *Wittgenstein's best known stage three writings*. These appeared posthumously as his *Philosophical Investigations*, G. E. M. Anscombe, Rush Rhees, and G. H. von Wright, eds.; translated by Anscombe. Oxford, 1953; 3rd edn. 1968.

Section 5. Moore on Common Sense

Page 21. *Contemporary British Philosophy*, 1st and 2nd Series. Edited by J. H. Muirhead, London, 1924 and 1925. Moore's widely anthologized essay appeared in the 2nd Series. (Later series of essays under the same title have been edited by H. D. Lewis, the third appearing in 1961 and the fourth in 1976; both New York and London.)

Page 23. *Nor can any combination of true statements entail a contradiction*. This assumes that they figure in a coherent conceptual scheme or system. The reason for this restriction will become apparent in Chapter 4. But let us give an illustration here which the reader may wish to check up on after reading that chapter. The combination of true statements constituting the islanders' incoherent scheme (p. 63) entails both that we can see various objects and that we cannot see any objects. The former entailment will be obvious from the combination itself as listed on p. 62, while the latter entailment is explained on p. 61.

Page 25. *Moore himself did a good deal of stage two epistemology*. See his lectures of 1910 and 1911 published as *Some Main Problems of Philosophy*, London and New York, 1953.

Section 6. Moore and Later Philosophy

Page 26. *Stage one arguments were rare before Moore*. Of course it was usually assumed that the skeptic must be wrong. But very few philosophers were prepared to assert that they knew the skeptic was wrong even when they were unable to point out any defect in his argument. Stage one consists in asserting such knowledge and then refuting the skeptic merely with a *reductio ad absurdum*; that is, by pointing out that at best his argument entails somethings known to be false and is therefore unsound.

Page 27. *If there are common-sense beliefs then there are people holding them in common.* It may be this sort of argument that has led some careless readers to say that Moore thinks all common-sense beliefs are necessarily true. The argument does show the necessary falsehood of a statement like "The common-sense belief that more than one mind exists is possibly false." But not all common-sense beliefs need be challenged by such obviously inconsistent statements, nor need they make any references to common sense itself. Furthermore, Moore explicitly acknowledges that some common-sense beliefs (beliefs that practically everyone takes for granted as obviously true) have been false in the past, and that some are no doubt false now, although we do not know which ones. There is no inconsistency between such an acknowledgment and Moore's statement that he knows certain common-sense beliefs to be true, and a good many of them.

But should not such an acknowledgement have led Moore to *question* his own knowledge concerning *any* given common-sense belief? No, not the most basic common-sense beliefs, as I shall argue in Chapter 3 and the beginning of Chapter 4.

Page 28. *Hume on the impossibility of skepticism in everyday life.* Two of the several places where he expresses this view are *Enquiry concerning Human Understanding*, Sec. XII, Part II (fifth paragraph), and Sec. V, Part I (second paragraph).

Section 7. Private Language

Page 29. *Wittgenstein's argument against private language.* This begins at Section 243 of the *Philosophical Investigations*, Part I, and runs for several dozens of these short sections, merging with a discussion of pain.

Section 8. A Critique and a Promissory Note

Page 35. *The fallibility of memory not a sufficient obstacle to private language.* For a development of this point and further references on the private language problem, see H.-N. Castañeda's article of that title in Edwards's encyclopedia. For a book-length discussion, see J. T. Saunders and D. F. Henze, *The Private Language Problem*, New York, 1967. More extensive references to Wittgenstein's writings and the secondary literature on his philosophy are given in the Notes to Chapter 6 below. See also the note to p. 52 below.

CHAPTER THREE

Section 9. Identification

This section is introductory, sketching some main ideas from the opening section of Strawson's *Individuals*, London, 1959.

Section 10. Re-Identification

Pages 41 – 42. *Strawson's reply to the skeptic in the re-identification puzzle.* The passage quoted is on page 35 of *Individuals* (pages 23-24 in the American paperback edition, New York, 1963).

Page 42. *A critic might ask the following question.* I owe this objection to Dr. John Sutula.

Section 11. A Skeptical Counterattack

Pages 45 – 46. *The Skeptic's counterattack.* This also was suggested, in substance, by Dr. Sutula.

Page 48. *A typical contemporary formulation of skepticism.* See, for example, Peter Unger's *Ignorance: A Case for Skepticism*, Oxford, 1975, at page 13f., and John Pollock's *Knowledge and Justification*, Princeton, 1974, at pp. 3 – 4. Not that Pollock defends skepticism. In fact he repeatedly emphasizes what I have been calling "stage one," and he also points out (at what I call "stage three") that the conceptual error underlying the skeptic's argument is often that of requiring an entailment between experiential data and what common sense claims to know. While both points have been more or less familiar to analytic philosophers since J. L. Austin's 'Other Minds' (1946), Pollock deserves credit for using them quite explicitly and systematically.

Section 12. A Final Paradox

Page 49. *Harman's formulation.* This appears at p. 148 of his book *Thought*, Princeton, 1973.

Page 52. *Only a cause for personal embarrassment.* It is reported (perhaps apocryphally) that Moore was embarrassed this way at a talk he once gave at an American university, saying that he knew a certain object in the ceiling of the lecture room was a skylight when in fact it was only a source of artificial light, etc. For reasons explained in the text, I believe that the possibility of being mistaken on any particular occasion in no way alters the indubitability of the general statements in Moore's list.

In a manuscript on which he was working at the end of his life, published as *On Certainty*, Oxford, 1969, Wittgenstein commented on Moore and objected that we do not *know* propositions like "The earth existed for many years before I was born," or "This is a hand" – at least not apart from very special situations that make it suitable to say such things, as where we might want to reject a suggestion that the hand in question is artificial. Rather than being items of knowledge, such things are more like rules for the whole "language-game" of common-sense knowledge, so that (apart from those special situations) it is simply out of order (against the rules) either to say that we know them or to question whether we know them. Now suppose we substitute some general statements in Moore's list for the singular statements Wittgenstein happened to use in this discussion. Then I think we can get the following results under his (Wittgenstein's) doctrine. (1) We can accept the rule of reason that we must *never* disregard all future evidence or arguments against something we properly claim to know. But (2) we *are* entitled to disregard skeptical arguments against statements of the kind Moore *improperly* claimed to know, including statements like "We are often able to re-identify objects," since skepticism is also a violation here. This way of making the point avoids having to qualify Harman's attractive principle, and it tips one's hat to Wittgenstein. But it is not clear whether we should follow Wittgenstein (and therefore Harman) in this matter. Perhaps it is a reasonable and unconfusing extension of ordinary uses of "know" to say that we know things like those in Moore's list. But whichever way we make the point, it seems to me correct.

Page 53. *Further skeptical attacks, however inane.* Here is an example of a further doubt which may seem rather absurd in the context of the present metaphysical problem, but which is *not* philosophically pointless. "Perhaps we are mistaken when we now seem to recall that Strawson's arguments were cogent; or perhaps we do not recall correctly what we said in (iii) and (iv)." This sort of doubt should be left for a descriptive inquiry into the concept of memory, and probably into the concept of reasoning as well – both of which are rich sources of philosophical perplexity, and both of which are crucial to many of our most fundamental beliefs.

But a further skeptical doubt which is sometimes heard and which I think is utterly inane, can be stated as follows. "Granted, we cannot change our most fundamental conceptual schemes without tearing human knowledge and thought to shreds; and granted, it would be impossible for humans, constructed as they are, to adopt some fundamentally different scheme for making their way in the world. Still, how do we know that our scheme is not seriously misleading or inadequate for gaining true access to the world, for acquiring 'real' knowledge? Perhaps the members of the inter-galactic civilization of the future will have a sensory apparatus and conceptual scheme far superior to ours for this purpose, a scheme we humans could not even learn. Now this mere possibility is enough to reinstate all the skeptical doubts which those two concessions may have seemed to invalidate."

It seems to me that philosophers who are impressed by this sort of objection need to develop a better sense of what is really germane to their enterprise. Skeptical doubts have much point and need to be attended to as long as they are an aid to the clarification and extension of knowledge, including knowledge of our own conceptual schemes. But when they reach the point where, by their own admission, they cannot be of any use at all, we no longer have any philosophical obligation to listen to them or answer them, however much we may happen to enjoy wondering (perhaps in a spirit of playful self-confusion) what the world must be like to those inter-galactic beings. Some good cold water is thrown on this "inter-galactic" objection by Richard Rorty in his wide-ranging article, 'The World Well Lost,' *Journal of Philosophy* **69** (1972). It seems to me that Garrett Vander Veer is not sufficiently aware of the foregoing methodological issue in his criticism of Rorty. See Vander Veer's interesting book, *Philosophical Skepticism and Ordinary-Language Analysis*, Lawrence, Kansas, 1978, at pp. 222 – 234.

CHAPTER FOUR

Section 13. Time Gaps

Page 56. *The non-arbitrary cut-off point.* I refer to D. M. Armstrong, *Perception and the Physical World*, London, 1961, at pp. 144 – 152, especially 145; and to W. A. Suchting, 'Perception and the Time-Gap Argument,' *Philosophical Quarterly* **19** (1969), at pp. 46 – 56, esp. 54. In the text I follow Suchting's way of making this point. Other discussions of the time-gap problem alluded to in the text are G. E. Myers, 'Perception and the "Time-Lag" Argument,' *Analysis* **17** (1957); F. Ebersole, 'How Philosophers See Stars,' *Mind* **74** (1965); R. G. Henson, 'Ordinary Language, Common Sense and the Time-Lag Argument,' *Mind* **76** (1967); and L. S. Carrier, 'The Time-Gap Argument,' *Australasian Journal of Philosophy* **14** (1969). For briefer discussions, see A. J. Ayer, *The Problem of Knowledge*, Baltimore, 1956, at pp. 93 – 95; and Roderick Chisholm, *Perceiving*, Ithaca, 1956, at p. 153.

Page 57. *Forced change in scientific concepts.* On p. xi of the Introduction, I referred to the undoubted fact that conceptual reform is sometimes necessary in science, whether or not it is required in order to resolve the traditional problems of metaphysics, or some of them. For a famous nonmathematical explanation of how certain basic propositions in pre-Einsteinian physics formed an inconsistent combination requiring "conceptual reform," as I have been using this expression, see Albert Einstein and Leopold Enfeld, *The Evolution of Physics*, New York, 1938; Part III. The result of this reform was the theory of relativity, of course, not the more limited reform discussed in the text: that concerning the time-location of objects seen in present time, as required by the discovery that light has finite speed.

Page 59. *No change is required in the everyday concept of seeing.* Another objection to the opinion expressed in the text might run as follows. "Although the time lags dealt with in modern astronomy are of no significance in everyday experience, a great many of the events dealt with in various scientific theories *do* occur within everyday experience. Well confirmed theories enable us to predict and control such events when we could not otherwise do so. The practical advantage of knowing and understanding theories of this kind cannot be enjoyed without importing into everyday thought some of the conceptual structures they use." But is this really so? Or is it true often enough to alter common conceptual schemes? In a rather narrow sense of "everyday thought," it may be true of the engineer whose work it is to design such controls. But I doubt whether careful analysis would show that it is true of nontechnical people who use the devices of technical culture. I would expect it to turn out that everyone but the scientist (at work) and the design engineer (at work) continues to get along very well without using such structures.

Perhaps it will be replied that we laymen may get along *fairly* well in this way, but that we could get along better — say, in the more intelligent design of public policy concerning the uses of technology — if we had more scientific culture. Having it, we would need to replace common-sense concepts with those of science at some point in our discourse about such policies. But would we really? Certainly we would need to *refer* to scientific theories and techniques when discussing, in ordinary terms, certain events and conditions of life which are unpleasant or harmful and thus to be avoided, or events and conditions which favor certain interests and are thus to be promoted by available means if the cost in our other interests is not too high. But would we need to *use* the theoretical concepts of science in such judgments of political ends and means? Indeed *could* we properly use them in that sort of discourse? It seems more likely that those who attempt to do so are not really employing scientific concepts, which have their meaning in scientific contexts, but scientific myths.

A familiar example from late 19th-century and early 20th-century politics is the use of terms from the theory of evolution when attempting to justify certain very broad public policies. These included the policy, advocated by certain Social Darwinists, of not interfering with the development of a superior human stock by helping weaker members of society survive and reproduce themselves. And they also included the policy, favored by certain other Social Darwinists, of doing just that in order to promote man's "evolutionary advance as a moral being." But of course the concept of biological evolution has neither of such moral implications. Nor are people *developing* that concept in a scientific way (that is, to explain events which otherwise remain unexplained) when they give it these implications. For an interesting discussion of these mattes, see Stephen Toulmin's essay, "Recent Scientific Mythologies," in *Metaphysical Beliefs*, A. MacIntyre, ed., London, 1956.

Section 15. The Theory of Stage Four

Page 64. *Giving our eyes access to the past*. See A. J. Ayer, *The Problem of Knowledge*, Baltimore, 1956, at p. 95.

Page 65. *Kant is intentionally revisionary*. I do not mean to suggest that Kant was working to Strawson's model! To say that he intended to correct the structure of common sense on one crucial point is not to imply that he had in mind the general distinction between revisionary and descriptive metaphysics that Strawson has pointed out.

CHAPTER FIVE

Section 16. Introduction to Part Two

Page 70. *Moore's 'Refutation of Idealism.'* The article appeared originally in *Mind* **12** (1903), and has been reprinted in his *Philosophical Studies*, London, 1922, and in various anthologies.

Pages 70 – 71. *Philosophy as logical analysis*. Here one can gather a little more specifically what Moore meant when he said that although he knew there are bodies and minds, etc., he did not know how to "give the analysis" of any of these truisms. (Section 5 above) He accepted Russell's view that the method of philosophy is analysis, though he did not accept the metaphysical atomism that Russell had advanced to justify that method. And only rarely did Moore make any use of logical symbolism when pursuing his own analysis.

Pages 71 – 74. *Mentioned works by Russell, Wittgenstein, Strawson, Quine, Donnellan, Kripke*. Bibliographical information on these works will be found in the notes to the next nine sections.

Section 17. Russell on Descriptions

Page 75. *Russell's account as a model of analysis*. F. P. Ramsey's much cited reference to "that paradigm of philosophy, Russell's theory of descriptions" is to be found in a note on p. 263 of his *Foundations of Mathematics and other Logical Essays*, London and New York, 1931.

Page 75. *The theory appears in several of his works*. First in his article 'On Denoting,' *Mind* **14** (1905). Then in *Principia Mathematica*, Cambridge, Eng., 1910–1913. Then in Chapter 16 of his *Introduction to Mathematical Philosophy*, London, 1919, the version on which our discussion in the text is mainly based. Then in the work which we are going to discuss in the next section.

Section 18. Russell's Atomism

Page 80. *'The Philosophy of Logical Atomism.'* These lectures were delivered in London in 1918, and were first printed in three issues of *The Monist* of that year. They are reprinted in Russell's *Logic and Knowledge* (Essays 1901–1950), edited by R. C. Marsh, London, 1956.

Page 81. *The Russell–Whitehead logic.* Often referred to in later sections as Russell's logic. The main ideas of the work were developed by Russell prior to his collaboration with Whitehead in writing it. However, some of the fundamental notions of mathematical logic incorporated in *Principia Mathematica* were first conceived by Gottlob Frege.

Page 86. *"Your atom has got to turn out,"* etc. Quoted from p. 274 of *Logic and Knowledge*, cited above.

Page 86. *Longer quotation on the justification of analysis.* The passage appears on p. 270 of *Logic and Knowledge*.

Page 87. *Russell's malice towards common sense.* Most of the quoted sentences and phrases appear at pp. 274–275 of the same book.

Pages 80–87. *Russell's philosophy.* For a general account of the development of his metaphysics and theory of knowledge during the 1905 to 1919 period, see D. F. Pears, *Bertrand Russell and the British Tradition in Philosophy*, New York, 1967. Another good account is Morris Weitz, 'Analysis and the Unity of Russell's Philosophy,' in *The Philosophy of Bertrand Russell*, Vol. I; P. A. Schilpp, ed., New York, 1963. Sections II and IV of Weitz's long essay are especially pertinent to this section of our text and the preceding section. The Schilpp volume, one of several in his *Library of Living Philosophers* series, contains many articles on special aspects of Russell's work, plus an autobiographical sketch and a 'Reply to Criticism' by Russell.

CHAPTER SIX

Section 19. Some Early Wittgenstein

Page 88. *Tractatus Logico-Philosophicus.* The work appeared in 1921 in the German periodical *Annalen der Naturphilosophie* under the title *Logisch-Philosophische Abhandlung*. The first English edition (C. K. Ogden, translator) appeared in 1922 under the Latin title which is said to have been suggested by Moore. A later translation was made by D. F. Pears and B. F. McGuinness, and was published at London in 1961; revised edn., 1974.

Page 88. *Some excellent commentaries.* See especially G. E. M. Anscombe, *An Introduction to Wittgenstein's Tractatus*, London and New York, 1959 (2nd edn. 1963); and Max Black, *A Companion to Wittgenstein's 'Tractatus'*, Ithaca, 1964. Two other very helpful works from the extensive literature on the *Tractatus* are *Understanding Wittgenstein*, G.

Vesey, ed. (the first several articles), Ithaca, 1974, and Anthony Kenny, *Wittgenstein* (about the first half of the book), Cambridge, Mass., 1973.

Page 89. *General statements can be eliminated from a complete description of the world.* Wittgenstein's reasoning for this is rather obscure and dubious. See Anscombe, *op. cit*, Chapter 11; and Black, *op. cit.*, Chapters LXI and LXII.

Page 89. *Truth function.* Two very simple examples: (1) Let T_1, T_2, and T_3 be any three statements, and let S be the compound statement made by conjoining them: "T_1 and T_2 and T_3". Then S is true if T_1, T_2, and T_3 are all true, and false otherwise. (2) Let S be the alternation of the first statements mentioned: "T_1 or T_2 or T_3." Then S is true if at least one of T_1, T_2, and T_3 is true, and false otherwise.

Page 93. *In the neighborhood of what commentators have said.* Compare the argument given at pp. 89 to 92 of our text with the interpretations by Anscombe, *op. cit.*, Chapter 2, and by R. M. White in the Vesey collection cited above.

Section 20. The Decline of Analysis

Pages 95 – 96. *Logical Positivism.* A short history of the movement and a collection of important articles by leading figures in it will be found in *Logical Positivism*, A. J. Ayer, ed., New York, 1959. Ayer's own *Language, Truth and Logic*, London, 1936 (2nd edn. 1946) was the earliest book-length presentation of Logical Positivism in English, and a very forceful one.

Page 96. *Other causes of the decline of older analytic philosophy.* For a thorough account, see J. O. Urmson's *Philosophical Analysis: its development between the two world wars*, Oxford, 1956, especially pp. 99 – 162.

Section 21. Critique of the Tractatus

Page 97. *The Blue and Brown Books.* The single volume bearing this title was published at Oxford in 1958. The two sets of mimeographed notes had been commonly identified by the color of their covers.

Page 97. *The difficulty of the Investigations.* The interpretive and critical literature on the work is very extensive. Some good pieces are conveniently available in *Wittgenstein: The Philosophical Investigations*, G. Pitcher, ed., New York, 1966; and items 8 through 13 of the Vesey collection cited above. Also, the second half of Kenny, *op. cit.*

Page 104. *Extreme and unpalatable speculations.* Unpalatable at least to those who dislike "grandiose philosophical myths." (Black, *op. cit.*, p. 19) Black's sentence is worth quoting in full. "Prolonged study of this remarkable work [the *Tractatus*] only deepens one's admiration for the man who could overcome in himself the fascination of the grandiose philosophical myth so memorably expressed in his great book."

Section 22. Strawson on Reference

Page 104. *Strawson's 1950 article*. Called "On Referring," it first appeared in *Mind*, vol. 59, and is reprinted in various collections, including *Essays in Conceptual Analysis*, A. Flew, ed., London, 1956, and Strawson's *Logico-Linguistic Papers*, London, 1971.

Page 104. *Russell's theory is now controversial*. It should be mentioned that some important philosophers still prefer it to Strawson's account. See the discussion of W. V. Quine on this point in Section 25 below. A more recent example is the article by Saul Kripke cited in the note to page 126, below.

Page 105. *Sentences, utterances, uses, and statements*. In earlier sections and chapters I have often ignored or violated the important distinctions made here. I wanted to preserve for the reader the illuminating effect of Strawson's points in the present context. It also would be somewhat anachronistic to use these distinctions when summarizing the work of writers who had not yet seen the need for them.

Page 105. *Meaning as general directions for use*. The word "directions" is perhaps not a very happy one here, suggesting, as it does, that rules have been laid down by some authority. Of course, Strawson intends nothing of the kind, but "conventions for correct use" might be better.

Pages 106 – 107. *He would not have managed to refer to anything* (point 3). It is true that in most (and perhaps all) scenarios in which a person might now seriously attempt to use the sentence, "The King of France is wise," to make a statement, he would indeed fail to refer to anything. But we shall see in Section 26 that it is often possible to refer to something or someone by using a definite description which does not truly apply to anything or anyone.

CHAPTER SEVEN

Section 23. The Analytic-Synthetic Distinction

Page 110. *Quine's 'Two Dogmas of Empiricism.'* The article first appeared in *Philosophical Review* **60** (1951) and is reprinted in many collections, including Quine's book *From a Logical Point of View*, New York, 1953, 2nd edn. 1961.

Page 110. *Hume on "relations of ideas" and "matters of fact."* The discussion in our text refers especially to Section IV of his *An Enquiry Concerning Human Understanding*, 1748. His related critique of metaphysics is fundamental to the whole of that work and to Book I of his *Treatise of Human Nature*, 1739.

Page 110. *Departing from Kant's doctrine*. He believed that some synthetic statements can be known *a priori*, and in the Introduction to the *Critique of Pure Reason* (1781, 1787) he announces his goal of showing how this is possible.

Page 112 *Rudolf Carnap.* Probably the most influential of the Logical Positivists. For many good studies of his work, see *The Philosophy of Rudolf Carnap*, P. A. Schilpp, ed., La Salle, Ill., 1963, another volume in the *Library of Living Philosophers* series.

Page 112. *Putnam on Quine's "bad argument."* The quotation is from Putnam's essay, ' "Two Dogmas" Revisited,' in *Contemporary Aspects of Philosophy*, G. Ryle, ed., London and Boston, 1976, at p. 204.

Page 112. *"Revolutions" in science, and "normal" science.* T. S. Kuhn has presented a widely discussed theory of the historical relation between the two in his book *The Structure of Scientific Revolutions*, Chicago, 1962, 1970.

Page 113. *The shift from Ptolemy to Kepler, Newton to Einstein,* etc. Quine mentions these truly revolutionary changes in connection with the thought that even the logical law of the excluded middle might have to be given up as a means of simplifying quantum mechanics. In his *Philosophy of Logic*, Englewood Cliffs, N.J., 1970, he questions (pp. 85 – 86) whether that particular change would in fact be economical. But he still holds (p. 100) that "Logic is in principle no less open to revision than quantum mechanics or the theory of relativity." Putnam continues to favor the idea that "quantum logic" – in which certain familiar logical laws are given up, though apparently not the law of the excluded middle, as things actually work out – may well turn out to be "the logic of the world." See his essay in the Ryle volume cited above, as well as his article 'The Logic of Quantum Mechanics,' 1968, reprinted in vol. I of his philosophical papers: *Mathematics, Matter and Method*, Cambridge, Eng., 1975, 1979.

Section 24. Time Gaps Revisited

Page 115. *Let us suppose that Z came before* V. Newton said that he discovered his "method of fluxions" (the calculus, which uses the idea of Z when dealing with motion) in 1665. Römer's demonstration that light has finite velocity was in 1676 (*V* for present purposes, where we do not need the value of 186,000 mps). But the method of fluxions was not published until years later. Newton's *Principia* uses the older geometric methods, though he discovered his results with the aid of the calculus. For a convenient discussion, see W. P. D. Wightman, *The Growth of Scientific Ideas*, Chapters IX and XIII; New Haven, 1953. Of course, the work of G. W. von Leibniz (1646–1716) will famously come into any discussion of the discovery of the calculus. For a very thorough account, see Carl B. Boyer, *The History of the Calculus and its Conceptual Development*, New York, 1949, esp. Chap. V. (The book appeared originally as *The Concepts of Calculus*, New York, 1939.)

The point of the present illustration in the text goes through just as well if we suppose that *V* came before *Z*. Thus: there was a time when the scientific concept (*and* the common-sense concept) of seeing could be represented as *A, E, H, O, not-P*, and *D*. Then if we add *V* to the scientific concept we get problems about seeing stars (*H*) even if not (in view of *D*) about seeing objects on earth (*E*). Then, adding *Z* a little later in place of *D* we only make matters worse. In either case we are forced to drop *not-P* for *P*.

Page 116. *The sample statement has ceased to be analytic.* It might be objected that we really are not dealing with the same statement, precisely because the meaning of the word "seeing" *has* changed. This may be true in some sense, but one wonders whether it affects the substance of the point at hand. For (1) we are dealing with the same English sentence; (2) we are using it to talk about the same part of our experience, visual experience; and (3) what we are now using the sentence to say is no longer true *a priori* but false.

Page 117. *A point emphasized by several critics.* The first to do so, I believe, were H. P. Grice and P. F. Strawson, in their article 'In Defense of a Dogma,' *Philosophical Review* **65** (1956). See the last two sentences of their third-to-last paragraph.

Section 25. Canonical Language

Pages 118–119. *Quine's objectives.* See especially Section 33 of his *Word and Object*, Cambridge, Mass., 1960. The long passage quoted on p. 119 is from this Section at p. 161.

Page 119. *The structure so well understood by logicians.* The quoted words are at p. 228 of *Word and Object*.

Page 119. *The same device Russell used.* The technical detail of Quine's treatment is different, but he uses the same device of including an existence assertion to assure that the sentence in which the description occurs will at least be false. *Ibid.*, pp. 183–84.

Page 121. *Quine's comments on those who reject Russell's theory.* These are quoted from pp. 260–61 of the same book.

CHAPTER EIGHT

Page 124. *Transformational grammar.* For a collection of critical articles on the best known philosopher-linguist in the field, see *On Noam Chomsky*, G. Harman, ed., New York, 1974. The book includes the excellent article by Searle from the *New York Review of Books*, mentioned in our general Introduction.

Page 124. *Logical form and deep structures.* Some relevant articles will be found in *The Logic of Grammar*, D. Davidson and G. Harman, eds., Encino and Belmont, Calif., 1975. The book also deals with the topic of *excluding* certain apparent implications from the purview of logic (H. P. Grice's "implicatures").

Section 26. Proper Names

Page 125. *A view characteristic of the later Wittgenstein.* See Section 79 of the *Philosophical Investigations*, Part I.

Page 126. *Donnellan's 'Reference and Definite Descriptions.'* The article appeared in *Philosophical Review* **75** (1966) and is reprinted in *Naming, Necessity, and Natural Kinds*, S. P. Schwartz, ed., Ithaca, 1977. Schwartz's 30-page Introduction to the topic is very helpful. Donnellan's distinction between the attributive use and the referential use of a definite description seems to have the following consequences for Russell's and Strawson's accounts, as he points out. (1) Russell's theory applies at most to the attributive use. That is, even if it is part of the *meaning* of any sentence having a definite description as its subject that there exists something which fits the description, this would be true in the attributive use but not the referential. (2) Not only is there an implication (Russell) or an presupposition (Strawson) that something or other fits the description , but in the referential use there is the further implication or presupposition that a *particular* person or thing fits it. (3) Consider Strawson's claim that no true or false assertion is made when nothing fits the description. Assuming Strawson is right about this as against Russell, the point only holds good for the attributive use, not the referential. (4) Strawson is mistaken when he says that if nothing fits the description there can be no reference.

For an argument that Donnellan's own account of descriptions is not entirely coherent – though like Strawson's and Russell's it undoubtedly includes some new and important points – see Saul Kripke, 'Speaker's Reference and Semantic Reference,' *Midwest Studies in Philosophy*, Vol. II: *Studies in the Philosophy of Language*, pp. 255 – 76; Univ. of Minnesota Press (Morris), 1977. New articles on the theory of descriptions continue to appear. Thus Richard Sharvey argues (in 'A More General Theory of Definite Descriptions,' *Philosophical Review* **89** (1980)) that Russell's analysis is all right for definite singular descriptions but not for descriptions containing mass predicates or plural predicates.

Page 127. *Donnellan's 'Proper Names and Identifying Descriptions'* appeared in *Semantics of Natural Language*, D. Davidson and G. Harman, eds., Dordrecht and Boston, 1972.

Page 127. *A complicated set of further circumstances.* The subject of the experiment, being an old hand at such matters, thinks he has an infallible test for determining whether the lenses have been reversed. He applies the test but gets the wrong result. Alpha appears to him to be on top, and he mistakenly concludes that it really is on top. Later, when the projector is turned off, we ask him which square he refers to as 'Alpha,' and he replies, "The square that turned color; the square on top." By this time he has forgotten where the square appeared to be, and exactly how he arrived at the conclusion that it was on top. So he is unable to supply the true description, "the square that appeared to be on top."

Page 128. *Donnellan has been joined by S. Kripke and H. Putnam.* For conventience of exposition I only discuss one of Kripke's articles and none of Putnam's. But all the points discussed seem to have been made independently by Putnam. See his 'Is Semantics Possible?,' which appeared in *Language, Belief, and Metaphysics*, H. Kiefer and M. Munitz., eds., 1970, and is reprinted in the Schwartz volume cited above. Also his 'Meaning and Reference,' *Journal of Philosophy* **70** (1973), reprinted in the Schwartz volume. Also his 'The Meaning of "Meaning",' *Minnesota Studies in Philosophy of Science*, vol. VII; Univ. of Minnesota Press (Mnpls.), 1975. Also his 'It Ain't Necessarily So,' *Journal of Philosophy* **59** (1962), reprinted in *Readings in the Philosophy of Language*, J. Rosenberg and C. Travis, eds., Englewood Cliffs, 1971. All but the second of these are to be found in Putnam's two volumes of philosophical papers published by Cambridge University Press, 1975, 1979.

Page 128. *Kripke's 'Identity and Necessity'* appeared in *Identity and Individuation*, M. Munitz, ed., New York, 1971, and is reprinted in the Schwartz volume cited above.

Section 27. Necessary Identity Statements

Pages 129 – 130. *Kripke's preliminary points.* There are other important preliminaries which I omit in the text. One of them is his reasoned denial that we need to have general criteria of identity "across possible worlds," and another is his illustrated claim that there are essential properties of individual objects: properties that the object has to have if it exists at all. In easy cases it seems obvious that we can make such identifications without possessing general criteria of identity. ("Imagine that this desk were now over against that wall instead of where it is.") And in more difficult cases Kripke thinks we can use essential properties for this purpose. To illustrate the latter claim, imagine a situation (possible world) in which Nixon is a member of a radical students' organization like S.D.S. It is not essential to Nixon – that very man – that he should have become and remained an arch-conservative politician; he might have been a radical over-aged graduate student. But now try this: "Imagine that Nixon were a 20-year old member of S.D.S. in 1970." That won't work because it is essential to Nixon that he developed from a particular ovum fertilized in 1912 or 1913. No 20-year old in 1970 can have that property. And anyone who lacks it cannot be Nixon even if he resembles Nixon in every other way.

Page 132. *This is our normal way of describing such a situation.* A critic of Kripke might reply, "Yes, we do say there is heat there, but only because we have it in the back of our minds that if we or other animals were there we *would* have the sensation. This shows that the idea of the sensation really is essential to the meaning of 'heat'." However this objection should be answered, there is one general point to be made in favor of the Kripke – Putnam account. With the growth of knowledge there is a tendency (in general culture, not just in the culture of scientists) to focus upon underlying structures rather than subjective phenomena in fixing the meaning of words. By now practically everyone knows that water is H_2O, for example, and this seems to explain why people who hear Putnam's "Twin Earth" example say without hesitation that the colorless potable liquid found in the rivers and lakes of Twin Earth (having some other chemical analysis X, Y, Z) is not water. See his "Meaning and Reference," cited in the note to page 128.

Section 28. Mind-Brain Identity

Page 133. *Kripke's Book, Naming and Necessity.* Published at Oxford in 1980, it appeared originally as a series of printed lectures in *Semantics, of Natural Languages*, cited in the note to p. 127, above.

Page 133. *The Mind-Brain Identity Theory.* For a collection of basic articles, see the book of that title edited by C. V. Borst, New York, 1970.

Page 136. *"For reasons that you have pointed out,"* etc. The possibility about the future course of science which is then described is one that Kripke refers to more than once in the book and article cited above. It appears to be the point that Harman used in formulating the "Kripke – Harman Paradox," discussed in Section 12, above.

Section 29. Retrospect

Page 139. *Clues supplied by a particular discipline.* Historians of philosophy often point out that the system builders of various periods have been powerfully influenced by the scientific achievements (or rediscoveries) of their own eras: Aquinas by Aristotelian science, Kant by Newtonian science, Herbert Spencer (1820–1903) by Darwinian science; the list could be extended. But the case of Wittgenstein (though not of Russell) seems to be rather unusual. His metaphysical theory seems to result *entirely* from reflection on mathematical logic, and not at all from epistemological criticism of common sense, or from other materials more typical of the philosophical tradition itself.

Page 140. *Criticisms of scientific popularizers.* Stebbing's well known book on this and related topics is *Philosophy and the Physicists*, London, 1937. And see Wittgenstein, *The Blue and the Brown Books*, p. 45f., Oxford, 1958.

CHAPTER NINE

Page 145. *R. M. Hare's book, The Language of Morals*, was published at Oxford in 1952. The most important chapters for present purposes are 4 through 9.

Page 146. *Recent ethical theorists who emphasize "the moral point of view."* As mentioned in the text, not all of these writers use this phrase in referring to the basic principle of morality, and some also try to marry it to the principle of rational egoism. Thus Rawls puts certain blinders on his rationally self-interested social contractors in order to guarantee impartial results. There are further references to this in the notes to Section 36 below. Some principal works are Kurt Baier, *The Moral Point of View*, Ithaca, 1958, rev. edn., 1965; Marcus Singer, *Generalization in Ethics*, New York, 1961; R. M. Hare, *Freedom and Reason*, Oxford, 1963; John Rawls, *A Theory of Justice*, Cambridge, Mass., 1971; William Frankena, *Ethics*, 2nd edn., Englewood Cliffs, 1973.

Section 32. True Values

Page 154. *"Justified in asserting that other things are equal."* A person might be so justified, for example, if he makes a thorough inquiry without turning up any plausible defeating conditions, at least where there is good reason to think that such an inquiry would bring them to his attention if they exist.

CHAPTER TEN

Section 33. The Problem of Moral Truth

Page 157. *Moral "reasons" are attempts to persuade by emotional appeals, etc.* This is the principal claim of the so-called Emotive Theory of ethics, classic statements of which are found in C. L. Stevenson's 'The Nature of Ethical Disagreement,' in *Readings in Philosophical Analysis*, H. Feigl and W. Sellars, eds., New York, 1949; and Stevenson's *Ethics and Language*, New Haven, 1944. For a later discussion, see J. O. Urmson's *The Emotive Theory of Ethics*, New York, 1968.

Section 34. Two Types of Moral Thought

Page 158. *Semantical rules for "wrong" and other moral value words.* This suggestion about the meaning of moral terms and the self-evidence of certain moral statements was made by R. W. Beardsmore in his *Moral Reasoning*, New York, 1969. See also D. Z. Phillips and H. O. Mounce, *Moral Practices*, New York, 1970.

Pages 161–162. *Some recognized moral principles do promote the general welfare.* The most obvious of these are the rules against murder, mayhem, theft, rape, etc., which are mentioned several times in this chapter as common to all or practically all societies. The most important condition of human welfare is no doubt the existence of organized society itself, and this would hardly be possible without generally accepted rules of these kinds. But many recognized moral rules do not have this kind of objective basis.

Page 167. *The problem of justice in Utilitarianism.* Some important modern discussions of this are collected in *Contemporary Utilitarianism*, M. D. Bayles, ed., New York, 1968. The question is treated extensively by John Rawls in *A Theory of Justice*, Cambridge, Mass., 1971.

Section 35. Reforming the Concept of Moral Truth

Page 163. The *book-length study* is my *Moral Reasoning and Truth*, Oxford, 1976.

Page 166. *Demonstrably good moral reasons.* Here the objection may be made that even if I have managed to identify, on the model of Sections 31 and 32, a valid standard for evaluating certain items which I have chosen to call "reasons," a person who merely gives good reasons in this sense does not thereby provide a "rational justification" of his judgment. For these so-called reasons are misnamed; they are only calculated to produce agreement and mutual respect, not to establish objective truth or probable truth. In chapter 5 of the book cited in the preceding note I have argued that this objection distorts the notion of rational justification, which is not exclusively concerned with the attainment of objective truth.

Page 166. *The only other relevant notion of evaluative truth and falsity.* There is also a *legislative* model of evaluative truth (explored in chapter 1 of the book just cited) which is irrelevant in the sphere of critical morality.

Page 167. *Our only inkling comes from theological ethics.* As far as I am aware, no secular philosopher since Locke has explicitly held the rather crude view (see the preceding note) that *X* is good because God wills it. I am merely suggesting that it is this fragment of myth at the back of our minds that makes the ethical Intuitionist's ontological suggestion seem at least intelligible and possible until we take a close look at it. ("What *are* those absolute ethical values-in-the-world? Why, God's preferences! What else?")

Page 167. *No other way of identifying or conceiving of such entities is known.* It is interesting to contrast the situation of a congenitally blind person with that of someone who doubts the existence of those absolute values-in-the-world. While the blind person has no more direct experience of light and color than I have of those alleged entities, he can learn the physical theory of light and even add to it, with the help of normally sighted people perhaps. But there is apparently nothing I can learn about the Intuitionist's value entities except that they are said to exist and render our moral judgments true or false.

Page 168. *Those principles and judgments which common sense would cite as obviously true are just the ones that would qualify as true under our conception of moral truth*. There is only space for one example. At p. 70 of his book *Contemporary Moral Philosophy*, London, 1967, G. J. Warnock mentions as an obvious moral truth that it would be wrong of him to cause his children to become addicted to heroin. Now this certainly is an obvious truth in the traditional morality of Warnock's society, and no doubt in many others. But it is also a consentient truth in the fully critical morality of autonomous persons. In view of the psychological and social harm (if not physical harm) that addiction would cause to the children, and in view of the very high likelihood that reasonable inquiry would fail to identify any substantial countervailing reasons why inducing such addiction would be morally permissible, practically anyone satisfying MPV (and probably everyone) would agree with this judgment. I have discussed the example in detail at p. 114f. of the book cited in the note to p. 163.

Section 36. The Economy of This Reform

Page 172. *The Utilitarian unwittingly sacrifices assumption 3*. To this it might be objected that the Utilitarian can claim to save assumption 3 in the same way the Intuitionist can. That is, it is no infringement of my autonomy to be obliged to conform to the truth once the truth is known, and the Utilitarian might claim to have had just *one* big intuition of *the* true moral principle: "It is always right to follow the rule that best maximizes welfare if generally followed" (or if generally accepted, in some versions). Since the Utilitarian also retains assumptions 1, 2, and 4, this would be advanced as a dissolution, not as a revisionary solution. But it has the same disadvantage that we saw in Intuitionism: total obscurity as to the ground of this truth which supposedly is being intuited. It also has the disadvantage of extreme moral eccentricity. If any seriously unjust rule were found to satisfy the principle (at least without purchasing a very *great* increase of happiness or decrease of unhappiness), practically everyone but the Rule Utilitarian would feel justified in rejecting it.

Page 173. *A weak sense of truth*. It also allows the (necessarily rare) situation in which a person might justifiably and persistently hold a moral opinion which he knows to be "false," i.e. one that would be rejected by practically all other people who might justifiably form a judgment on the same moral question. This would be rare by the very meaning of "consensus," and it is made rarer still by the fact that where there *would* be such a consensus contrary to one's well-considered view, one would sometimes not be in a position to know this. For example, the question might be a novel one, and of course no survey of properly informed and reflective people will have been made about it. Indeed the situation referred to can be seen to be much rarer still in light of the following point. If anyone satisfied MPV and discovered that practically everyone else satisfying it would hold a certain view on the moral question at hand, he would be strongly influenced to adopt that view himself if he had not already done so. But while such a situation would thus be extremely rare among all the occasions on which people make moral judgments, it might not be uncommon in the moral life of a particular person (if there could be such a person) who (a) had eccentric moral views on various common moral questions, and (b) typically satisfies MPV when adopting or deciding whether to retain such views. I accept this result as the price of retaining any notion of truth in the second type of moral thought.

It might appear that there is another and closely related paradox entailed by our solution. I have said that a person who substantially satisfies MPV may be justified in rejecting some moral principles or judgments which are true in the first type of moral thought. Thus our solution might be thought to license such a statement as "I know that such and such a moral statement is true but I am justified in rejecting it." But I have already provided against this by distinguishing the two types of moral thought and discourse. Such a statement would be nonsense if made *in* discourse of the first type about a moral statement which is true in that type of thought. And it would be confused or misleading if made in discourse of the second type, unless the context made it clear that the truth being attributed to the moral statement in question is that proper to statements in the first type of discourse only. If that were clear from the context or from further statements by the speaker, there would be no paradox, real or apparent. For then the quoted statement would say no more than that the speaker is justified in rejecting some moral principle or judgment traditionally accepted in the community.

Pages 171 – 175. *The relative economy of our solution.* As mentioned earlier in the text, this solution belongs to a family of ethical theories which has been very prominent in recent moral philosophy. Perhaps the best known members of the family are the theories found in R. M. Hare's *Freedom and Reason*, Oxford, 1963, and John Rawls's *A Theory of Justice*, Cambridge, Mass., 1971. They too will be found to preserve assumptions 1, 2, and 3, while significantly qualifying 4. In the book cited in the note to p. 163, I have attempted to explain at some length why I believe Hare's theory is less efficient than the one summarized here. But perhaps a comment on Rawls will be of some use.

In his qualification of assumption 4, the nearest thing to objective truth that Rawls recognizes is that our moral judgments should correctly apply principles which are adopted in a reasonable way. His reasonable way is called the "original position," and it includes a theoretical "veil of ignorance" about various kinds of facts the knowledge of which could lead to *undue* self-interest when choosing principles. It should be noted in passing that this "original position" is an invention of his social-contract political theory, not a commonly standard like MPV, which any morally reflective person can try to live up to. (No one can literally take the veil of ignorance.) But this may not be a very important difference; the "veil of ignorance" may only be a device to remind us of the restrictions we ought to impose on ourselves in adopting moral principles. The really important difference is that Rawls does not attempt to demonstrate the objective validity of the "original position," something we have attempted to do for MPV. He merely offers some "philosophical considerations" which he hopes will "persuade" other theorists to accept the reasonableness of the requirements which he imposes on his theoretical contractors. It is true that in the concluding section of his book he does add another argument for these requirements. But it seems to me that there are so many weak points in this argument that it gives them little real support. In briefest outline the argument runs as follows. Since the two principles of justice which the contractors would (allegely) adopt when restricted by these requirements are (allegely) in close agreement or "reflective equilibrium" with "our" (anyone's?) considered judgments of which social arrangements are just and which are not, the requirements, like the principles themselves, are confirmed by this equilibrium. A number of convincing attacks on these claims and "allegations" will be found in the articles and critical reviews collected by Norman Daniels in *Reading Rawls*, New York [1975].

Our own solution would thus appear to preserve more of the structural assumptions of critical morality *if* it succeeds in *showing* the truth of the common assumption that MPV is a valid standard binding on all who make moral judgments of the second type.

Page 174. *Of course many moralists will object that our solution does not explain how objective moral truth is possible.* It may be worth adding that this solution does not commit the familiar sin of converting objections into favorable evidence without giving independent reasons why they do constitute such evidence (a complaint often brought against psycho-analysis, for example). We have given a general theory of stage four solutions in Chapter 4, and we have attempted to show how the present conceptual problem falls under that theory. We have not, of course, offered the present objection as evidence for that theory, and we have argued independently for our description of the existing conceptual scheme of fully critical morality, a scheme in which one does insist that moral statements can be objectively true.

CHAPTER ELEVEN

Page 176. *Moral philosophers turning from general studies to practical problems.* In the middle third of the century they were much concerned with "metaethics," defined as the study of the meaning of moral terms and the methods of moral reasoning, as distinguished from "ethics," defined as the attempt to find true theories of right and wrong conduct. Since the traditional theories of the latter type are quite vague by recent standards, this emphasis was probably desirable for a time. But critics soon pointed out that there can be no sharp separation between ethics and metaethics. The discussion of substantive moral questions is illuminated by purely conceptual inquiries and in turn helps to advance such inquiries.

Page 176. A good many articles have appeared on almost every one of these topics. The leading journal in the field is *Philosophy and Public Affairs*, founded in 1971 and published at Princeton, but many of these articles have appeared in various other periodicals and co-operative volumes.

Section 37. A Problem of Privacy

Page 178. *The article by Thomson* appeared in *Philosophy and Public Affairs* **4** (1974 – 75).

Page 179. *Exchange of computerized information by government agencies.* One of the better studies in this field is Arthur R. Miller's *The Assault on Privacy: Computers, Data Banks, and Dossiers*, Ann Arbor, 1971. See also *Records, Computers, and the Rights of Citizens* (Report to the Secretary of Health, Education, and Welfare), Cambridge, Mass., 1973.

Section 38. Some Descriptive Inquiries

Page 180. *The articles by Scanlon and Rachels* appeared in *Philosophy and Public Affairs* **4** (1974 – 75).

Pages 181 – 184. *Reiman's article* appeared in *Philosophy and Public Affairs* **6** (1976 – 77).

Page 182. *Benn's article* appeared in *Privacy: Nomos XIII*, R. Pennock and J. W. Chapman, eds., New York, 1971. It is reprinted in *Today's Moral Problems*, Richard Wasserstrom, ed., New York and London, 1975.

Section 39. Constructing the Right

Page 187. *The right to social practices under which we are able to feel that we own our lives.* This raises one of the many difficulties attaching to the notion of a human right. On the one hand, we do want very much to say that people have a right to social practices which are necessary for the satisfaction of basic needs. But on the other hand, there is no one in particular *against* whom one holds this right to action on the part of others, and this does not jibe with the structure of most of our talk about "rights."

Pages 186 – 189. *Conceptual elements that have to be added to existing moral thought.* It hardly needs saying that the precise argument and structure which I have buiilt up by adding to Reiman's argument may not be the best that could possibly be devised for the general right to privacy. But there are two very general features of this structure which would seem to be required if any argument for that right is to succeed: (1) that facts of *some* kind should be found to obtain concerning the needs or crucial interests of people, and (2) that *some* sort of ground-floor warrant should exist to support a normative inference moving from needs to rights.

It might be objected to what I say in the text that whatever psychological, biological, or other relations may need to obtain for the first of these features to be present, they might very well obtain whether or not the people who engage in moral-political discourse believe they obtain or possess the concepts necessary to form such a belief. But it seems clear to me that the second feature *must* somehow be present in our social practices and discourse if any argument for the right to privacy is to be complete and sound. For it warrants the truth of a basic normative premise, and I assume that such warrants must exist in the agreements or other practices of human beings if they are to exist at all.

Section 40. The Metaphysics of Politics

Page 190. *Radical reconstructions like hard determinism.* At various places in this book I have spoken of an "old city" of the mind whose structures must be presumed to be coherent and are beyond deliberate alteration, and of "suburbs" whose structures may not always be coherent and may be alterable. In evaluating hard determinism, it may be helpful to change the figure and distinguish three broad segments of a continuous scale extending from (1) the psychologically impossible, through (2) the excessively costly, to (3) the relatively economical. I would doubt that any revision of moral or political concepts would be located at (1), where we had to place the fundamental revision of spatial notions discussed in Chapter 3, along with the denial or doubt of Moore's general truisms. The rejection of naive moral traditionalism, or of theological ethics, or both of them together, would no doubt be of sufficient "structural" importance at certain stages in the history of culture to count as conceptual changes. But I would locate them at (3) rather than (2). Various philosophical proposals concerning morals must be located at (2), however, and rejected accordingly. The hard determinist's claim that we are never responsible for our actions is a prime example, and it should probably be placed quite close to the border between (2) and (1). If such a revision of common sense is not quite the flat impossibility for human creatures that we encountered in Chapter 3, its general adoption would render impossible anything resembling human social life as we know it. An interesting argument to this effect will be found in the title essay of P. F. Strawson's *Freedom and Resentment*, London, 1974.

Page 191. *Emotivism as the mere beginning of philosophical reflection on morals.* This is not to deny the philosophical usefulness of spelling out this skeptical position very forcefully, as in the books and article cited in the note to p. 157.

CONCLUSION

Pages 198 – 200. *A pessimistic point of view.* Many readers will recognize this as a sketch of the position defended by Richard Rorty in his widely discussed book, *Philosophy and the Mirror of Nature*, Princeton, 1979. Like any two-page sketch of a philosophical work running to almost 400 pages, it cannot be offered as an adequate outline of the arguments. Rather it is intended as a handy foil for certifying the present good health of philosophy against one kind of short obituary which has been written often enough by some of the admirers of the later Wittgenstein and is encountered again in Rorty's main conclusions. While he says "there is no danger of philosophy's 'coming to an end' " – since some form of discussion will no doubt continue to bear the name philosophy – he also repeatedly says that philosophy *as we have known it during the whole modern period* is over. For he thinks we can and should *stop discussing* "the traditional problems of modern philosophy." (both quotes are from p. 394.)

BIBLIOGRAPHY

Acton, H. B.: 'George Berkeley', *The Encyclopedia of Philosophy*, New York & London 1967.

Anscombe, G. E. M.: *An Introduction to Wittgenstein's Tractatus*, London and New York: Hutchinson Univ. Library, 1959.

Armstrong, D. M.: *Perception and the Physical World*, New York: Humanities Press, 1961.

Austin, J. L.: 'Other Minds', in *Philosophical Papers*, Oxford: Oxford Univ. Press, 1961.

Ayer, A. J.: *Language, Truth, and Logic*, London: V. Gollancz Ltd., 1936.

Ayer, A. J.: *The Problem of Knowledge*, Baltimore: Penguin, 1956.

Ayer, A. J. (ed.): *Logical Positivism*, New York: Free Press, 1959.

Baier, Kurt: *The Moral Point of View*, Ithaca: Cornell Univ. Press, 1961.

Bayles, M. D.: *Contemporary Utilitarianism*, New York: Doubleday, 1968.

Beardsmore, R. W.: *Moral Reasoning*, New York: Schocken, 1969.

Benn, S. I.: 'Privacy, Freedom, and Respect for Persons', in *Privacy: Nomos XIII*, Ed. by R. Pennock and J. W. Chapman, New York: Atherton, 1971.

Berkeley, George: *The Works of George Berkeley, Bishop of Cloyne*. Ed. by A. A. Luce and T. E. Jessop, 9 Vols., London and New York: Thomas Nelson & Sons, 1948–57.

Black, Max: *A Companion to Wittgenstein's 'Tractatus'*, Ithaca: Cornell Univ. Press, 1964.

Borst, C. V. (ed.): *The Mind-Brain Identity Theory*, New York: St. Martin's Press, 1970.

Boyer, Carl B.: *The History of the Calculus and its Conceptual Development*, New York: Hafner Pub. Co., 1949.

Carrier, L. S.: 'The Time-Gap Argument', *Australasian Journal of Philosophy* 14 (1969).

Castañeda, H.-N.: 'The Fallability of Memory not a Sufficient Obstacle to Private Language', *Encyclopedia of Philosophy*, 1967.

Chisholm, Roderick: *Perceiving*, Ithaca, Cornell Univ. Press, 1956.

Copleston, Frederick C.: *A History of Philosophy*, London: Oates & Washbourne, 1946, Vol. 5.

Daniels, Norman: *Reading Rawls*, New York: Basic Books, 1975.

Davidson, D. and G. Harman (eds.): *The Logic of Grammar*, Encio and Belmont, Calif.: Dickenson Publ. Co., 1975.

Descartes, René: *The Philosophical Works of Descartes*, Transl. by E. S. Haldane and G. R. T. Ross, Cambridge, Eng.: Cambridge Univ. Press, 1967.

Donne, John: *Complete Poetry and Selected Prose*, Ed. by John Hayward, London: Nonesuch, 1962.

Donnellan, Keith: 'Reference and Definite Descriptions', *Philosophical Review* 75 (1966).

226

Donnellan, Keith: 'Proper Names and Identifying Descriptions', in *Semantics of Natural Language*, Ed. by D. Davidson and G. Harman, Dordrecht and Boston: D. Reidel, 1972.

Ebersole, F.: 'How Philosophers See Stars', *Mind* **74** (1965).

Einstein, Albert and Leopold Infeld: *The Evolution of Physics*, New York: Simon & Schuster, 1938.

Flew, A. (ed.): *Essays in Conceptual Analysis*, London: Macmillan, 1956.

Frankena, William: *Ethics*, 2nd ed., Englewood Cliffs, N.J.: Prentice-Hall, 1973.

Fried, Charles: *An Anatomy of Values*, Cambridge, Mass.: Harvard Univ. Press, 1970.

Grice, H. P. and P. F. Strawson: 'In Defense of a Dogma', *Philosophical Review* **65** (1956).

Hare, R. M.: *The Language of Morals*, Oxford: Oxford Univ. Press, 1952.

Hare, R. M.: *Freedom and Reason*, Oxford: Oxford Univ. Press, 1963.

Harman, Gilbert: *Thought*, Princeton: Princeton Univ. Press, 1973.

Harman, G. (ed.): *On Noam Chomsky*, New York: Anchor Press, 1974.

Henson, R. G.: 'Ordinary Language, Common Sense, and the Time-Lag Argument', *Mind* **76** (1967).

Hicks, G. Dawes: *Berkeley*, London: E. Bean Ltd., 1932.

Hume, David: *Enquiry Concerning Human Understanding*, Ed. by L. A. Selby-Bigge, Oxford: Oxford Univ. Press, 1975.

Hume, David: *Treatise of Human Nature*, Ed. by L. A. Selby-Bigge, Oxford: Oxford Univ. Press, 1978.

Kant, Immanuel: *Critique of Pure Reason*, Transl. by Norman Kemp Smith, London and New York: Macmillan, 1929.

Kant, Immanuel: *Prolegomena to any Future Metaphysics*, Transl. by Lewis White Beck, New York: Liberal Arts Press, 1950.

Kenny, Anthony: *Wittgenstein*, Cambridge, Mass.: Harvard Univ. Press, 1973.

Kiefer, H. and M. Munitz (eds.): *Language, Belief, and Metaphysics*, Albany, N.Y.: SUNY Press, 1970.

Kripke, Saul: 'Identity and Necessity', in *Identity and Individuation*, Ed. by M. Munitz, New York: New York Univ. Press, 1971.

Kripke, Saul: 'Speaker's Reference and Semantic Reference', in *Midwest Studies in Philosophy*, Vol. II: *Studies in the Philosophy of Language*. Ed. by Peter A. French, Theodore E. Uehling, Jr., and Howard K. Wettstein, Morris: Univ. of Minn. Press, 1977.

Kripke, Saul: *Naming and Necessity*, Oxford: Oxford Univ. Press, 1980.

Kuhn, T. S.: *The Structure of Scientific Revolutions*, Chicago: Univ. of Chicago Press, 1970.

Leroy, A. L.: *George Berkeley*, Paris: Presses Universitaires de France, 1959.

Lewis, C. I.: *An Analysis of Knowledge and Valuation*, LaSalle, Ill.: Open Court Press, 1946.

Lewis, H. D. (ed.): *Contemporary British Philosophy*, 3rd and 4th series, London: George Allen & Unwin, 1961 and 1976.

Miller, Arthur R.: *The Assault on Privacy: Computers, Data Banks, and Dossiers*. Ann Arbor: Univ. of Michigan Press, 1971.

Miller, Arthur R.: *Records, Computers, and the Rights of Citizens*, Report to the Secretary of Health, Education, and Welfare. Cambridge, Mass.: MIT Press, 1973.

Moore, G. E.: 'The Refutation of Idealism', *Mind* **12** (1903).

Moore, G. E.: *Some Main Problems of Philosophy*, London: George Allen & Unwin, 1953.

Muirhead, J. H. (ed.): *Contemporary British Philosophy*, 1st and 2nd series, London: George Allen & Unwin, 1924 and 1925.

Myer, G. E.: 'Perception and the "Time Lag" Argument', *Analysis* **17** (1957).

Pears, D. F.: *Bertrand Russell and the British Tradition in Philosophy*, London: Collins, 1967.

Perry, Thomas D.: *Moral Reasoning and Truth*, Oxford: Oxford Univ. Press, 1976.

Phillips, D. Z. and H. O. Mounce: *Moral Practices*, New York: Schocken, 1970.

Pitcher, G. (ed.): *Wittgenstein: The Philosophical Investigations*, New York: Anchor, 1966.

Pitcher, G.: *Berkeley*, London: Routledge & Keegan Paul, 1977.

Pollock, John: *Knowledge and Justification*, Princeton: Princeton Univ. Press, 1974.

Putnam, Hilary: 'It Ain't Necessarily So', *Journal of Philosophy* **59** (1962).

Putnam, Hilary: 'Is Semantics Possible?', in *Language, Belief, and Metaphysics*, Ed. by H. Kiefer and M. Munitz, Albany: SUNY Press, 1970.

Putnam, Hilary: 'Meaning and Reference', *Journal of Philosophy* **70** (1973).

Putnam, Hilary: 'The Meaning of "Meaning",' in *Minnesota Studies in Philosophy of Science*, Vol. VII: *Language, Mind, and Knowledge*, Ed. by Keith Gunderson, Morris: Univ. of Minn. Press, 1975.

Putnam, Hilary: 'The Logic of Quantum Mechanics', in *Philosophical Papers*, Vol. I: *Mathematics, Matter, and Method*, Cambridge, Eng.: Cambridge Univ. Press, 1975.

Putnam, Hilary: ' "Two Dogmas" Revisited', in *Contemporary Aspects of Philosophy*, Ed. by G. Ryle, London and Boston: Oriel Press, 1976.

Quine, W. V. O.: 'Two Dogmas of Empiricism', *Philosophical Review* **60** (1951).

Quine, W. V. O.: *From a Logical Point of View*, Cambridge, Mass.: Harvard Univ. Press, 1953.

Quine, W. V. O.: *Word and Object*, Cambridge, Mass.: MIT Press, 1960.

Quine, W. V. O.: *Philosophy of Logic*, Englewood Cliffs, N.J.: Prentice-Hall, 1970.

Rachels, James: 'Why Privacy is Important', *Philosophy and Public Affairs* **4** (1974–75).

Ramsey, F. P.: *Foundations of Mathematics and Other Logical Essays*, New York: Harcourt, Brace & Co., 1931.

Rawls, John: *A Theory of Justice*, Cambridge, Mass.: Harvard Univ. Press, 1971.

Reiman, Jeffrey: 'Privacy, Intimacy, and Personhood', *Philosophy and Public Affairs* **6** (1976–77).

Rorty, Richard: 'The World Well Lost', *Journal of Philosophy* **69** (1972).

Rorty, Richard: *Philosophy and the Mirror of Nature*, Princeton: Princeton Univ. Press, 1979.

Rosenberg, J. and C. Travis (eds.): *Readings in the Philosophy of Language*, Englewood Cliffs, N.J.: Prentice-Hall, 1971.

Russell, Bertrand: 'On Denoting', *Mind* **14** (1905).

Russell, Bertrand: *Introduction to Mathematical Philosophy*, London: George Allen & Unwin, 1919.

Russell, Bertrand: 'Reply to Criticism', in *The Philosophy of Bertrand Russell*, Ed. by P. A. Schilpp, Evanston, Ill.: Northwestern Univ. Press, 1944.

Russell, Bertrand: 'The Philosophy of Logical Atomism', in *Logic and Knowledge: Essays 1901–1950*, Ed. by R. C. Marsh, London: George Allen & Unwin, 1956.

Saunders, J. T. and D. F. Henze: *The Private Language Problem*, New York: Random House, 1967.

Scanlon, Thomas: 'Thomson on Privacy', *Philosophy and Public Affairs* **4** (1974–75).

Schilpp, P. A. (ed.): *The Philosophy of Bertrand Russell*, Evanston, Ill.: Northwestern Univ. Press, 1944.

Schilpp, P. A. (ed.): *The Philosophy of Rudolf Carnap*, LaSalle, Ill.: Open Court Press, 1963.

Schwartz, S. P. (ed.): *Naming, Necessity, and Natural Kinds*, Ithaca: Cornell Univ. Press, 1977.

Searle, J.: 'Chomsky's Revolution in Linguistics', in *On Noam Chomsky*, Ed. by G. Harman, New York: Anchor Press, 1974.

Sharvey, Richard: 'A More General Theory of Definite Descriptions', *Philosophical Review* **89** (1980).

Singer, Marcus: *Generalization in Ethics*, New York: Knopf, 1961.

Stebbing, L. Susan: *Philosophy and the Physicists*, London: Methuen, 1937.

Stevenson, C. L.: *Ethics and Language*, New Haven: Yale Univ. Press, 1944.

Stevenson, C. L.: 'The Nature of Ethical Disagreement', in *Readings in Philosophical Analysis*, Ed. by H. Feigl and W. Sellars, New York: Appleton-Century-Crofts, 1949.

Strawson, P. F.: 'On Referring', *Mind* **59** (1950).

Strawson, P. F.: *Individuals*, London: Methuen, 1959.

Strawson, P. F.: *Logico-Linguistic Papers*, London: Methuen, 1971.

Strawson, P. F.: *Freedom and Resentment*, London: Methuen, 1974.

Suchting, W. A.: 'Perception and the Time-Gap Argument', *Philosophical Quarterly* **19** (1969).

Thomson, Judith: 'The Right to Privacy', *Philosophy and Public Affairs* **4** (1974–75).

Toulmin, Stephen: 'Recent Scientific Mythologies', in *Metaphysical Beliefs*, Ed. by A. MacIntyre, London: Ryerson Press, 1956.

Unger, Peter: *Ignorance: A Case for Skepticism*, Oxford: Oxford Univ. Press, 1975.

Urmson, J. O.: *Philosophical Analysis: Its Development Between the Two World Wars*, Oxford: Clarendon Press, 1956.

Urmson, J. O.: *The Emotive Theory of Ethics*, New York: Hutchinson, 1968.

Van der Veer, Garrett: *Philosophical Skepticism and Ordinary-Language Analysis*, Lawrence, Kan.: Regents Press of Kansas, 1978.

Vesey, G. (ed.): *Understanding Wittgenstein*, Ithaca: Cornell Univ. Press, 1974.

Warnock, G. J.: *Berkeley*, London: Penguin, 1953.

Warnock, G. J.: *Contemporary Moral Philosophy*, London: Macmillan, 1967.

Wasserstrom, Richard (ed.): *Today's Moral Problems*, New York and London: Macmillan, 1975.

Weitz, Morris: 'Analysis and the Unity of Russell's Philosophy', in *The Philosophy of Bertrand Russell*, Ed. by P. A. Schillp, Evanston, Ill.: Northwestern Univ. Press, 1944.

Whitehead, A. N. and Bertrand Russell: *Principia Mathematica*, Cambridge, Eng.: Cambridge Univ. Press, 1910–13.

Wightman, P. D.: *The Growth of Scientific Ideas*, New Haven: Yale Univ. Press, 1953.

Wittgenstein, Ludwig: *Tractatus Logico-Philosophicus*, Transl. by D. F. Pears and B. F. McGuinness, London: Routledge & Keegan Paul, 1974.

Wittgenstein, Ludwig: *The Blue and Brown Books*, Oxford: B. Blackwell, 1958.

Wittgenstein, Ludwig: *Philosophical Investigations*, Transl. by G. E. M. Anscombe, Oxford: B. Blackwell, 1953.

Wittgenstein, Ludwig: *On Certainty*, Oxford: B. Blackwell, 1969.

NAME INDEX

231

SUBJECT INDEX